CLOSING THE LOOP
SYSTEMS THINKING FOR DESIGNERS

Sheryl Cababa

NEW YORK   2023

"Design helps people by offering thoughtful solutions, which can also bring unintended consequences. Sheryl's book urges us to broaden our perspective and provides valuable guidance to bring in to daily practice."

—Hung-Hsiang Chen,
Head of UX & HF at ConvaTec

"Cababa's book comes at a crucial moment for design, and points the way toward a more inclusive, meaningful future for our work."

—David Dylan Thomas,
author, *Design for Cognitive Bias*

"Cababa reminds us of what design was intended to be: a force for positive impact. Through relatable examples and frameworks for thinking plus doing, this book is a guide for designers to practice the design we all want."

—Masuma Henry,
Design Director, Google

"As an anthropologist, I know the value of bringing a systems perspective to designing for change. Sheryl's book is a thoughtful guide for designers seeking to bring more systems thinking to their craft."

—Tracy Pilar Johnson,
Design Anthropologist, Bill & Melinda Gates Foundation

"More than ever, designers are poised to play higher-impact roles. Sheryl Cababa reveals how systems thinking will be the powerful new skill to get us there."

—Brandon Schauer,
Rare.org's leader of Climate Culture

"This is a must-have book for practitioners developing products and services at every level."

—Jose Coronado,
Executive Director Digital Experience Design, JP Morgan Chase

"Cababa provides a fresh perspective on how design research and practice can meet the needs of a complex and sometimes contentious 21st century."

—Beth Kolko, Professor,
University of Washington

"In her comprehensive, insightful, and actionable guide, Sheryl Cababa draws from real-time and historical global events, expert insights from across industries, and her depth of expertise, challenging us to use systems thinking to shift our own perspectives and assumptions about how to envision and design for a better future."

—Kristin Skinner,
Chief Experience Officer at &GSD and
co-author *Org Design for Design Orgs*

Closing the Loop
Systems Thinking for Designers
By Sheryl Cababa

Rosenfeld Media

125 Maiden Lane

New York, New York 10038

USA

On the Web: www.rosenfeldmedia.com

Please send errata to: errata@rosenfeldmedia.com

Publisher: Louis Rosenfeld

Managing Editor: Marta Justak

Interior Layout: Danielle Foster

Cover Design: Heads of State

Indexer: Marilyn Augst

Proofreader: Sue Boshers

ISBN: 978-1-959029-88-5

ISBN 13: 1-959029-88-6

LCCN: 2022943944

Printed and bound in the United States of America

For Rebecca and Ernesto,
who always supported my curiosity

HOW TO USE THIS BOOK

Who Should Read This Book?

This book is for practitioners who want to incorporate systems-thinking methods into their practice. Design researchers, strategists, and experience designers, as well as those from domains such as technology, healthcare, education, and other spaces in which human-centered design is often incorporated, will benefit from this book's tools and instruction that help broaden perspectives.

What's in This Book?

This book includes the rationale for incorporating systems thinking into your design practice. You'll find examples and stories that support that rationale, as well as interviews with experts who engage with systems thinking in their own practice. In order to make the systems-thinking perspective accessible and actionable, you'll also find practical tools and frameworks that you can include in your practice right away. Prompts, examples, and advice about how to use those tools will help facilitate their use.

This book is designed in three parts. In Chapters 1 through 3, I introduce the rationale for combining design with systems thinking. In Chapters 4 through 6, the focus is on tools and methods to understand the problem space and map the status quo. Lastly, in Chapters 7 through 9, you will learn about tools and methods for envisioning the future.

Within the various chapters, you'll find some common elements:

- **System Spotting:** Throughout the book, I've included sidebars that are examples of visible systems. These sidebars have events, objects, symbols, and words that you might see in your own cities, in the news, history, or the language that you use. They are good exercises in determining what patterns, structures, and mindsets sit beneath the events you experience and the things you see in the world.

- **Interviews:** I end many chapters with an interview with an expert design practitioner who engages in systems thinking. I admire and have learned from each of them, and they each have inspiring ways to think about systems, concepts that drive their practice, and tools that you can likely use as well.

This is your plastic hour. From digital technology to global health, you, as a designer, have already been problem-solving in ways that are great and small. By using systems thinking, you can shift your perspectives and assumptions about what you should design and why. Finally, you'll have a chance to build upon your skills to create an even greater impact. I hope these tools, frameworks, and approaches will help you facilitate that shift.

What Comes with This Book?

This book's companion website (https://rosenfeldmedia.com/books/systems-thinking-for-designers/) contains a blog and additional content. The book's diagrams and other illustrations are available under a Creative Commons license (when possible) for you to download and include in your own presentations. You can find these on Flickr at www.flickr.com/photos/rosenfeldmedia/sets/.

FREQUENTLY ASKED QUESTIONS

What do you mean by systems thinking?

This is a very good question because you'd be surprised at how many different answers there are to this question. For example, there are ideas and practices oriented around hard systems methodology, which is focused primarily on finding and enacting efficiencies within a given system. This includes approaches such as systems engineering.

In this book, your main concern will be oriented around soft systems methodology, which can be described as understanding a problem space, creating a holistic view of it, and considering where intervention can happen to create certain outcomes.

I feel intimidated by systems thinking as a practice. Can I really use systems thinking as a designer?

Designers sometimes tell me that they feel like systems thinking requires complex software to be able to model causal loop maps and simulate how systems will change. This often feels like a barrier to being able to engage.

The tools that are the focus of this book mostly involve various forms of visual mapping. If you, as a designer, use outputs such as user journeys, service blueprints, or other forms of mapping as analysis, then this approach should resonate with, and feel accessible, to you. You do not need complex software to engage in the mindset of systems thinking and make it actionable in your process. It could be helpful to engage with experts in systems analysis if that's what your project work requires, but I do not view it by any means as a necessity. As you grow as a systems-thinking-oriented designer, your practice might shift to involve different tools and collaborations with other experts, but this is not a requirement from the beginning.

If you know how to facilitate workshops, engage a diversity of stakeholders, use sticky notes, and create visual maps on paper or in tools like Miro and Mural, then you are already well on your way to being able to incorporate many of the mapping tools and frameworks within this book.

Can systems thinking work with design disciplines such as service design and user experience design?

Systems thinking can absolutely work with these design practices. In Chapter 3, "Systems Thinking and Design Thinking," you will find a framework that describes how systems thinking intersects with the typical design-thinking approach. The key thing to remember is that systems thinking is much more of a mindset than a codified set of practices, so you can employ a systems-thinking lens to your existing practice and tools, as well as enhance your current practice with some of the tools and frameworks introduced to you in this book. For example, mapping outputs such as service design blueprints could be paired with outcomes mapping or theory-of-change frameworks to broaden the perspective of how to enact change. (See Chapter 7, "Creating a Theory of Change," for mapping tools that are oriented toward envisioning the future.)

Are design systems and systems thinking the same thing?

A design system is, as described by Nielsen Norman Group, "a set of standards to manage design at scale by reducing redundancy while creating a shared language and visual consistency across different pages and channels." This includes components of the system and ways of using them.

Systems thinking is a mindset and approach that helps you consider and analyze systems as a whole, consider the relationships within them, and investigate cause and effect that leads to specific outcomes.

So design systems and systems thinking are not the same thing. However, because creating design systems involves creating a pattern language and acknowledging how components affect each other, a systems-thinking mindset intersects with the mindset required to create a design system. The creation of design systems has more alignment with hard systems methodology, whereas soft systems methodology is the main focus of this book. (The Chapter 2 sidebar,

"The System of Systems Thinking," is good for understanding systems methodology.)

Design systems are not addressed in this book as most of the tools and frameworks are oriented around more broad practices of systems thinking combined with design strategy, but if you are interested in the mindset required for creating good design systems, see the interview with Nicole Sarsfield at the end of Chapter 3.

Do I need to use all the tools and frameworks in this book in order to engage in systems thinking?

You can use whatever tools in this book you find useful for the kind of problem-solving you are engaging with. If, for example, you are using systems thinking to facilitate how your own company or organization can change, you might find analysis tools such as the iceberg model a good way to gain alignment on the problem space. (See Chapter 6, "Mapping Forces," for more systems-thinking tools to model the status quo.)

The tools and frameworks outlined in this book are not by any means a codified set of tools that all systems thinkers use. They have been collected from various forms of systems practices, and represent those that I've found most useful for design practitioners. There are many more tools out in the world, and I encourage you to continue exploring and growing your practice.

CONTENTS

FOREWORD

What does it mean to serve people in today's converging world where change is a constant? If the last few years have shown us anything from COVID-19, societal imbalance, and climate change, the playbooks that explain how we should serve people need to change. How might we revisit our institutions and industries to instigate systemic, positive change?

Despite advances in the proliferation of design thinking and human-centricity over the last couple of decades, the business world continues to suffer from a cloud of ambiguity concerning design's application in business. This ambiguity is exacerbated when the speed of the clock becomes exponentially faster, thanks to digital technology and increasing global connectivity.

Enter *Closing the Loop* where Sheryl Cababa leverages her more than two decades of diverse experiences to offer us clarity about this dilemma. While many design practitioners cite the virtues of being human-centric and making the end user the hero, Sheryl helps us understand the potential cascade of unintended consequences from every design and business decision. She opens our aperture.

As a design practitioner myself, I love that Sheryl implores us to question our own positionality, power, and privilege with a healthy dose of humility. Because, if we resort to the typical design-thinking process of empathizing with "end users" and imagining "solutions," we probably filter what we hear from people through our own myopic biases and create further harm.

Instead, by integrating system thinking into our approach, we can leverage alternative techniques, like using causal loop maps to study counterintuitive effects to really test our foundational assumptions. We can also push back on the prevalence of techno-optimism that doesn't consider unintended consequences, by leveraging tools like the futures wheel to study first- and second-order effects.

To rise above the fray of marketers marketing and consumers consuming, *Closing the Loop: Systems Thinking for Designers* provides us with a plethora of accessible frameworks to systematically address the "who, what, why, and how" behind our work. Consequently, we stand a better chance of shaping our preferred futures with better tools in hand through the rubrics that Sheryl provides.

The bottom line: This is probably the best body of work on systems thinking that I've run across in quite a while. Kudos to Sheryl!

—Kevin Bethune
Author, *Reimagining Design: Unlocking Strategic Innovation,*
and founder, dreams • design + life

INTRODUCTION

The Plastic Hour

For the first time in my generation, the COVID-19 pandemic is the first truly global event that has touched every single person in one way or another. The whole series of events and their impact on every layer of society is a reminder of how interconnected everything is. It shines a light on how the systems around us, from logistics to education to media to finance, are fragile and ill-designed to handle catastrophic events. In addition, some systems didn't even exist in the past. The COVID-19 virus spread undetected for months because most countries, including the U.S., lacked virus surveillance networks and other tracking mechanisms that might have curtailed the contagion.

With catastrophe, however, comes opportunity. The world is now recognizing the importance of shared global health communication, government and community social safety nets, and flexibility and adaptability in their economic systems. Moments of hope spring from moments of darkness, and a window opens that allows societies to question the way things work and to work toward something better. The philosopher Gershom Scholem referred to moments like this as "plastic hours": "Namely, crucial moments when it is possible to act. If you move then, something happens." The writer George Packer elaborated on this idea by saying, "In such moments, an ossified social order suddenly turns pliable, prolonged stasis gives way to motion, and people dare to hope."

For designers working in technology, this is a moment to act. Perhaps you are a UX designer working on digital products, or a service designer crafting experiences. You might be wondering how your work connects to the greater good, or how you as a designer can use design as a skill to work toward a world that is more fair, safe, equitable, and joyful for everyone, and not just those who hold power.

I've worked as a human-centered design practitioner for years, in product design, design research, and design strategy, both in-house and in consultancy. I've been a staunch believer that design, because of its focus on human connection, is a powerful force for impact. However, a few years ago, I came to realize that the tools we use in human-centered design are fairly narrow and may even cause harm. These tools can be used to consolidate, rather than disrupt power, to reinforce the status quo, and to harm those at the margins of society. On top of that, design methods are often used to employ, as the RSA noted, "efficiency innovations" rather than "empowering innovations."[1]

In response, I started broadening my lens and my methods to integrate tools, such as causal loop diagrams, that are typically associated with systems thinking. This has benefitted my practice in centering analysis on understanding problems by extending who I think of as stakeholders, broadening the ideas of what constitutes problem-solving, and gaining a more holistic view than I ever had as a UX designer. In practice, this means creating and using visual frameworks to map relationships and causality, essentially extending skills that many designers already employ, but through a systems lens. There's a quote that is often (I assume apocryphally) attributed to Albert Einstein: "If I had an hour to solve a problem I'd spend 55 minutes thinking about the problem and 5 minutes thinking about solutions."

There are times in which I combine ideas that are not necessarily explicit within systems-thinking literature. One of those concepts is positionality. Researcher positionality has been acknowledged, for example, by Horst Rittel and Melvin Webber in their foundational paper about wicked problems (though using different terms). It basically means that researchers and designers need to acknowledge their own background, perspectives, and biases in order to engage in the work accordingly. Additionally, systems thinking pushes designers to acknowledge other peoples' expertise—lived expertise as well as professional expertise—and involve and facilitate that knowledge. Participation in the process is key. Designers have the power to further empower others, and with this, they can all have a greater impact.

---

1   Rowan Conway, Jeff Masters, and Jake Thorold, "From Design Thinking to Systems Change: How to Invest in Innovation for Social Impact," The RSA in partnership with Innovate UK, July 2017.

CHAPTER 1

The Shortcomings of User-Centered Design

As a designer working in technology, I never thought I would see *Black Mirror,* the BBC show focused on a future of dystopian technologies, used for product inspiration.

I was in an ideation workshop with a client team that was working on a design strategy for augmented reality. We were talking about potential features and adding sticky notes with ideas to a whiteboard. During our discussion, we started talking about potential unintended consequences to features and design decisions. One of my colleagues brought up an example from the show *Black Mirror* in which soldiers, implanted with an augmented reality system, saw other humans as monsters that must be killed.

We discussed it for a bit, and everyone was quiet. Finally, one of our clients spoke up.

"Yeah, that's a good idea—add it to a note on the whiteboard."

"Add what?" my colleague asked.

"You know, the idea that people can use avatars and disguise themselves."

It was one of the key moments in which I realized that our methods—our user-centered design methods—were failing us.

We reminded our client that, no, *Black Mirror* wasn't meant to be a feature inspiration—rather, it's a cautionary tale. We reminded him that it's a good example of showing the ramifications of technology—that not all scenarios are good. And that even if he were thinking of it strictly from the technical problem-solving perspective, that the horror of it should give him pause.

It showed me that the ideation process was too myopic, too idealistic, and way too technology-solution-centered.

And so is the rest of user-centered design.

The design practice is experiencing a critical moment in time. Designers design products and services, especially in technology, that often have millions, and even billions, of users, yet they often fail to see design beyond individual users and the immediacy of their interactions with the products and services they work on. They often fail to anticipate and design for the impact on those who are not the direct users of their products, or for long-term effects on those they design for. And before that, they fail to clearly understand the problem space and the context in which their products will live.

In order to address the problems of user-centered design, you first need to understand what it is, why this is an approach that is widely used, and why it's so problematic in the first place.

The Beginnings of User-Centered Design

If you've ever seen a Dutch bike, known as an *omafiets*, you might notice that it's got quite a different design than the typical racing bike or modern commuter bike. Its handles are swept back, curved toward the rider in a way that keeps your arms and wrists free of pressure when you are sitting upright on the bike (see Figure 1.1). This type of bike is a good example of user-centered design: it's meant to make the act of riding the bike more comfortable and enjoyable. It's designed for the context in which these types of bikes are used, such as getting to work, carrying kids, running errands, all while wearing street clothes, which is quite a different context than, say, a racing bike. It's a design decision made more than a century ago that prioritizes how the rider experiences the bike. It does not appear to have prioritized a more efficient manufacturing process, or cheaper materials, although perhaps with the popularity of this design over time, these processes may have responded to the demand. Ultimately, it's a design that puts the user first.

IMAGE: TODD FAHRNER

FIGURE 1.1
A Dutch omafiets is a good example of a product designed with the user experience in mind.

This type of design, which prioritizes the user's experience, is certainly not new. However, a user-centered approach has not been inherent to, nor codified within, the design process, particularly in digital technology, until fairly recently. Much of the user-centered approach to design in the technology industry was pioneered by designers in the 1980s, and the spread of its ideas can be attributed to the writings of Donald Norman.

In his 1988 book, *The Design of Everyday Things*, Norman referred to a conceptual model that has three parts: a designer, a user, and a system. The interaction between the designer's decisions and a user's actions is facilitated through what he called a *system*, which, in this case, are objects and products. This book popularized the notion of conducting user-centered research and framed "good design" as that which is intentionally directed toward, and considerate of, a user's mental models of how things should work.

These ideas shaped the tenets of the modern user experience design practice. Designers in recent decades have rallied around and emphasized the importance of these ideas: *Designers must develop an understanding of end users by engaging with them directly through the course of their design decisions! They should emphasize ease of use and efficiency as it maps to a user's expectations!*

These were much needed advancements in the philosophy of product design, particularly as many products entered the digital realm. For example, think about many products—particularly electronics—that existed before the popularization of user-centered design: the first personal computers or VCRs when they initially appeared on the market. They were barely usable, with buttons and interfaces that were impossible to decipher. The approach that has brought us the iPhone, and the obsession with user-friendliness, was a much needed shift that users of digital products have all benefited from.

This approach has been built upon and articulated in a process known as *design thinking*, popularized by the Hasso Plattner Institute of Design at Stanford (also known as the *d.school*). The process was borrowed from a method called *challenge mapping* developed by Min Basadur, which sought to emphasize problem generation and concep-tualization prior to solution development.[1]

---

1   Min Basadur et al., "Discovering the Right Questions About the Management of Technology Using Challenge Mapping," Management of Innovation and New Technology Research Centre, 1998.

The five parts of the design-thinking process are typically articulated in the following way:

- **Empathize:** This phase emphasizes gaining empathy with your user and their situation, in order to understand the context in which your product or service will potentially solve something. It involves conducting foundational user research.

- **Define:** This phase is focused on taking your insights from the Empathize phase and synthesizing them to create problem statements, user journeys, or other aspects that will serve as a foundation for your ideas for solutions to your user's problems.

- **Ideate:** This phase is where designers brainstorm on possibilities for solving for the problems identified and articulated in the first two phases. Often, designers ask "How might we [solve for X]? to spur creative thinking around potential solutions.

- **Prototype:** Core to the design-thinking process is experimentation. This phase occurs when designers create quick versions of design solutions—they could be paper prototypes, digital, physical, or anything that is lightweight—to take to end users for testing purposes.

- **Test:** In this phase, designers test the prototypes with end users, so they can continue to learn, iterate, and refine.

This process has helped many organizations take a user-centered approach to product and service design and development. It has also gained broader appeal as business leaders can see their return on investment for user-centered design. Apple is a good example of a company whose products have had wild success due to their user-friendliness, and many apps and services, such as Airbnb, which was founded by designers, have become prominent and widely used. User advocacy has become core to business decision-making, which has been an advancement from the bad old days in which users of products were poorly understood, seen as just buyers, or considered to be an obstacle to a business's profits. An understanding of users has become essential.

And yet… this philosophy, with its thoughtful approach to how people interact with products, has led to a myopia in which designers—and others within organizations—have failed to recognize other consequences that fall outside the realm of the *direct use of the products they are designing*. There have always been outsize effects to both good and bad design. However, there is a growing sense among user-centered designers that the process does not address contextual understanding of people beyond just users, nor take into account impact at scale, nor acknowledge the complexity of the technology for which they are designing.

To clarify, there is nothing inherently wrong, per se, with the design-thinking process articulated previously. And, in fact, much of the criticism directed at the design process is actually related to how this process is *practiced*. For example, for the Empathize phase, the process itself does not necessarily prescribe *who* you need to empathize with. But in the practical and common execution of the Empathize phase, most practitioners are focused on one type of stakeholder only: the end user of a product. And this particular way, in which design thinking and UCD are commonly understood, informs how design is typically practiced far and wide.

Ultimately, there are three key problems with the approach and process of user-centered design that contribute to its shortcomings and lead to shortsightedness and potential unintended consequences.

- Users are viewed as nothing more than users.
- A user-centered approach does not acknowledge or address potential harm, and it limits the potential impact of design.
- A user-centered process does not inherently take into account the systemic forces.

Users Are *Not* Just Users

Users are multifaceted humans who affect others and are affected themselves by contexts that go beyond their relationship with the products they are designing.

Yet the approach in design is often oriented toward only the direct benefit of usage. Think about the tools that designers often use to create understanding about people: personas, user journeys, and user stories are common frameworks for synthesizing insight about users into something that can be used to make design decisions (see Figure 1.2).

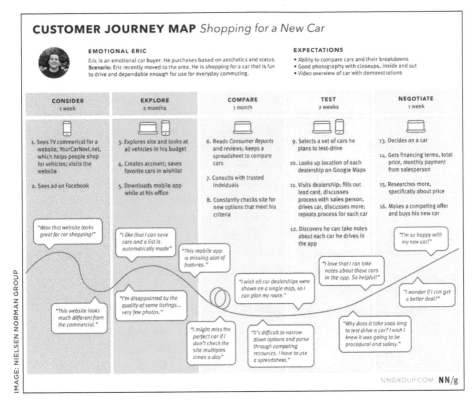

FIGURE 1.2

A typical user or customer journey map articulates the direct relationship between a person and the product.

These tools, such as the customer journey map, provide nuances about an individual's contextual situation as it applies to how they might perceive and interact with your product. They help articulate customer pain points when it comes to that product relationship, and they can be used to identify opportunities for making the product experience better. The commonality is that they tend to focus exclusively on an individual who might buy or use a specific product.

Take a mad lib that is popular in the product design process: As an [individual], I want to [do something] so that [I can achieve something]. Although it seems to take an outcome into account (the "so that" part of the statement), this mad lib is most often used to define software features. In most design processes, people are defined solely by their relationship with your product. This is the most efficient way to think about people—as users—but it narrows your purview of the ways their lives and situations interconnect with other people and circumstances.

In addition, designers tend to only design for a "typical" user. By focusing on a typical user, and trying to solve for their immediate needs, they can go through the motions of being a user advocate. Let's take a designer working on a social media platform. She's been tasked with designing a fun experience that allows users to look at their past year and enjoy photos and posts they may have forgotten about. Surfacing this experience keeps the users engaged and makes it fun and interesting for them to keep returning. She creates an experience: fun celebratory illustrations that include text that says, "It's been a great year! Thanks for being a part of it!" She engages evaluative testing to see which versions resonate most, and the feature goes live.

Although this is hypothetical, it is actually close to a feature that Facebook launched and continues to run. You may be familiar with the fallout from the platform's "Year in Review" feature. In 2014, designer and developer Eric Meyer wrote a blog post addressing his experience with this feature. Rather than surfacing a fun party, an amazing trip, an excellent meal, or any of the other scenarios that Facebook's designers may have considered, the Year in Review feature surfaced Meyer's most-interacted-with post: the photo that he posted when his six-year-old daughter, Rebecca, died of cancer. Instead of celebrating, he was forced to relive his grief over and over again every time he logged into Facebook, because this feature con-tinually surfaced in his feed for weeks on end. In writing about this experience, Meyer said, "The design is for the ideal user—the happy, upbeat, good-life user. It doesn't take other use cases into account."

The designers who worked on this feature almost certainly did not intend to cause this type of trauma for Meyer or other users like him. But they failed to consider people at the margins, who might not be having what they assumed to be the typical user experience.

The tools that designers use contribute to this "flattening" of people into users viewed in isolation of others. In addition, the narrow focus on ideal users, and a failure to recognize additional contexts, contrib-utes to unintended consequences time and time again.

User-Centered Harm and the Limited Impact of Design

In November 2020, design researcher Erika Hall tweeted, "This is all too often how UX design is considered and practiced." The image she referred to was an anglerfish, with its glowing lure marked "UX" and its mouth marked "business model" (see Figure 1.3).

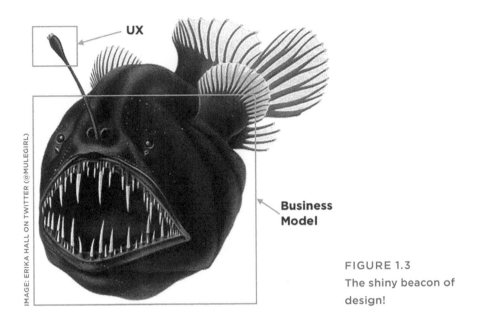

IMAGE: ERIKA HALL ON TWITTER (@MULEGIRL)

FIGURE 1.3
The shiny beacon of design!

When you consider many tech industry products, particularly those based on ad tech such as Facebook, this is an apt and depressing metaphor. Designers often create shiny, wonderfully interactive experiences that can lead to detrimental outcomes.

The UCD process does not take into account the impact that designers have on their users beyond their direct use of their product, and in fact, there are no codified tools that help designers think specifically about harm. The repercussions of this are vast, particularly in tech.

Take, for example, Instagram's infinite scroll. Aligning with tenets of persuasive design, Instagram's feed provides what twentieth century psychologist B.F. Skinner referred to as *variable rewards*.[2] The three components are described by writer Nir Eyal, a former proponent of addictive technology.[3] He outlined them as rewards of the tribe (validation by others), rewards of the hunt (satisfaction gained by searching for information), and rewards of the self (gratification through stimulation). Instagram's feed provides all of these things, with a touch of randomness that keeps its users engaged and interested.

Although users are constantly entertained by scrolling through for seconds, minutes, and hours, other outcomes aren't so wholesome. Teens are less happy, misinformation thrives, and users experience addiction to these products.

If you asked designers whether Instagram's infinite scroll constitutes good design, well, it would be hard to say *no* based on what makes user experience design successful. Is it easy to use? Yes. Does it satisfy and keep users engaged? Yes. Does it give people what they want from the product? Yes.

And yet, this feature, in keeping users glued to the product, can lead to harmful behaviors. Aza Raskin, who is often credited with (or blamed?) for the concept of infinite scroll, has said, "One of my lessons from infinite scroll: that optimizing something for ease-of-use does not mean best for the user or humanity."[4]

In another example, Tony Fadell, a former executive at Apple and founder of the thermostat company Nest, once remarked that he now regrets the design choices that his team made while designing the iPhone because of the destructive patterns of distraction,

---

2 Nir Eyal, "Variable Rewards: Want to Hook Users? Drive Them Crazy," nirandfar.com.

3 Nir Eyal wrote his book *Hooked: How to Build Habit-Forming Products* in 2014, before an increase in scrutiny directed at addictive, attention-capitalizing technologies. I describe him as a proponent of addictive technology because the book is an example of the kind of mindset that has encouraged designers and technologists to engage in brazen manipulation of their users. It honestly feels kind of gross to read in light of more recent studies about attention and technology. Though Eyal has since tried to address the problems of addiction, his more recent writing still puts the onus on technology users to address the problems of usage rather than technology companies.

4 András Juhász, "Is Infinite Scroll the Slot Machine of the New Generation?" Medium, September 19, 2020.

interruption, and digital addiction with which the device has been associated: "I wake up in cold sweats every so often thinking, what did we bring to the world?"

From a user-centered design perspective, those very decisions for the iPhone are wildly successful: engagement, ease of use, its fulfillment of users' needs and desires. On a societal level, it's a much more nuanced story: there are problems of distraction and addiction, as well as a pattern, particularly with teens, of deteriorating mental health associated with relationships with their smartphones. Unfortunately, the tools and methods of user-centered design make designers ill-equipped to address those nuances.

A key aspect worth acknowledging is that these examples are not about design gone wrong. It's very different when a product is created, and people are harmed because of flaws in the product or misunderstandings of how people might use it. These examples are not like Samsung phones catching fire. The technologists who worked on that did not intend for exploding phones to be an outcome. The difference between the Samsung phones and something like infinite scroll is that technologists intended the outcomes of infinite scroll to be a user spending more and more time in the product. In prioritizing the short-term goals that benefitted their product financially, they failed to account for the long-term harmful outcomes for individuals as well as for society.

It's important to recognize that the responsibility to do better does not just sit on the shoulders of designers. Everyone in an organization, particularly those empowered to make fundamental business decisions, is responsible for whether or not products have a positive impact on humanity. To return to the anglerfish metaphor, a fundamental problem is that a designer's influence only extends to the glowing lure, and the lure sits within the context of a harmful business model. It's not just a designer's job, but everyone's job, to consider context and actively strive to create less harmful products and services.

If organizations were shaped differently to prevent this deterministic use of design, then designers could be more empowered to use their skills to question the purpose of their work and think holistically about it.

UCD and Outside Forces

When conducting work with communities with whom I lack familiarity, whether in global health or regionally, I typically partner with practitioners from those communities to help give cultural context to our research work. This approach is not inherent to the user-centered design process, and adherents to the process are often willfully agnostic to the problem spaces and contexts for which they will later be tasked to design. This is hubris.

Although you can learn a lot by using the design process to "empathize" and "define," designers often fail to acknowledge their own blind spots and assumptions.

In his Medium article entitled "Stop Designing for Africa,"[5] designer Chris Elawa discussed the failure of the XO laptop, the device from the famed "One Laptop Per Child" initiative in the early 2000s. The initiative failed for a myriad of reasons. One key reason was that the designers and distributors did not understand the context of ownership: "The XO laptop was rejected by adults in African [low income economies] because it focused on empowering one child as opposed to providing value to a family or entire community." In addition, "Factors such as marketing, distribution, and funding do play a role in the relative success of a product designed for the socio-economic development of African [low-income economies]."

These factors are not typically considered through the course of user-centered design. An understanding of individual users can only take you so far. Now that designers, particularly in tech, are often designing in contexts for millions, and in some cases, billions of individuals, the practice needs better tools and processes to consider these challenges of consequence, context, and scale.

---

5   Chris Elawa, "Stop Designing for Africa (Part 2)," Medium, February 29, 2016.

CITY WARRENS VS. CITY GRIDS

If you've ever been to Belgium, you may have been charmed by the small medieval cities such as Bruges. These cities have canals and lovely little warrens of streets, none of which fall into any kind of discernible grid (see Figure 1.4). It's easy to get lost unless you know your way around.

IMAGE: THIERRY LEMAITRE

FIGURE 1.4
The narrow streets in Bruges are human-scaled.

continues

In contrast, you might visit a large American city, such as Chicago, and notice that the grid is a series of straight intersecting streets, wide arterial streets and straight, smaller residential streets. Often, you might not even need a map to figure out where you're going, as streets are in numerical order.

Why do these cities look like this?

In *Seeing Like a State*, James C. Scott pointed to the underlying reasons why each of these cities look the way they do. Medieval cities like Bruges were designed with the local resident in mind, and purposefully for confounding intruders. Those who most benefited from the small winding streets, close quarters, and strong external city walls were its residents. Its design was also reflective of a period in time when everyone traveled by foot. Fast forward a few centuries to when Chicago was first being developed. The grid benefitted residents to a certain extent (as it was easier to get around), but more importantly, it benefitted the government and its services and utilities: sewer and electrical grids, postal delivery, law enforcement, and activities such as census-taking.

A major example of this grid approach was the redesign of Paris between 1853 and 1869 by Baron Haussmann. In this huge public works project, his plan led to a razing of many dense and twisting neighborhoods to accommodate a series of boulevards: wide streets whose primary purpose was to expedite military units to tamp down insurrection.

Scott also pointed out that medieval cities, from a map view, look like a jumbled mess, whereas cities with a grid, such as New York or Chicago, almost appear to be designed primarily for a view from above, i.e., a God view. In a system, this points to whom the design benefits most: those who make decisions from the God view—politicians, bureaucrats, developers—and hold the most power; or those from the street view, who hold little power, and just live there.

Prompts to consider:

On one hand, a city grid prizes efficiency and can benefit citizens with order and quick responsiveness, such as mail delivery and sanitation. On the other hand, it can facilitate authoritarian control, such as deployment of the military or law enforcement in quashing dissent.

Imagining that you were involved in city planning, what could you ask yourself?

- How might you design to prioritize equity?
- How might you design to prioritize efficiency?

A Change in Perspective: Systems Thinking

Knowing about the variety of pitfalls in user-centered design, what is a designer to do? Given that so many tools of the practice represent the narrow philosophy inherent in UX and user-centered design, it's difficult to shift your mindset without also shifting the tools you use for problem-solving. Broadening your lens requires both a mindset shift and a shift in the tools that you use. Systems thinking is that mindset and contains your requisite set of tools and methods.

So, what is systems thinking? In *Systems Thinking for Social Change*, David Peter Stroh describes the practice as "the ability to understand ... interconnections in such a way as to achieve a desired purpose." What he acknowledges through this definition is that systems often do the opposite of achieving a desired purpose: sometimes the system achieves a purpose that is unintended, undesirable to most, or both unintended and undesirable.

For example, picture, as a system, a city's desire to decrease homelessness within its borders. The city spends money and resources toward attempts to solve the problem. Yet, unfortunately, homelessness continues to increase in the city, and despite its efforts, the city continues to increase its spending in this area. In this instance, the stakeholders within the city's government may need to ask themselves: Is our spending having an impact? Are there other interventions, or addressing of root cause, that we need to engage in? Are there actions that are exacerbating the problem? If homelessness continues to increase, then, harkening back to Stroh's definition, the system is not achieving the desired purpose.

Designing for Greater Impact

One of the most famous myths in animal lore is that lemmings collectively kill themselves by jumping off cliffs. It's a fanciful idea that definitely fascinated me in elementary school, leading my vivid imagination to picture cute little hamster-like animals dutifully marching toward a cliff edge, robot-like, and quietly plummeting to their deaths. (I never imagined them screaming because I had zero notion of what a lemming might sound like.) In case you were wondering, according to the Alaska Department of Fish and Game, this myth began after the release of a Disney nature documentary in the 1950s. Apparently, during the filming, "The lemmings supposedly committing mass suicide by leaping into the ocean were actually thrown off a cliff by the Disney filmmakers."[6] Monsters!

Despite its questionable origins, the lemming myth is often used as a metaphor for human behaviors. I find it useful to explain the benefits of systems thinking, a thought exercise around solving more broadly for certain problems. If, as a designer, you were faced with the problem of lemmings throwing themselves off a cliff en masse, you could take a couple of different approaches to reducing the harm. You could set up a lemming clinic at the bottom of the cliff and treat lemmings that were injured, or had survived the fall, maybe even catching some as they were falling. Or, you could build a barrier, a fence, at the top of the cliff to prevent them from falling in the first place.

It's a good parallel for the way that many of our institutions, both public and private, often approach complex problems. Lots of investment is spent at the bottom of the cliff, treating symptoms or the results of problems, rather than at the top of the cliff, on preventive measures. This plays out in many domains that have "wicked problems," a term coined by Horst Rittel, a design professor at Ulm School of Design in 1973.[7] Wicked problems include unique, multidimensional issues such as climate change, homelessness, public health crises, and extreme poverty. As the Interaction Design Foundation described it, they are often "problems with many interdependent factors making them *seem* impossible to solve."

Often in the design practice, the course of problem-solving is already determined. I've had multiple client organizations clarify—as my team and I were conducting foundational research to understand a problem space—that they already knew that the solution would take a digital form, that it would solve a specific acute problem, and that inquiry into other spaces was not needed because of that. This narrow and deterministic focus often leads to solutions that have minor impact.

Take, for example, solutions that are meant to reduce youth homelessness. One can treat the issues that young people face *once they are homeless*: a lack of shelter and safety, inaccessibility to healthcare and other resources, and a myriad of services that are confusing and

---

6 I love that Alaska's Department of Fish and Game have addressed the issues of Disney's lies in an article on their website. Riley Woodford, "Lemming Suicide Myth," Alaska Department of Fish and Game, September 2003.

7 "Wicked Problems" definition from Interaction Design Foundation: www.interaction-design.org/literature/topics/wicked-problems#.

dispersed. In the lemmings metaphor, this would be positioning the solutions at the bottom of the cliff. A preventive approach would be to address the issues that would keep young people from becoming homeless in the first place: increased housing or family stability, financial and educational support, a culture that protects LGBTQ youth, an end to institutional racism, and many other interventions, both narrow and broad.

The beauty of systems thinking is that it allows designers to access multiple forms of potential intervention as possibilities, even if, as a designer, you may have the skill set to design for only some areas of intervention. Acknowledging the diversity of possible interventions within a problem space, both preventive and treatment-focused, enables designers and their stakeholders to take a broader lens, and perhaps consider alternate areas of investment or direct ideas oriented toward policymaking and other domains, involving the appropriate experts. In the meantime, if a designer is, for example, a digital experience expert, she can more accurately focus on the most meaningful execution of her intervention space, while understanding the broader context in which that digital solution or experience will sit.

What Systems Thinking Is Made Of

In relation to the ability to understand interconnections, there are several methods that comprise systems thinking. The act of systems thinking, according to researchers Samir Patel and Khanjan Mehta in their comparative study on design frameworks, is focused on "not any one thing, but a set of tools, habits, and practices that help in mapping dynamic complexities. Systems thinking focuses on the cyclical cause and effects, as opposed to linear cause and effect relationships."[8] Often, in the methods employed in the design practice, designers are essentially required to engage in linear thinking. For example, in product design, think about the typical product lifecycle process. From a high level, it consists of four steps: introduction, growth, maturity, and decline. Similarly, many expressions of user journeys or experience mapping follow a linear process of product use. Systems thinking, through its focus on cycles, as well as radiating effects, extends designers' thinking beyond just the linear format. It requires you to recognize that problems aren't solved

---

8   S. Patel and K. Mehta, "Systems, Design, and Entrepreneurial Thinking: Comparative Frameworks," *Systemic Practice and Action Research* 30.5 (2017).

and done: in fact, solutions feed back into a cycle of effects, and could cause problems themselves, or create cycles of positive outcomes.

If you connect these ideas to some of the outcomes of user-centered design, this approach of focusing on system goals and intercon-nectedness can help avoid the shortcomings—the narrow view of "users," the limited impact, the unacknowledged outside forces—and create very different conversations from the outset, which automati-cally prioritize multiple views of a problem space. And, in fact, when designers consider systems, they can utilize their skills in design thinking to further and more thoughtfully think about how to *change* the system.

Takeaways

- User-centered design, when it was first developed, was a much-needed advancement in prioritizing the users of products and services. As time progressed, and prod-ucts and services became more complex, its limitations became apparent.

- Some of the shortcomings of user-centered design include: an assumption that users are only users, that the practice of user-centered design fails to acknowledge potential harms and limits the potential impact of design, and that it fails as a process to account for wider forces.

- A response to the shortcomings of UCD is combining design with systems thinking, which prioritizes a focus on understanding interconnections, recognizes multiple forms of intervention, and articulates whether system goals are meeting the outcomes we want as a society.

A Systems-Thinking Mindset

When my daughter was a toddler, she had a picture book with a fable of seven mice and an elephant. The mice could not see, and as each of them approached the elephant, they each thought it was a different object. The mouse closest to the elephant's ear thought the elephant was a fan. The trunk was a snake to another mouse, the back was a cliff to the third mouse, and the tail was a vine to the fourth. Each mouse was absolutely convinced it was correct, and that the other mice were completely wrong. Unable to grasp that these parts might make up something bigger, the mice were literally unable to see the elephant in the room.[1] (See Figure 2.1.)

FIGURE 2.1
Surprise! It's an elephant!

As you've seen in Chapter 1, "The Shortcomings of User-Centered Design," the typical user-centered design approach focuses on the user alone. It aims to gain an understanding of the individuals who

---

1   A couple of things worth knowing about this fable. First, it is based on a traditional parable from Hindu, Jain, and Buddhist texts, often referred to as *The Blind Men and the Elephant*, used as a metaphor to explain people's relationships to the truth. Second, it's not a very kind story about a disability, so a less ableist version of the story involves seven men at night, encountering a statue and trying to figure out what it is. I like to think that the mice in my daughter's book were encountering the elephant at night as well.

use a product or service: their context, needs, and challenges. It's a good example of *bounded rationality*, a systems-thinking concept that you'll learn about in Chapter 5, "Synthesis and Mapping Stakeholders." In many ways, these designers are like the mice, because they only focus narrowly on the one area that they understand. Yet with complex problems like those in healthcare, education, and technology, the user is just one part of a larger ecosystem of stakeholders—a single player in a series of causal and correlating events. For designers, the first step is to reach beyond user-centered design and approach systemic problems with systems thinking.

Systems thinking recognizes the elephant for what it is: a whole system. It is a methodology for considering the whole problem space, rather than seeing problems in isolation. Examining challenges through a comprehensive and multidisciplinary lens helps designers identify root causes and create interventions with the most impact.

So why is it important to understand problems and context more broadly? Why can't designers just solve the problems right in front of them? As you've seen in Chapter 1, this type of narrowly focused approach can lead to problematic outcomes, and worse, because of the scale at which many technology products operate, negative societal impact and unintended consequences. Knowing that many design decisions happen within a larger system of decisions helps designers not only make better choices, but also activates a combination of their design skills and systemic understanding to align and facilitate other stakeholders to drive change.

We've all seen what happens when systems go awry. That knowledge should motivate designers to want to effect positive change.

A Real-World Case

Take, for example, the beginning of the global pandemic in March of 2020. The world had a huge problem on its hands: COVID-19, a coronavirus that originated in the vicinity of Wuhan province, China. Countries began shutting their borders, and before anyone could digest what was happening, many cities, states, and countries initiated wide-ranging lockdowns of schools, businesses, and institutions to prevent the spread of the deadly virus.

As the virus continued to spread, hospitals and healthcare settings in cities like New York and regions like Lombardy, Italy, experienced a flood of COVID patients, and as a result, experienced enormous pressure not only to care for these patients in crisis, but also to keep their employees safe through minimizing their exposure to the virus. What was clear was that because of the sudden demand, there was not enough personal protective equipment (PPE), such as high-filtration masks, gloves, gowns, and face shields to go around.

In Belgium, where COVID cases were soaring and COVID-related deaths among the elderly were statistically some of the highest anywhere in the world, the lack of PPE was clearly a crisis.

An organization of designers, led by artist and designer Dries Verbruggen, decided that they could use their skills to help increase the production and distribution of PPE. Calling themselves Creatives tegen Corona (in English, Creatives Against Coronavirus, CtC for short), they created open-source patterns for PPE that could be used in automated manufacturing processes.[2] (See Figure 2.2.) Connecting their skills with their networks in textiles, fashion, manufacturing, and medical fields, they were able to coordinate the manufacturing of more than 100,000 pieces of PPE.[3] They worked with small local ateliers as well as larger companies such as Bioracer, which typically makes cycling performance wear, to respond to the demand for protective gear.

This approach is a form of systems thinking. CtC saw a complex problem with potentially dire outcomes—a lack of PPE caused by a myriad of issues, from supply chains to political barriers—that could literally lead to death. And their approach as designers was interesting: rather than thinking about designing and creating the PPE themselves, they sought out a more effective point of intervention by providing the patterns for PPE to organizations that could be better equipped to mass-produce them. An essential aspect of systems thinking for designers is going beyond the usual design output—making an end product—and considering various points of intervention, some of which may require the expertise of others. CtC took an approach that applied their design creativity with a systems lens.

---

2   Dries Verbruggen, "Open Source Protective Garments by Creatives tegen Corona," Wikifactory.com, 2020.

3   Nick Compton, "Paola Antonelli and Alice Rawsthorn on Design as a Powerful Tool of Change," *Wallpaper**, September 25, 2020.

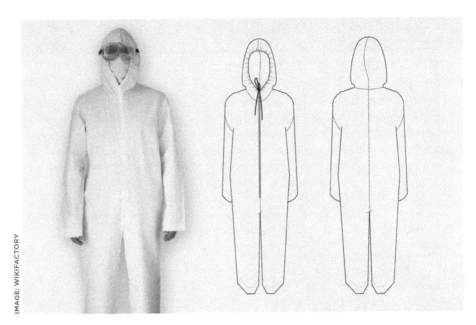

FIGURE 2.2

An innovative pattern for PPE was created by Creatives tegen Corona.

As Alice Rawsthorn, design critic and curator of the *Design Emergency* interview series, said, "The ingenuity, resourcefulness, courage, dedication, and generosity displayed by so many designers—professional and otherwise—has demonstrated what design can do to change our lives for the better."[4] She went on to describe design as a practice that can have value by "tackling complex social, political, and ecological problems."

Many designers express an interest in improving societal conditions, in having a positive impact through their work. Systems thinking is a way for you to increase your impact as a designer by broadening your lens to include the types of problems, solutions, and stakeholders that are normally outside of the purview of your practice.

---

4   Meghna Mehta, "Design Emergency Discusses Innovations That Are Crucial in the Age of Pandemic," *StirWorld*, August 11, 2020.

THE SYSTEM OF SYSTEMS THINKING

Lots of formal and semiformal forms of systems disciplines exist. In *Systems Thinking for Social Change*, Stroh lists some of these schools of systems thinking: "general systems theory, complexity theory, system dynamics, human system dynamics, and living systems theory." You could pile even more theory and framework on top of this: systems engineering, ecological systems theory, biological systems engineering, and system design. Many of these disciplines have some overlap with the more generalized form of systems thinking that you will encounter in this book, but it is important not to conflate them, particularly because some, such as systems design or systems engineering, are specific to scientific fields of engineering.

Systems thinking is often divided into two categories: hard systems-thinking methodology and soft systems-thinking methodology. According to management scientist Peter Checkland, hard systems thinking includes concepts such as systems engineering. This approach is "based upon the assumption that the problem task they tackle is to select an efficient means of achieving a known and defined end."[5] Examples include taking a systemic approach to creating efficiencies for manufacturing or military planning.

Soft systems methodology, on the other hand, is focused on understanding the problem space and creating a holistic view of it and possible ways to improve it. "A 'problem situation' is first analyzed and a 'rich picture' of the situation is built up. The aim is not to delimit particular problems 'out there' in the real world, but to gain an understanding of '...a situation in which various actors may perceive various aspects to be problematical.'"[6] (See Figure 2.3.)

In addition, Checkland points to "making drawings" through activities like Rich Picture Building to be a core aspect of soft systems methodology: "Pictures can be taken in as a whole and help to encourage holistic rather than reductionist thinking about a situation."[7]

---

5   Peter B. Checkland, "The Origins and Nature of 'Hard' Systems Thinking," *Journal of Applied Systems Analysis* 5.2 (1978).

6   Michael C. Jackson and P. Keys, "Towards a System of Systems Methodologies," *Journal of Operational Research Society* 35 (1984).

7   Peter Checkland, *Systems Thinking, Systems Practice* (Wiley, 1999).

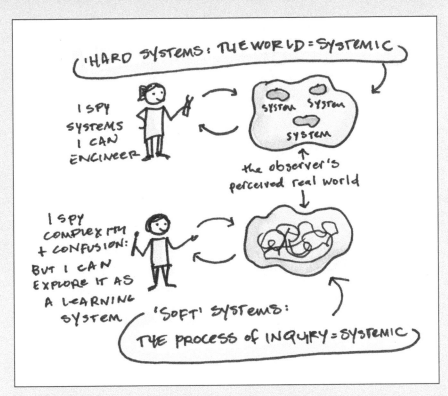

'HARD SYSTEMS: THE WORLD = SYSTEMIC

I SPY SYSTEMS I CAN ENGINEER

SYSTEM SYSTEM
SYSTEM

the observer's perceived real world

I SPY COMPLEXITY + CONFUSION: BUT I CAN EXPLORE IT AS A LEARNING SYSTEM

'SOFT' SYSTEMS: THE PROCESS OF INQUIRY = SYSTEMIC

FIGURE 2.3
Checkland drew the difference between how practitioners perceive hard systems versus soft systems, and how it results in differing approaches.

With this definition, the focus of the methods in this book fall into the category of "soft" systems, as they reflect the idea that building an understanding of the complexity of existing systems, of the problem space, is fundamental to figuring out ways of improving the status quo. The idea is that mapping, or "making drawings" as Checkland described it, also aligns with the types of visual facilitation skills and strengths that designers can employ when engaging in systems thinking.

The Benefits of Systems Thinking

Throughout this book, you will learn about tools that you can incorporate in your design practice to integrate systems thinking in your approach. However, it is critical to remember that it starts with a mindset. Systems thinking shifts your perspective and assumptions—through the course of your work as a designer, and about what you should consider and why. Once you adopt the systems-thinking mindset, then the tools become a vehicle for being able to act on that mindset.

Core to the systems-thinking mindset are two themes.

- Problem spaces are often more expansive than what you might typically consider as a designer.
- Questioning the framing of a problem space is central to broadening your lens.

Expanding the Problem Space

In the classic movie *Enter the Dragon*, Bruce Lee said, "It's like a finger pointing a way to the moon. Do not concentrate on the finger, or you'll miss all the heavenly glory" (see Figure 2.4). When you, as a designer, focus on immediate users and needs, you are concentrating on the finger. If you broaden your outlook and understand the system and design for it, you are shooting for the moon, and you can have a greater societal impact.

The systems-thinking mindset begins with the view that, for whatever it is you're designing, be it a product or service, platform or communication, users are just one small part of the wide universe of stakeholders you should be considering. Likewise, designing intentionally for just direct experiences by an individual user is only one small part of the impact you could be having, whether positive or negative.

Systems-thinking theorist Russell Ackoff created interactive planning, a framework to respond to how organizations can address what he called "messes": systems of interdependent problems. One of the principles of interactive planning is what he described as "the participative principle." This framework encourages the involvement of all possible system stakeholders within various phases of the planning process. These stakeholders include not just organizational stakeholders, but also those who are within the system and affected by its problems. Putting this tenet in experience design terms, these stakeholders could be those whom you think of as users, or broadened to those who are affected by various parts of the system, those who have an impact on the system, decision-makers, and those who are potentially harmed by, or benefit from, the way the system works.

IMAGE: BRUCELEE.COM

FIGURE 2.4
Bruce Lee explains systems thinking to a student in *Enter the Dragon*. (Or at least that's what I'd like to think.)

In addition to expanding whom you involve and seek to understand, systems thinking also shifts and expands your area of focus as a designer. Designer Boon Yew Chew created a comparison of user experience design versus systems thinking that helps position the difference in mindset (see Figure 2.5).

In essence, systems thinking helps you recognize factors that may have been invisible to you as a designer, but have impact on your outcomes. This recognition helps you become better at broadening your problem-solving.

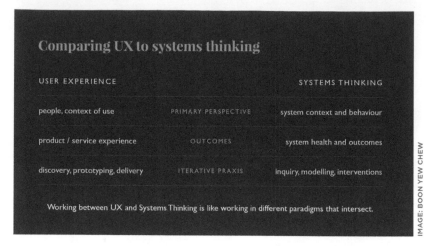

Comparing UX to systems thinking

USER EXPERIENCE		SYSTEMS THINKING
people, context of use	PRIMARY PERSPECTIVE	system context and behaviour
product / service experience	OUTCOMES	system health and outcomes
discovery, prototyping, delivery	ITERATIVE PRAXIS	inquiry, modelling, interventions

Working between UX and Systems Thinking is like working in different paradigms that intersect.

FIGURE 2.5

While user experience is focused on the context of use around a product or service, systems thinking is focused on understanding the context of a system and its outcomes.

Questioning the Framing

Between 2017 and 2018, Seattle had as many as four different dock-less bike share programs operating in the city. Walking through my neighborhood near the University of Washington, you might encounter orange, bright green, yellow, and red bikes that were parked anywhere and everywhere. A subscriber to one of the bike share programs could unlock a bike by using an app, and after their ride, park and lock it in various neighborhoods throughout the city (see Figure 2.6).

As a cyclist, I liked having the bikes around. A friend of mine thought otherwise. "They're in piles all over the place," he said. "They're basically litter!"

I asked him what he thought of cars parked all over the neighborhood. "I mean, think about the space that cars take up on the street versus the bikes," I said. He thought about it for a minute. "It's true, the bikes take up a lot less space when you compare them to cars." He explained that he hadn't thought about it that way, and concluded that maybe the bikes weren't as bad as he initially thought.

FIGURE 2.6
A variety of Seattle bikeshare bikes in 2018.

My friend was thinking of the bikes as a nuisance, as stationary objects. I had always looked at them as transportation, as an easy-to-access replacement for cars. He wasn't necessarily wrong about them being kind of messy, parked all over the place, but reframing helped him look at the issue in a more nuanced way.

This kind of consideration of how issues or problems are framed is important in systems thinking. It helps you think beyond a deter-mined set of solutions, or a simplistic read of the problem space. It also helps designers imagine possibilities beyond their own capabili-ties. You've probably been in ideation sessions with other designers. If the room is filled with designers who primarily work in the digital space, you can guarantee that, even if the ideation prompt is oriented around, say, improving transportation, there will be half a dozen ideas that primarily revolve around mobile apps. This issue is incred-ibly common in tech and design.

The pervasiveness of this technology-determinant mindset is exemplified by a story from *Being Mortal* by doctor and writer Atul Gawande. In it, he describes the results of an 18-month study focused on geriatric care for patients older than 70. As compared to patients who received standard care, patients who had received care from a geriatric team were "a quarter less likely to become disabled and half as likely to develop depression. They were 40 percent less likely to require home health services."[8]

Gawande continues:

> These were stunning results. If scientists came up with a device—call it an automatic defrailer—that wouldn't extend your life but would slash the likelihood you'd end up in a nursing home or miserable with depression, we'd be clamoring for it... Medical students would be jockeying to become defrailulation specialists, and Wall Street would be bidding up company stock.
>
> Instead, it was just geriatrics.

Geriatric care is an example of a different way of looking at and solving the problem, as opposed to what is typical in the UX design practice. Integrating different points of problem-solving—things like incremental care and wraparound services—are often beyond a UX designer's capabilities. So what is a designer to do? If, within the course of analysis and synthesis, designers uncover potential design approaches that are beyond UX design, they need to engage a diversity of stakeholders with expertise aside from those within design and technology. For example, in healthcare, these stakeholders could include experts in public health policy, researchers, and lived experts: those who operate within and are affected by the system.

Designers should use their skills oriented around design as a form of problem-solving to go beyond techno-solutionism. Understanding a system and all its potential touchpoints, as well as points of intervention, is a way of questioning the framing of both the problem space and where you as a designer can intervene.

---

8 Atul Gawande, *Being Mortal: Medicine and What Matters in the End* (Metropolitan Books, 2014).

A TREE-LINED STREET

In June of 2020, a deadly heat wave descended on the Pacific Northwest. Cities including Portland and Seattle experienced temperatures higher than 104°F/40°C during the course of three days. Given that cities in the Northwest are those in North America with the least amount of air-conditioning in residential environments, hundreds of people died as the result of the oppressive heat in Oregon, Washington, and British Columbia.

In Portland, for example, some neighborhoods clocked outdoor temperatures exceeding 116°F/46°C. The neighborhoods with the highest temperatures correlated with lower-income neighborhoods, many of which were also populated by Black residents. In Lents, one of the city's poorest communities, the temperature was as high as 124°F/51°C.

Why were these neighborhoods so much hotter than others? There are simply many more trees in wealthier and whiter neighborhoods than in poor Black, Latino, and Asian neighborhoods. Alejandra Borunda wrote in *National Geographic*, "A well-placed tree...can keep a building 18 degrees cooler than if it were fully exposed to the sun." And trees that provide shade can lower surface temperatures by up to 45 degrees (25 in Celsius) on a hot day.

The reason that lower-income Black, Latino, and Asian neighborhoods have fewer trees is the result of years and years of systemic decision-making by cities. For example, in Los Angeles, trees in public spaces were just not prioritized over the last century, confining much of urban foliage to private property. Wealthier property owners could afford the planting, maintenance, and upkeep of city trees, while dense, poorer areas relied on public spaces to provide foliage. In addition, "Trees were felled or trimmed to allow street surveillance by L.A. police helicopters." The result was that in the poorest neighborhoods like Huntington Park, there was less than 10 percent tree coverage, whereas in more affluent Los Feliz, there was approximately 40 percent coverage (see Figure 2.7). Vivek Shandas, an urban ecologist at Portland State University, has written about "urban heat islands": places that have lots of asphalt, lack foliage, and are close to parking lots and freeways.

continues

IMAGE: BART JAILLET

FIGURE 2.7
In the richer areas, like Los Feliz, California, trees are plentiful.

What does this lack of greenery correlate with? It correlated with housing discrimination, specifically redlining, which refers to the discriminatory city maps that prevented people in predominantly Black neighborhoods, from being able to get mortgages, and existed in more than 200 U.S. cities for much of the twentieth century. That practice, designed by the U.S. federal government, has resulted in lasting racial disparities, including, of course, fewer trees in nonwhite and immigrant neighborhoods. Shandas said, "You just don't see green in the areas that were redlined."

Having access to nature, greenery, and the positive health effects of being near greenery are benefits that everyone should have, regardless of their race or income.

Prompts to consider:

- What does your neighborhood look like when it comes to trees and other foliage? Does this align with the racial makeup of your town or city?

- If you were a city planner, what might you do to improve the conditions in neighborhoods that lack foliage?

- What are other visible signs of systemic discrimination in your city?

Three Concepts of Systems Thinking

Key to systems thinking are three concepts. As a systems thinker, you are concerned with analyzing and designing for contexts beyond just the product, features, or service on which you, as a designer, typically focus. These three concepts—wholeness, causality, and interconnectedness—are essential to this broader lens you will be applying to your work (see Figure 2.8).

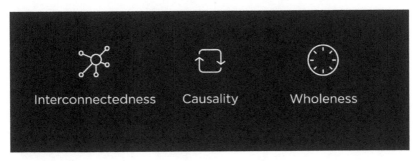

Interconnectedness   Causality   Wholeness

FIGURE 2.8
Three concepts that are central to systems thinking are interconnectedness, causality, and wholeness.

These three concepts shift the focus of the design process from the user and the product to the system and outcomes. Each one is critical to the systems-thinking mindset.

Wholeness: How Parts Create the Whole

The first concept of systems thinking is the consideration of the whole of a system and not just the parts.

An example of a large system is global shipping logistics. Our access to goods the world over is dependent on global shipping. You only need to look at the labels of your clothing, appliances, and electronics to understand that much of what you have in your home has come from somewhere else, and likely, via boat or freight. If you are worried about global warming, this should concern you. Global shipping accounts for at least three percent of global carbon dioxide emissions, and in fact, if global shipping were a country, it would be the sixth largest polluter on earth.[9]

---

9   Isabelle Gerretsen, "Shipping Is One of the Dirtiest Industries. Now It's Trying to Clean Up Its Act," CNN, October 3, 2019.

In 2017, a student named Mirjam de Bruijn at Design Academy Eindhoven thought about this problem and how she, as a designer, could help solve it.[10] She considered how much of common household and beauty products were water: for shampoo and conditioner, for example, it could be anywhere between 80 and 95 percent water.[11] Her creative thinking led her to consider how the design of these products could shift if they were shipped without water, and if instead, water were added by the person who purchased the products for use. The result of her investigation was a project called *Twenty*, which was intended to provoke thinking about how the design of products needs to take into account the cost of shipping (see Figure 2.9).

FIGURE 2.9
Mirjam de Bruijn's Twenty project. The shapes are solid products to which water needs to be added. Practical and beautiful!

10 Katharine Schwab, "This Incredibly Simple Packaging Idea Could Reduce Global Emissions," *Fast Company*, October 16, 2017.

11 Amanda Ogle, "5 Reasons to Ditch Your Shampoo Bottle for a Shampoo Bar," *National Geographic*, August 16, 2018.

Her project is a good example of how designers can go beyond the act of designing products or packaging for use. While she still considered the aesthetic appeal of the products to consumers, her primary concern was how she could use design to have an impact on the system of shipping and improve outcomes by shrinking the carbon footprint of the products she designed. She took a more holistic view of the space in which her product would sit.

What should designers ask themselves in order to take a similar approach? You might want to better understand, as systems-thinking scholar Donella Meadows said in *Thinking in Systems*, whether you are looking at a system or "a bunch of stuff." A good metaphor that she used described the elements of a system as the elements of a tree: roots, trunk, branches, and leaves. These elements aren't just sitting in the same place; they play a role with one another and affect one another. A prompt that can help clarify whether something is a system: Do the parts together produce an effect that is different from the effect of each part on its own?

In Mirjam de Bruijn's project, the shape and contents of a product's packaging have an effect on the ease, cost, and weight of shipping. The weight of shipping has an impact on fuel use. The fuel use has an impact on carbon emissions. This is a way of considering different elements as a whole: a holistic look at the context in which your decisions as a designer might sit.

Systems-Thinking Pluralism

It is possible that there could be conflicting views of what constitutes a holistic view of a system. This idea refers to the concept of systems-thinking pluralism: that the boundaries of a system can be disputed, and that they rely on the differing perspectives of various stakeholders. Systems scientist Michael C. Jackson, who theorized that systems thinking itself contains a system that he called *system of system methodologies* (SOSM for short),[12] considered pluralism an important aspect of postmodern systems practice. He argued that systems practitioners need to think critically about their own positionality and perspective:

---

12 It's not a surprise that a practice like systems thinking, which has a focus on increasing levels of abstraction, would have multiple layers of meta analysis directed at the practice itself!

> A critical approach [is] more suitable "to social systems where there are great disparities in power and in resources and which seem to 'escape' the control and understanding of the individuals who create and sustain them."[13]

Essentially, there are decision-makers—and even you, as a practitioner—who may be unaware of how you benefit from or are incentivized by how the system currently works, and in order to engage in proper analysis, you need to understand your positionality. He goes further, noting that "pluralism needs the support and 'ethical alertness' if it is to be able to justify the recommendations for improvement it delivers."

In short, if this perspective were to be applied to designers acting as systems practitioners, it contributes to your and your stakeholders' perspectives on what constitutes a holistic view of a system. It is critical to resolve the various boundaries and biases that stakeholders bring to the table, to examine your own position, and to consider what will be ethically correct when it comes to making change. (See Chapter 3, "Systems Thinking and Design Thinking," for further discussion on designer positionality and privilege.)

Interconnectedness: How Elements and Efforts Are Connected

The second concept central to systems thinking is interconnectedness, which is how you consider how elements and efforts are connected.

Here's an example of how built systems and nature are connected. Architect Julia Watson studies indigenous building systems. These often involve ancient technologies that promote integration with nature. For example, she points to how the Khasi, an indigenous community in the forests of northern India, build natural bridges from woven tree branches.[14] (See Figure 2.10.) People train the roots to grow in a certain direction collectively and over time. Watson describes this effort as generational thinking: "So people are planning where these trees are growing generations before. And once they reach a large enough height, then they start this process of the weaving and the

---

13 Michael C. Jackson, "Pluralism in Systems Thinking and Practice," in *Multimethodology: The Theory and Practice of Combining Management Science Methodologies*, ed. John Mingers and Anthony Gill (Wiley, 1997), chapter 13.

14 Amy Frearson, "Indigenous Technologies 'Could Change the Way We Design Cities' says environmentalist Julia Watson," Dezeen, February 11, 2020.

scaffolding and the training across the actual river. And then it's up to everybody to take care and maintain how that growth happens until about 50 years. And then you can start to walk across them."[15]

FIGURE 2.10
A bridge built by the Khasi people, Meghalaya, India, is a good example of the theme of interconnectedness.

According to Watson, "This is about symbiotic relationships, which are the fundamental building blocks of nature. These LO–TEK technologies are born of symbiotic relationships with our environment, humans living in symbiosis with natural systems."

The indigenous groups building these structures are constantly thinking about connections: the way nature and humans are networked together, as well as the way human generations connect with each other. Their stakeholders are much broader than those typically considered in a typical industry-based design project: they include nature and its elements, as well as future generations.

---

15 Manoush Zomorodi, Diba Mohtasham, and Sanaz Meshkinpour, "Julia Watson: What Can We Learn from Indigenous Design Developed over Generations?," TED Radio Hour, NPR, February 5, 2021.

In addition, natural systems—ecosystems—serve as inspiration for thinking about interconnectedness. If you think about a single tree, it has its elements: roots, trunk, branches, and leaves. Beyond that, trees form a root network with other trees, and effectively communicate through their roots to sustain and repair the trees, or parts of the network. Each of these elements connect with and rely on how the other elements function, and also balance in a way that sustains itself.

If you are a UX designer working on large digital technology systems, all the elements of the system in which you are designing probably have an effect on each other. You are also likely considering your user, and not necessarily the rest of a network of stakeholders. Designers within the industry can benefit from thinking like the Khasi people: understanding the variety of stakeholders who are affected by your design decisions, both positively and negatively, helps strengthen your design decisions, as well as expand your thinking in a way that goes beyond the direct benefit of use.

Causality: How One Thing Leads to Another

There is a running joke in my practice that some of my colleagues tease me about as I'm talking about outcomes and unintended consequences in my speaking engagements. When it comes to the Q&A that follows my talks, designers often ask about things like why tech companies have certain business models, or why companies don't make better decisions when it comes to societal outcomes. In the way that all roads lead to Rome, my answers eventually go down the same path: "Because capitalism!" (See Figure 2.11.)

This is an example of root cause, which is something that you will likely uncover through your systems analysis. Root cause analysis is an aspect of causality, which is the third concept central to systems thinking. Arriving at root cause is the result of thinking about cause and effect several degrees away from your area of focus. You might not be able to do anything about the system of capitalism, but you can go further in your analysis than you might typically consider, opening up avenues for change that you might not have previously imagined.

FIGURE 2.11
My "Because Capitalism." sticker reminds me that all roads lead to Rome.

As you attempt to understand a system, the concept of causality can lead you in two different directions, depending on your starting point. For example, you might start with an event and move backward from that event to uncover the root cause. You might also move in the opposite direction, starting with the same event and identifying other further events caused by that starting event. These are called *radiating effects*.

Here's an example. In 2020, in the midst of the global coronavirus pandemic, the world was jarred awake by the murders, at the hands of police, of Breonna Taylor and George Floyd. George Floyd's murder, in particular, was the catalyst for worldwide protests against police brutality and demands for racial justice. In the midst of this awakening, I noticed an image circulating on Twitter. It depicted an iceberg: at the top of the iceberg, above the water, the description read "George Floyd." Beneath the water, a series of conditions were listed, including "no universal healthcare," "racist justice system," "mass incarceration," among others (see Figure 2.12). The anonymous author of this graphic concluded that the events that you saw above the water—George Floyd's murder, followed by "riots and looting"—were the visible results of the underlying conditions that made up the majority of the iceberg.

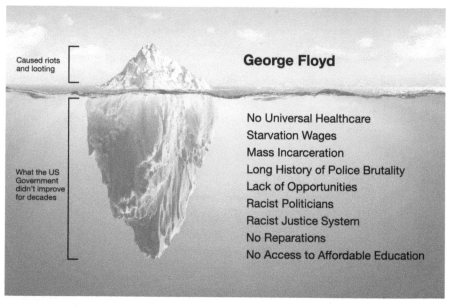

FIGURE 2.12

A systems-thinking iceberg focused on systemic racism that made the rounds on social media in 2020.

The iceberg metaphor is common in systems thinking as a way of, according to Stroh, "distinguishing problem symptoms from underlying or root causes."[16] By understanding root cause in the example from the events related to George Floyd, you can see that in order to effect meaningful change, you cannot just react or respond to the events. You must address the system structure: the trends or patterns of behavior that led to those symptomatic events.

---

16 David Peter Stroh, *Systems Thinking for Social Change: A Practical Guide to Solving Complex Problems, Avoiding Unintended Consequences, and Achieving Lasting Results* (Chelsea Green Publishing, 2015).

Likewise, you may need to understand the radiating effects that stem from potential changes to the system structure. What other symptoms are revealed by, for example, a racist justice system? In addition, what have been, and might be, the radiating effects from the racial justice protests of the summer of 2020? This type of analysis focused on cause-and-effect can increase your ability to think more broadly about understanding the problem space and how to effect change on multiple levels.

Expanding the Potential for Change

In OpenLearn's "Strategic Planning: Systems Thinking in Practice" course, they point to a good example of how systems thinking can expand your view of causality. At the turn of the twentieth century, rail crashes in England were killing far too many people. As a governmental response, draconian speed limits were imposed on trains, meant to prevent further loss of life. As an alternative to the slow trains, many people chose to use cars instead. Because, by orders of magnitude, cars have a higher probability of accidents than trains, overall fatalities increased when considering both types of transportation together. "A decision taken about the safety of the railway system may well have had completely the opposite effect to that intended when considered in relation to the wider transport system."

A good systems practitioner, when viewing cause and effect by several degrees, can better design for outcomes in multiple ways, and account for what incentivizes certain behavior. (See Chapter 8, "Anticipating Unintended Consequences," for more on the Cobra Effect, which is a good example of perverse incentives and unintended consequences.)

How to Engage in Systems Thinking

So now that you have a good understanding of the systems-thinking mindset, how do you put it into practice?

To a designer, it may sound obvious, but the most direct way to analyze systems is by mapping them. In *The Decision Book*, which is a book of various analysis models, the authors describe the purpose of mapping: "When we encounter chaos, we seek ways to structure it, to see through it, or at least to gain an overview of it. Models help us to reduce the complexity of a situation by enabling us to dismiss most of it and concentrate on what is important."[17]

As my work as a designer has shifted from someone who designs products and services to someone who facilitates alignment between stakeholders in order to address broader problems, I find it is important to use visual tools that communicate complex and varying layers of information. In the subsequent chapters, you will encounter several forms of mapping that you can integrate at various points of your design process. These are the tools of systems thinking.

As someone who designs products or services, you might be wondering whether this is relevant to you. Designers and design researchers can be incredible facilitators of change. Rather than thinking about your skills as limited to products and services, systems thinking encourages you to consider how you can use those skills to engage in meta-design: conducting research, designing experiences for alignment, and thoughtfully facilitating decision-making among diverse stakeholders. You can think of yourself as designing systems, tools, and methods for designers to design, and for other stakeholders to use to develop shared understanding.

The idea of other stakeholders is important to systems thinking: ultimately, it is a mindset and a set of tools for facilitating change that you as a designer cannot do alone. It's kind of like being a conductor. As a designer, perhaps you were a virtuoso—you were first violin! As a conductor, you are helping others align, to make beautiful coordinated music together. And by coordinating the musicians, you will inspire change beyond the orchestra—others in the audience might take up music, and maybe there will be education programs that make music more accessible. This is all to say that engaging various stakeholders—nondesigners, powerful decision-makers, lived experts, and folks from various organizations—is important to the systems-thinking process and methods.

---

17 Mikael Krogerus and Roman Tschappeler, *The Decision Book: Fifty Models for Strategic Thinking* (Norton, 2017).

The Tools and Process of Systems Thinking

Systems-thinking tools can be broken down into two key categories:

- **Mapping the status quo:** This is the part of the design process in which you use mapping methods such as ecosystem mapping and causal loop mapping, techniques like "the five whys," and methods such as qualitative research to understand the status quo, which are the current conditions within the system that you are analyzing.

- **Envisioning the future:** Based on your analysis and synthesis of the status quo, you will then use tools that focus on where to intervene and address problems within the system. This includes mapping and alignment frameworks, such as theory-of-change mapping, futures wheel, and outcomes mapping; and it also encompasses methods that drive the imagination of future scenarios, such as speculative design.

Chapters 4, 5, and 6 provide guidance and methods for mapping the status quo, and Chapters 7, 8, and 9 introduce methods that focus on using design tools to model opportunity areas and intervention. The practical application of these tools and methods should help you facilitate change, adopt the systems-thinking mindset, and hopefully inspire you to integrate systems mapping into your processes. It's a bit like a finger pointing a way to the moon.

Takeaways

- Systems thinking requires a mindset shift: expanding your thinking about what constitutes problem-solving and reframing problem spaces.

- Three concepts are core to systems thinking: wholeness, causality, and interconnectedness.

- Combining a design approach with systems thinking from a process perspective should include mapping the status quo and envisioning the future.

CHAPTER 3

Systems Thinking and Design Thinking

One of the most famous examples of user-centered design is IDEO's shopping cart. In 1999 the television news program *Dateline* aired a segment in which the *Dateline* producers commissioned IDEO to develop an idea for a new and improved shopping cart. The segment showcased the design studio's process, with a constraint of a five-day timeline. The team conducted user research in stores with customers and staff, generated ideas based on what they'd learned, narrowed ideas to those innovative enough to prototype, and created a final prototype that they unveiled and shared with grocery store staff. If you are a designer, you are very likely familiar with this example (and probably a bit tired of it as well!). Love it or hate it, it is an iconic example of the user-centered design process, which is what IDEO would eventually call "design thinking."

Design thinking and systems thinking have a relationship in that they are both ostensibly focused on gaining a better understanding of the world in order to change it for the better. Author Christina Wodtke describes the act of design as consisting of two parts: modeling the world as it is, and modeling the world as it could be. "Designers create mental models and system models to document the current state of their corner of the world. Designers model both the object of the design challenge and the ecosystem it resides in. Design Thinking is Systems Thinking."[1]

As a designer, you're likely well-versed in the process of design thinking. In a framework popularized by Stanford's d.school, it is often represented as a series of five steps that designers (and those who want to think like a designer) conduct sequentially in their work (see Figure 3.1).

This design-thinking framework well articulates the design process in general, as it contains two key parts: exploration of a problem space (*empathize, define*) followed by focused action (*ideate, prototype, test*). Or to reiterate Wodtke's summary, the world as it is, and the world as it could be. The five steps outline the following mindset and activities:

- **Empathize:** Designers build empathy by conducting research that is focused on people who will likely be end users of products or services within a problem space. This phase is described as *empathize* because a core aspect is using qualitative research techniques that uncover people's behaviors, pain points, and motivations. (See sidebar "The Role of Empathy.")

---

1   Christina Wodtke, "How I Stopped Worrying and Learned to Love Design Thinking," *Medium*, August 26, 2017.

Understanding and gaining
contextual insight

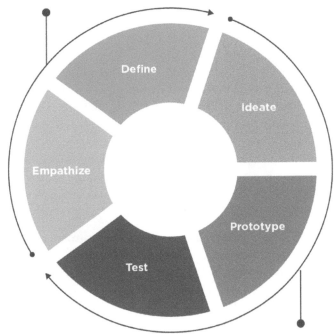

Designing products,
services, and interventions

FIGURE 3.1
The five parts of the design-thinking process articulate a process of
gaining understanding (*empathize* and *define*) and taking action by
designing (*ideate*, *prototype*, *test*).

- **Define:** Designers engage in sensemaking, or synthesizing their findings from the *empathize* phase. This includes creating visual artifacts such as experience or journey maps, personas, design principles, and other synthesis and insights frameworks that set up the move into the action phase.
- **Ideate:** Designers facilitate expansive ideation with their teams, generating lots of potential solutions in low-fidelity formats such as sketches. They then narrow their ideas to those that can be prototyped.
- **Prototype:** In this phase, designers prototype the most promising solutions from the previous phase. They create versions of the solutions that could be anything from paper prototyping to elaborate digital prototypes.

- **Test:** The prototypes are now tested with real end users, eliciting input and feedback for further iteration. Iteration can lead to further ideation and prototyping as a feedback loop.

Within this process, typically the problem space is narrow enough that you can focus on specific types of users. What this means in practice is that the solution developed in the design phase is already predetermined as you enter the *empathize* phase. In short, you already know the problem that you'll be solving. Returning to the shopping cart example, the IDEO team knew they were being hired to redesign a shopping cart, so that's what their process was focused on. To apply the idea to the digital realm, if you are working on, say, an app for photo enthusiasts, you know you will, in the end, be creating or modifying a digital app, and that will be the form your solutions will take.

In many product design contexts, this idea of determinism is generally okay, and reflects the reality of how the world often works when it comes to problem-solving. If you are hiring an industrial designer to "fix" a shopping cart, then you probably do not have the power or experience to, say, change how people shop in general, or even how stores are designed.

The problem that arises is when this narrowed design-thinking process is applied to large scale systems or wicked problems. For example, there is no single avenue for solving the problem of a lack of civic engagement or racial inequity. The process does not account for multifinality: the idea that rather than a single solution, multiple ways of addressing problems exist.

In addition to multifinality, the design-thinking process does not account for the kinds of systemic changes—that lie outside of a design solution—that need to shift in order for that design solution to be successful. In the RSA's report "From Design Thinking to System Change," the authors pointed to the need to shape the systems that surround design innovations: "[I]n order for a service innovation to flourish, you may need to push for a complementary governance innovation, such as altering procurement frameworks or regulatory rules."[2]

---

2   Rowan Conway, Jeff Masters, and Jake Thorold, "From Design Thinking to Systems Change: How to Invest in Innovation for Social Impact," The RSA in partnership with Innovate UK, July 2017.

As you learned in Chapter 1, "The Shortcomings of User-Centered Design," the design-thinking process includes inspiration from challenge mapping, particularly in its adoption of "How might we?" as a prompt for ideation. What it leaves out is a more extended analysis of the "why"; in challenge mapping, this analysis is represented by prompts that include "Why must we do this?" and "What's stopping us from doing this?" that both broaden and narrow the consideration of the areas in which you can solve problems.[3]

Thus, as the UK Design Council wrote, design thinking as a process can "reframe social and environmental issues like healthcare or climate change as creative opportunities" and successfully center problem-solving and innovation on users. Its shortcoming is its determinism, as well as a narrowness of what kinds of innovations and interventions are potentially needed within a problem space.

Beyond User-Centeredness

A critical feature of the design-thinking process is its emphasis on foundational research during the Empathize phase. If you are a design researcher, you've almost certainly found yourself having to convince others of the value of conducting foundational research for UX design projects. Typically, the rationale is to understand the challenges of the people who are, or will be, the customers or users of your product or service, or the context in which your product will sit. In addition, foundational research helps you understand what problems you should be solving. Jesse James Garrett summarized it succinctly in a tweet from August, 2019 (see Figure 3.2).

> **Jesse James Garrett** ✓
> @jjg
>
> The designer's first and most essential task is choosing the correct problem to solve. Because if you get that wrong, every choice you make after that is irrelevant.
>
> 8:40 PM · Aug 7, 2019 · Twitter for iPhone
>
> **529** Retweets   **1.7K** Likes

FIGURE 3.2
Jesse James Garrett sums up the rationale for good foundational design research.

---

3   Min Basadur, "Reducing Complexity in Conceptual Thinking Using Challenge Mapping," *The Korean Journal of Thinking & Problem Solving*, 2003.

Design thinking is often described as an empathy-centered process. Psychologist Judith Hall describes how most people view empathy as "having something to do with understanding what other people are going through and being concerned about them."[4] This notion, that through a bit of user research you can develop a deeper understanding of a user's context, problems, motivations, and behaviors, is widely accepted as truth in the UX design practice. However, as designers, it's important to be aware of the limitations of both the designer's ability to build empathy through the design process, as well as the limitations of empathy itself.

Designers seek to gain empathy with end users by utilizing research methods such as interviews and situational observation of research participants, as well as simulation exercises. These can be good ways for designers to gain insight into the user experience, but it can lead to not only asymmetrical power between researcher and participant, but worse, actually further distance designers from users.

In their ACM CHI Conference on Human Factors in Computing System's 2019 paper about empathy,[5] Cynthia Bennett and Daniela Rosner pointed to how empathy-centered processes in design thinking may

---

4   Judith Hall and Mark Leary, "The U.S. Has an Empathy Deficit. Here's What We Can Do About It," *Scientific American*, September 17, 2020.

5   Cynthia L. Bennett and Daniela K. Rosner, "The Promise of Empathy: Design, Disability, and Knowing the 'Other'," CHI 2019.

The importance of understanding the problem space, and what it is that you as a designer are trying to solve, is a broadly accepted principle of design thinking. Again, the limitation of user-centered design thinking is a focus on individual users and their direct interaction with a product. Systems thinking extends the idea of understanding a problem space to the realm of understanding current conditions beyond just users. With this alignment on developing foundational understanding of context, systems thinking and design thinking can philosophically work well together.

be counterproductive to designers' attempts to humanize those they are designing for, particularly those with disabilities.

First, when designers seek to build empathy by involving research participants in exercises such as interviews and prototype-testing, these participants' perspectives are often filtered through the designer, leaving "the voices of those with disabilities for the non-disabled designer to explain." In addition, designers often conduct simulation exercises, such as wearing a blindfold to simulate the experience of those who are blind to gain empathy. This then replaces the firsthand experience of lived experts with a "restaging of the disabled experience." These approaches end up "othering" those whom designers are attempting to understand.

To correct for this, designers can work to ensure that they work in partnership with lived experts, not only extracting their experiences, but empowering them throughout the design process, ensuring there is representation on the design team and holding space for lived-expert advisors.

Empathy can be a great motivator and a powerful tool; designers must be aware of its power and ensure that it's not counterproductive. Bennett and Rosner wrote that designers must "grapple with how to minimize harm while still reaping the benefits of human contact that inform design." Ultimately, designers need to experience a mindset shift: empower those who benefit from design from those you are "designing for" to those you are "designing with."

Systems thinking involves using a broader lens than user-centered design thinking. With systems thinking, in order to truly respond to large gnarly problems, you have to reach beyond a user, their problems, and a solution. The problem spaces are many, and a single solution does not exist. Rather, there are design approaches that can serve as a response to problems. Typical design thinking also lacks focus on circumstances changing over time and the impact on others beyond just the user or potential user of a product or service. As a result, the idea of a "problem space" and a "solution space" are too narrow.

WHY I AVOID USING THE TERM *SOLUTION*

In *The Fifth Discipline*, systems-thinking expert Peter Senge's first law of organizational systems thinking is "Today's problems come from yesterday's solutions." This idea acknowledges that deliberate change—design—affects outcomes in a way that feeds back into the system.

With this context in mind, the term *solution* feels both fixed and final. In addition, it feels arrogant to assume that the singular way in which you are engaging in problem-solving will lead to a solution that will never have repercussions, nor require change. It also limits problem-solving to those who have the power and privilege to drive fully realized and stand-alone solutions.

Antoinette Carroll, founder of Creative Reaction Lab, prefers the term *approaches* rather than *solutions*. She stated, "I like the word 'approach' because it shows this is not a finite type of solution—it's flexible, it's agile."[6] In addition, a term like *approaches* acknowledges that many people—the community—can and should be given the opportunity to approach problems, not just those who hold privilege and power. The people who are "solutioning" are often not the people who have to *experience* those solutions.

I suggest using terms like *approach, intervention*, and *initiative* to imply the kind of flexibility that Carroll is referring to. Approaches, interventions, and initiatives are things that you continue to work on, to change, and to adjust. They are terms that do not imply finality. It speaks of humility within the design process and that we, as designers, are facilitators, not "solutioners."

---

6   Meg Miller, "Want to Fight Inequality? Forget Design Thinking," *Fast Company*, February 16, 2017.

In order to broaden your problem-solving beyond the narrow idea of identifying singular problems and then creating solutions for them, you will need to think further about who your stakeholders are within a system, how the system works beyond discrete problems, and the possibility that there are multiple ways to address problems. Beyond the idea of modifying the design process to accommodate this mindset, you will need to extend it by mapping the status quo and then envisioning the future. This process is distinct from design thinking alone, and is also different from typical systems-thinking processes because of its combination with design.

Combining Systems Thinking with Design

So where does systems thinking fit? Systems thinking can integrate with those design thinking methods that help designers understand where the problems are and which ones require intervention.

In the standard design-thinking process, a designer sees a problem and uses design as a creative method for solving that problem. In systems thinking, the goal is to understand interconnectedness, causality, and wholeness. Thus, it's important to understand the status quo, literally "the present situation," or the existing state of affairs. In *Systems Thinking for Social Change*, David Peter Stroh wrote that examining the status quo allows you to "help people compare the benefits of change with the benefits of the status quo—and then help them make a conscious choice between the payoffs they are now getting and the espoused purpose they say they want the system to accomplish."[7]

It's possible that you may not want to change many aspects of a system, even one that is dysfunctional, because it rewards stakeholders in a way that reinforces positive outcomes. It's also possible that you might pinpoint clear areas of intervention within a system and be able to confidently design for change. Either way, understanding the status quo—the way things work now—is a critical aspect of being deliberate, clear, and strategic about the changes you may want to make.

Some of the ways to think about a system are: Where are the relationships? How are they affecting each other? Do diverse problems trace back to a root cause that has many different outcomes?

If you think back to the design-thinking process, you might integrate systems thinking at the beginning and end of the process, with the assumption that the process as a whole is circular rather than linear (see Figure 3.3).

---

7   David Peter Stroh, *Systems Thinking for Social Change: A Practical Guide to Solving Complex Problems, Avoiding Unintended Consequences, and Achieving Lasting Results* (Chelsea Green Publishing, 2015).

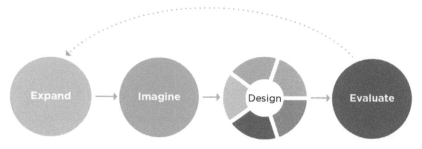

FIGURE 3.3
What's not to love about a process that includes "Imagine"?

- **Expand:** In this phase, you, the designer, will attempt to understand the system, rather than diving straight into understanding a specific problem space. For example, if you are thinking about designing educational software for high school students, you would need to understand what is currently happening in the education system in which the software would sit. Expanding your understanding involves using research, analysis, and mapping to broaden your lens beyond the typical area of focus for the standard design-thinking process.

- **Imagine:** Here you will identify potential points of intervention in the system and ask yourself, "Are there different levels at which interventions can occur?" Interventions could include possibilities beyond the realm of user-centered design, such as policy, business models, services, or long-term strategy. This concept is often described as "multifinality": making change depends on multiple—and different—forms of problem-solving. Developing a theory of change is key to design and implementation of varying types of intervention. In addition, the designer imagines and considers futures—scenarios in which future changes might sit.

- **Evaluate:** After interventions have been designed and implemented, they must be evaluated in the world for their effectiveness, and to ensure that they are leading to desired outcomes. This process involves monitoring the changes that interventions have made, as well as potentially looping back to "expand" to further conduct systems analysis in order to understand consequences and radiating effects.

It's tempting to describe these systems-thinking steps as dovetailing into design thinking, but describing it as a linear process does not acknowledge the cyclical nature of systems thinking, nor the multifi- nality of possible problem-solving. It makes sense to represent it as a series of circular processes intersecting with each other: understand- ing the system, making change to the system, evaluating the change, and understanding the system once again (see Figure 3.4).

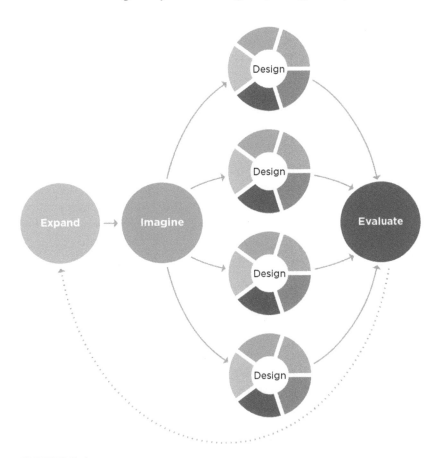

FIGURE 3.4
There are lots of possibilities for potential interventions, and some can go through the design process. In this diagram, you can picture four different interventions, identified during the *imagine* phase, that would now enter the design process. The key is that there are multiple pos- sibilities for problem-solving and intervention.

Addressing the Flaws of Design Thinking

Before being able to combine design thinking and systems thinking in an effective way, design thinking itself needs to be re-examined. A growing number of design practitioners are recognizing not just its practical shortcomings, but also inherent problems with the mindset that design thinking is a universal form of problem-solving, and that the designer is a universal problem-solver. In addition, the typical approach to design thinking fails to acknowledge the privilege of the designer. Natasha Iskander, associate professor of Urban Planning and Public Service at NYU, described design thinking as a process that "privileges the designer above the people she serves, and in doing so limits participation in the design process."[8] She continued that this approach "limits the scope for truly innovative ideas, and makes it hard to solve challenges that are characterized by a high degree of uncertainty—like climate change."

Systems thinking requires engagement with an extended set of stakeholders and their perspectives, and is fundamentally an appropriate approach for seeking to understand and solve challenges that are complex and uncertain. So how can you, as a designer, better address the shortcomings of design thinking? You need to reflect on your privilege and then work to disrupt power imbalances.

Reflecting on Your Privilege as a Designer

First, it's important to acknowledge your privilege as a designer. The idea of privilege includes aspects of your experience and identity, such as your access to higher education and your racial and socioeconomic background. In addition, your role in problem-solving as a designer is usually a privileged position in comparison to people who are most affected by problems in a system. Many of those in the industrialized design practice (including myself) can be categorized as coming from a "WEIRD" background: Western, Educated, Industrialized, Rich, and Democratic.[9] Ask yourself: What kind of power do I hold in comparison to those who might be most affected by design and systems decisions?

---

8   Natasha Iskander, "Design Thinking Is Fundamentally Conservative and Preserves the Status Quo," *Harvard Business Review*, September 5, 2018.

9   Michael Muthukrishna et al., "Beyond Western, Educated, Industrial, Rich, and Democratic (WEIRD) Psychology: Measuring and Mapping Scales of Cultural and Psychological Distance," *Psychological Science* 31.6 (2020).

A good way to reflect on your position is by considering your personal proximity to power and privilege. The Power Wheel is a framework used by organizations such as the Canadian Council for Refugees to help people reflect on the privileges they have. Using the framework in Figure 3.5, you can check the categories within which you fall.

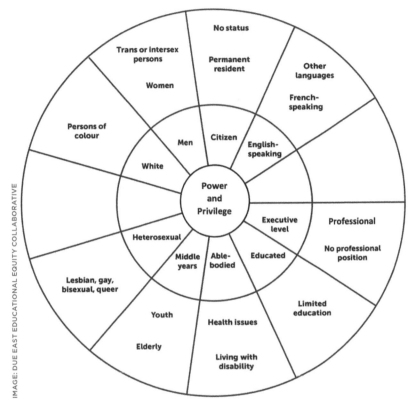

FIGURE 3.5
The Power Wheel shows your proximity to power and privilege.

Many designers will likely find themselves mostly in the inner wheel categories. Understanding and acknowledging your privilege helps you have a clear view of how to actively understand the power dynamic between yourself and your system stakeholders. For example, if you are conducting research in education, and you know that teachers and students will be most affected, you will want to reflect on the power dynamic between you and your research participants. This awareness helps you find better ways of disrupting the power imbalance between you and your stakeholders.

Disrupting Power Imbalances

In addition to reflecting on your privilege, you need to find clear opportunities to disrupt the power imbalance between you as a designer and those who, in a traditional design-thinking process, you would be designing "for." Typical design research, for example, uses methods such as interviewing end users and extrapolating insights from their input. As Iskander put it, this results in "whatever needs of product users and communities [you] perceive are refracted through [your] personal experience and priorities."

Ways of shifting the power imbalance include actually empowering community stakeholders to engage in participatory design. Iskander refers to the type of interaction where power is more distributed as "interpretive engagement." It's an opportunity for stakeholders who are usually just "researched" to actually participate in the design process. Design approaches are more open to incremental adjustment, which allows the community to take ownership and make change.

In "An Intersectional Approach to Designing in the Margins," authors Sheena Erete, Aarti Israni, and Tawanna Dillahunt discussed the challenges of conducting research and design with underserved communities.[10] One challenge is the difficulty of adapting design and research methods to support those communities. For example, seemingly participatory methods such as prototyping may be intimidating to those with limited exposure to digital technology. Other barriers include community ownership of design project goals and outcomes, as well as limited investment in the time it takes to build trust with community stakeholders.

Erete, Israni, and Dillahunt identified three calls to action for designers and researchers. First, designers must understand, and attend to, context: "HCI researchers and designers should consider design methods, or even icebreaker activities, that delicately expose the various identities present, the historical oppression that may have been faced as a result of those identities, and the resilient ways in which members of underserved communities have overcome those challenges." In other words, ensure a strengths-based approach rather than a deficit-based approach when it comes to the context of your stakeholders. Second, researchers and designers must self-reflect on

---

10 Sheena Erete, Aarti Israni, and Tawanna Dillahunt, "An Intersectional Approach to Designing in the Margins," *Interactions*, May-June 2018.

their own identity, positionality, and biases. Lastly, researchers and designers must attend to and disclose dissent: "Attuning to... voices of dissent and any tensions that may occur... helps to ensure everyone's interests are represented."

In essence, through engaging with systems thinking and making the process more equitable for other stakeholders, you are shifting both your mindset and approach from that of a producer to that of a facilitator.

Design as Facilitation

Integrating systems thinking into your processes as a designer not only expands your analysis, but also changes the purpose of your activities. Typically, those in the design field would describe their activities as using their design skills to deliver something. This could be the UX design work for a digital product, the design of a physical object, or perhaps the visual communication design of information.

Your role, and the way you apply your design skills, shifts when you engage in systems thinking. Rather than delivering design outputs, you can think of yourself as facilitating the knowledge—often the knowledge of other stakeholders—that leads to outputs. You yourself might design and deliver those outputs, but first, you need to surface the information that leads to an understanding of a system and the potential changes that need to be made to a system.

There will be forms of problem-solving and intervention that do not fall into the design-thinking process. Design-thinking methods such as facilitation, participatory design, and sensemaking can be used to draw out and integrate other stakeholders' expertise and experiences. In the Expand and Imagine phases of the process shown in Figure 3.4, you, as a designer, can help articulate potential avenues for intervention that could fall into categories outside your expertise. These avenues could be as diverse as policy change, further analysis and study, logistics, or other areas of study and action that others have more experience with than designers. You might not be a subject matter expert, but you are an expert in design-thinking methods. Through systems thinking, you can use those methods to collaborate with other stakeholders and draw out, articulate, and visualize their expertise, which leads to a shared understanding of problems and how to create change. As Arturo Escobar explained in *Designs for the Pluriverse*, "In between problem solving and meaning making, and diffuse and expert design, there opens a space for rethinking 'design in a connected world.'"[11] This approach helps folks from varied disciplines tackle chronic, wide-ranging, and complex problems.

Let's take an example of what your activities might look like as a designer and systems thinker. Imagine that you are a service designer working with your city. The city has a goal of having zero fatalities on the city's roads. (Many cities have this as a goal, and it's called *Vision Zero*, a global movement, originating in Sweden, to end traffic-related fatalities.) Your role is to understand the space and the stakeholders involved, engage others with expertise to inform your understanding, and come up with potential solutions. If you were to design an approach to this project that emphasized systems thinking, you might go through this process in the following way:

- **Expand:** You could identify stakeholders to help you build your understanding of the status quo in the system: city planners, traffic specialists, pedestrian advocacy groups, car owners, cycling advocacy groups, public transportation representatives, and delivery companies. In addition to literature review and secondary research on the topic, you could convene these diverse stakeholders in workshops or interviews to start systems mapping. You could continue this phase by developing a detailed systems map and conducting research with multiple stakeholders to answer key questions about the status quo and better understand why things are the way they are.

- **Imagine:** Once you have a shared understanding with your stakeholders about the different points in the system, you could start identifying where to intervene. Should the city design traffic calming patterns on the city's deadliest streets? Does there need to be further investment in certain types of public transportation so that fewer people feel compelled to drive? What about punitive measures against car usage, such as increases in parking fees? Could technology help increase pedestrian awareness of vehicle danger? This phase shows different ways of intervening in problems identified in your systems mapping from the Expand phase, as well as imagining futures for long-term planning. Although not all of the potential interventions will fall into the design process (for example, policy decisions may not), you might have a handful of ideas that could potentially be designed and tested through the design-thinking process.

---

11 Arturo Escobar, *Designs for the Pluriverse: Radical Interdependence, Autonomy, and the Making of Worlds* (Duke University Press, 2017).

For some of the interventions identified in the Imagine phase, you could then use a design-thinking process to use creative thinking to follow through on certain ideas. For this example, imagine that one avenue of investigation is figuring out ways of improving crosswalks that could lead to better outcomes, and design for it, if so. If you were then to dovetail into the design-thinking process for this one intervention, your process might look like the following:

- **Empathize and Define:** In this combined phase, you would conduct research with a narrower set of stakeholders, specifically oriented around improving crosswalks. This phase could involve conducting interviews and participatory design sessions with pedestrians of varied demographics: commuters, schoolchildren, crossing guards, etc. You would then take your findings and synthesize them into journey maps, personas, or archetypes that could inform your design principles.

- **Ideate:** In this phase, you might get the diverse stakeholder band back together to focus on ideation for crosswalks. Urban planners, technologists and developers, designers, and participants from your Empathize and Define phases could come together and generate ideas. You could focus on involving implementers because this is where you will start narrowing based on feasibility.

- **Prototype and Test:** A handful of ideas will move from your ideation into prototyping. For example, there could be digital approaches such as an LED crosswalk idea that seems promising as both safe and cost-effective. You and your team might prototype it and test it at varying spots in the city. With iteration, if this plan works, you'll find yourself guiding its implementation.

Continued prototyping and testing will eventually lead to implementation, in which continued evaluation would take place. Evaluating the different avenues of intervention and their impact is important to systems thinking because you and your stakeholders can see which changes are meaningful, which aren't, and which changes need to change or adjust in order to lead to preferable outcomes.

- **Evaluate:** Now that some of these nifty crosswalks are installed at various intersections throughout the city, you as a systems-thinking service designer, could help the city make a plan to collect feedback, measure its success, and iterate. Ideally, this intervention would be one of many different ideas explored and implemented. You would start evaluating these varying interventions and measuring their collective impact, or start

CARP AND OTHER "SOLUTIONS"

In the 1960s and 1970s, a species called Asian carp was introduced into the Mississippi River to control invasive weeds and algae within the aquaculture industry in the Mississippi Delta (see Figure 3.6). In response to the previous pollution in the region's waterways, they were employed as a nonpoisonous way of solving the problem with weeds. The fish themselves became invasive, proliferating at alarming rates and working their way to other bodies of water via forms of water engineering such as canals. Because the species of Asian carp, including bighead and silver carp, consume large amounts of plankton, they now threaten the native species of the Great Lakes, with engineers now building electric barriers to keep the invasive species out.

IMAGE: ADAM RHODES/USPLASH

FIGURE 3.6
A fisherman holds up a common carp.

identifying ineffectiveness or worse, unintended consequences that are having a negative impact. You may even revisit your original systems maps to see how cause and effect, behavior, and connections have changed. And then you would potentially start the process again.

Through this process, you've engaged in the two key aspects of systems thinking in relation to the design process: mapping the status quo and envisioning the future. The process can be messy,

There is a long history of introducing invasive species to "solve" problems, or just for human enjoyment. For example, Nile perch were introduced by colonial officials in Uganda to Lake Victoria in 1962 as a food source, aiming to boost the local fishing industry. As a large predator, its introduction has driven native lake species to extinction, and has played a role in the lake's changing ecosystem. Cane toads, native to South America, were introduced to Australia and Pacific countries such as the Philippines to combat sugar cane pests. They are now considered one of the world's worst invasive species. In Texas, millions of Eurasian wild hogs—originally introduced by early colonizers and again in the 1930s for hunting—are considered to be one of the most destructive invasive species, devouring fields, fish, and contributing to soil erosion.

These are all examples of man-made ecological problems. Aside from preventing the spread of invasive species to begin with, there are different ways that societies can intervene. In the case of Asian carp, one idea is promoting the idea of overfishing (a typically bad idea when it comes to native species but attractive for invasive ones), with the goal of making it attractive for eating. The same goes for feral hogs, with chefs promoting the idea of the meat as a delicacy. If you can't beat 'em, eat 'em.

Even with creative forms of intervention in mind, in the end, the best way to solve for the problem of invasive species is to prevent their introduction to begin with.

ambiguous, and of course, not as cleanly mapped as I've outlined here. However, you now have a decent idea of where, tactically, you could engage in systems-thinking methods, once you've adopted the mindset.

In the next chapter, you'll dive into the research methods and facilitation activities that serve as a foundation for mapping the status quo of the system.

Takeaways

- Systems thinking can be combined with design thinking to create a powerful approach to multilayered problem-solving and intervention.

- Adding Expand and Imagine to the front end of the typical design-thinking process of Empathize, Define, Ideate, Prototype, and Test, and Evaluate at the end of the process, extends the design-thinking process to integrate a systems-thinking lens.

- In order to engage fully in systems thinking, designers must acknowledge the problems with traditional systems-thinking and interrogate their own privilege and power. The designer's role as a systems thinker is as a facilitator.

- Systems thinking plus design thinking can be considered in two parts: *mapping the status quo* and *envisioning the future*. The first part refers to understanding the current context and landscape, and the second part involves considering and taking action to change the existing system.

Nicole Sarsfield is a lead designer at Breville. She has previously led design practices at Work & Co, Oracle, Artefact, and Deloitte.

Author's Note: Although I don't think about design systems as a systems-thinking framework, I do think that working on them requires a mindset that is fundamental to systems thinking. For anyone who has read Alexander, Ishikawa, and Silverstein's foundational book *A Pattern Language*, you will recognize that being thoughtful about components of a system and how they connect is essential for the system as a whole.

You have a focus on design systems in UX design. Tell me a bit about the difference between designing a design system versus a more traditional approach to UX design.

The key to creating an effective design system is probably to fix whatever patched-together system you have in place and start from scratch: you need to build at the component level and then build the flows. You will then have a stronger architecture that will support change. The goal of a design system is to be as efficient as possible, and there are points where you have to negotiate for efficiencies. If you do this the right way, then if you want to hold space to make special moments in the design that are not component-oriented, you can still have room for that.

In traditional UX, some of the decisions could feel very arbitrary: just designing things like forms or flows in isolation means creating a one-off solution, and that is hard to reuse later. Ultimately, thinking about making something that can respond to change, that is flexible, and can apply to many use cases makes you a better designer.

I've seen design systems established, and then kind of start shifting, or lose relevance. What do you do in your practice to ensure sustainability of a design system?

The thing about design systems is that you need to keep working on them. For example, I was once working on a list view component. It started out with us designing and building in isolation without knowing where it was going to go, so we had to keep making updates. It's important to understand the context in which components are going to be used.

This means that you basically need a team that works on the system all the time. This requires thinking about the system of the design team itself: how do you assign people to work on a design system, but still have the context in which the components are going to sit? A good model for this is the elevator model for design teams. This is where you have designers switching roles based on what's needed: they may be deployed to work on certain features, or they might be working to maintain and update the design system. This flexibility allows for people to understand both the parts of a design system and how a design system is used.

A design system is a living thing. If you design parts of it without context in mind, then it's design in isolation.

Are there any perceived tensions when it comes to design systems? And if so, how do you resolve them?

Now that working within design systems is so common, you have some junior practitioners who have never had to work outside of an established design system. This sometimes limits their ability to think about design in a "blue sky" kind of way. I think a benefit of the design practice is being able to explore, to step out of the confines when you are trying to be generative. I think those organizations that have strong design systems need to provide the space to innovate so that the design system is not a barrier to creativity. It's finding that balance between thinking holistically and optimizing for efficiency, and then giving room to explore beyond those confines.

CHAPTER 4

Collecting Your Data

Integrating systems thinking into your design practice starts with using its methods as a form of analysis when learning about your problem space. And because you need data to analyze, you're going to have to conduct research.

Typically, in user-centered design, you would conduct research with, well, users. The objective would be to understand their context and formulate insights about how your products would fit into that context. The process is focused on individual end users and their relationships with a product.

In a systems-thinking project, you need to extend your understanding to a much wider set of stakeholders. End users are relevant (if there are products involved), but the center of your focus is a system, not a product. As a result, stakeholders are more diverse in many ways. You can ask yourself:

- Who has lived experiences within the system, and how do I consider their context?

- Who are the decision-makers within a system? Specifically, who holds power?

- What are the organizations and communities that both affect and are affected by the system?

Understanding the diversity of stakeholders within your problem space requires multiple forms of data collection.

In order to plan your project, you'll need to figure out what you need to understand, what research methods you'll use, and when you will use each method.

The Purpose of Your Systems-Thinking Research

First things first, you'll need to formulate your research goals. What are you trying to understand about a given system? The questions are similar to those you might ask yourself in a typical design research project. As Erika Hall puts it in *Just Enough Research*, "You'll need to know what decisions are in play (the purpose) and what you're asking about (the topic)."[1]

---

1 Erika Hall, *Just Enough Research* (A Book Apart, 2013).

For thinking about how you might design your systems-thinking research, imagine that you are working on a project focused on K–12 (kindergarten to 12th grade) education in the United States. You are working on a project for an education nonprofit in which the objective is to understand the experience of math for multilingual learners, specifically middle school students in the U.S. Secondly, you want to identify potential opportunity areas or points of intervention for improving outcomes for them.

If you consider the purpose and the topic of your systems-thinking analysis, it would be to understand what kinds of decisions are being made within the system that have an impact on multilingual learners and their experience with math.

With a design research project, your focus would often be on a specific type of solution. For example, if you were conducting product-focused design research for an educational software company, solutions would be presupposed as software. In a systems-thinking process, the shape of interventions and approaches would be broader: they could be anything from policy, to funding, to programs, to, yes, even software.

However, even if you are a researcher working on a narrower problem space, you can benefit from broadening your data-collection process with a systems lens in mind. By planning nearly any design research project with a systems-thinking perspective, you could discover relevant context that could inform your problem-solving.

What you'll find as you plan your research is that even seemingly simple problem spaces are, in reality, complex. You can benefit from understanding this complexity, acknowledging lots of diverse stakeholders, and realizing that cause and effect are not necessarily direct.

Within your systems-oriented research, your job is to gain insight into challenges, relationships, and incentives within the existing system, and to eventually map those insights.

Types of Data Collection

When starting a systems-thinking-oriented design research project, you are seeking as holistic a picture as possible. That requires multiple levels of inquiry. It makes sense to integrate two core forms of research: primary research and secondary research.

In primary research, you are directly conducting research with stakeholders, whereas in secondary research, you are immersing yourself in research that others (experts, academic scholars) have conducted. Both types of research have multiple methods you can employ, and they frame your job as a designer who facilitates other people's input and knowledge, as you learned in Chapter 3, "Systems Thinking and Design Thinking."

Some forms of design research are articulated in Table 4.1. You would typically start with a review of existing research in the field (secondary research) and build upon—or even challenge—that information with primary research.

TABLE 4.1 TYPES OF PRIMARY AND SECONDARY RESEARCH.

Secondary Research (Immersion)		Primary Research (Discovery)		
Literature Review	Statistical Analysis	Interviews and participatory design with lived experts	Interviews and participatory design with subject matter experts (SMEs)	Interviews and participatory design with decision-makers and organizational stakeholders
Surveying existing research from academic experts and publications	Reviewing existing statistical data within the problem space	Conducting interviews and participatory design with those who are affected in the system and often have the least power or influence.	Involving or collaborating with SMEs and practitioners throughout the course of your analysis and design work	Conducting interviews and co-designing with those who are making decisions about interventions or changes to the system

You don't necessarily need to conduct all forms of research for your data collection, but you should consider which kinds of research will best inform a broader systemic understanding of the problem space. It's important to involve a mix of people with expertise in the system you are trying to understand, especially as a design generalist, who likely does not have deep knowledge about that domain.

Although designers bring a new lens based on their unfamiliarity with a domain, it is wise to acknowledge that important stakeholders, such as researchers and practitioners, have spent years, and maybe even decades, building a deep, meaningful understanding of the system. For example, returning to the example of your multilingual learners research project: on research projects focused on education, in addition to conducting research with students and teachers, you can learn from education policymakers, researchers, curriculum developers, and administrators in order to better formulate your understanding of the system and learn from how they perceive it.

Starting with Secondary Research

I once worked on a K–12 education project focused on culturally relevant teaching. My team began by spending a few weeks examining the most influential white papers and journal articles in the domain of culturally relevant education, and started familiarizing ourselves with the most important themes, theories, and frameworks. Later in the project, I had an opportunity to interview one of the preeminent scholars in the field. The foundational understanding I had gained from reading her book, and learning the names and theories of other eminent scholars through other materials, put her at ease and allowed her expertise to shine through. It kept her from having to give me a "101" on the most basic of ideas, and built trust that, even though I was a designer and not a formal education scholar, I was equipped to engage in this work.

Most projects will ideally open with an *immersion* phase, a time for you to gain a baseline understanding of the problem space. A good start is a deep dive on existing research, conducting a literature review of academic articles, books, and other media that support a broader understanding of the subject area on which your system is focused. This is secondary research. During this *immersion*, you could also analyze statistical data that is relevant to the system space. Quantitative data are a good supporting mechanism if your primary research is entirely or mostly qualitative in nature.

Secondary research is especially important if, as a designer, you have little knowledge about the domain you are analyzing. In your multilingual learner project example, if you haven't worked in U.S.-based K–12 education, or even more specifically, with multilingual learners within that system, you will want to know what the common knowledge is in the field. For example, what theories are considered foundational to this particular system space? What ideas are controversial versus those that the scholarly field agrees upon?

Gaining this overview of the field gives you a baseline understanding of the terminology, theories, and thought leaders you'll encounter. When you eventually engage in primary research, it will provide you with the baseline language and understanding to have meaningful conversations with subject matter experts (SMEs).

In design research, it's unlikely that you'll be going through this process alone. The organization that you're working with, your colleagues, and other decision-makers can often point you to the most salient research in the field. For example, when I've worked on education projects much like our multilingual learner example, I've relied on policy experts and scholars who have deep knowledge in K–12 education to guide me to existing research, as well as potential subject matter experts.

If you don't have direct access to folks, it might be worthwhile to reach out to academic experts at various universities to see if you can chat with them about your project work and what you are trying to learn, and they can lead you to good starting points for your literature review. Twitter is an excellent resource for finding scholars and asking them questions directly about their research (particularly if you don't have access to research they've authored that is behind paywalls). ResearchGate is also a good resource for finding relevant articles and papers.

Conducting Primary Research

Primary research refers to the data that you will collect yourself. In the design research process, this often includes talking to people through interviews, focus groups, and workshops. It could also involve quantitative methods, such as surveys. In a typical user-centered research project, you will usually focus your research on end users of products or services. In a systems-thinking project, you will conduct primary research with a variety of stakeholders that might include end users of products or services, but also other system stakeholders (such as those who benefit and those who are harmed), decision-makers, and system experts.

These are people who will inform your view of the system, and who should even be collaborators in the process. Through your qualitative approach to understanding the system space, you can think of all these informants as experts: lived experts (these are people who, in a traditional research project, would be your research participants), academic experts, practitioner experts (those who work within the system), and policy experts (those who make decisions that affect the way the system works).

It's critical not only to collect information from these stakeholders, but also to figure out how to engage in co-design with them. As mentioned in Chapter 3, facilitating a more participatory approach to research is an important way to distribute power to those who are most affected by the system. In the multilingual learners example, you could interview students and teachers to learn about their current experiences, and then when it comes to envisioning the future (Chapters 7-9), you would once again involve them to imagine what kinds of approaches could solve some of the system problems that were identified through systems analysis. This approach ensures that you and other decision-makers are designing *with* lived experts, rather than designing *for* them. A participatory approach results in a more resilient system, as well as greater equity throughout the systems-thinking process.

> **NOTE** A NOTE ON THE TERM *STAKEHOLDERS*
>
> Often in traditional user-centered design projects, those who are referred to as *stakeholders* are usually members of your organization who have an interest in the decisions, activities, and outcomes of a project. These people could be a project sponsor, the team that's working on the project, or executives within the company or organization. In the world of social impact, stakeholders can be those who are affected by a system, which is a much broader definition. It could include everyone who has a stake—either positive or negative—in the system, including end users and end beneficiaries, and actors who have a hand in the current system dynamics.

The Data Collection Process

The data collection phase of your project can take anywhere from three weeks to several months, depending on your resources, schedules, and objectives. The process of data collection might take shape as follows (see Figure 4.1):

1. **Kickoff and alignment workshop:** Start the project with an opportunity for key project stakeholders and decision-makers to align on your immersion and discovery objectives and activities.

2. **Immersion (secondary research):** Spend the first few weeks of the project conducting a literature review and viewing available data of the problem space, as well as connecting with your project stakeholders about their domain knowledge.

3. **Subject matter expert (SME) interviews (primary research):** Interview people who have subject matter expertise in your systems space. They could include academic scholars, policy experts, and people from companies and organizations that create products and solutions within the system space, investors, etc.

4. **System stakeholder (lived expert) interviews (primary research):** Interview people who are affected by the system. For a healthcare project, they could include patients and their families. For an education project, they could include students, teachers, district leadership, and community members.

5. **Stakeholder workshops (primary research):** Bring together diverse stakeholders to conduct early analysis toward the end of your data collection. This allows stakeholders to work together, hear one another's perspectives, and collectively think about the system as a whole, rather than just the parts on which they are typically focused.

Research activities leading up to systems analysis

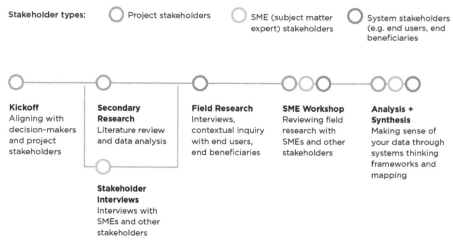

Stakeholder types: ◯ Project stakeholders ◯ SME (subject matter expert) stakeholders ◯ System stakeholders (e.g. end users, end beneficiaries

Kickoff
Aligning with decision-makers and project stakeholders

Secondary Research
Literature review and data analysis

Stakeholder Interviews
Interviews with SMEs and other stakeholders

Field Research
Interviews, contextual inquiry with end users, end beneficiaries

SME Workshop
Reviewing field research with SMEs and other stakeholders

Analysis + Synthesis
Making sense of your data through systems thinking frameworks and mapping

FIGURE 4.1

A typical research phase of your systems-thinking project might look like this from a process perspective, engaging a variety of stakeholders along the way.

These activities will be followed by your analysis and synthesis, in which you make sense of your data through systems-thinking frameworks and mapping.

Kickoff and Alignment Workshop

Kicking off your project by aligning with your key decision-making stakeholders is a good way to ensure that you have a shared idea of expectations, as well as what success looks like for your project. Often, people with various levels of knowledge, expertise, behaviors, and incentives may hold different assumptions about the expectations for your project, as well as the desired outcomes. A kickoff workshop is an opportunity for group alignment on these expectations and outcomes.

Returning to the example of a project focused on K–12 multilingual learners, imagine that you are closely working with a nonprofit that makes investments in education. Again, your project objective is to understand the experience of math for multilingual learners, specifically middle school students in the U.S., and to identify potential opportunity areas or points of intervention for improving outcomes for them.

You would first need to ask yourself:

- Who are the key decision-makers on this project with whom I need to align?
- Who are the system stakeholders I need to better understand through this research?

The stakeholders you would want to engage during a kickoff workshop are:

- Your own project team who will be carrying out the work of research and analysis.
- Those from the nonprofit who will be working with you day-to-day on your project, as well as main decision-makers within that organization.
- Partners on whom success is dependent for varying types of interventions and actions (for example, representatives from government entities that they are collaborating with).
- If you have access to them at the beginning of your project, system stakeholders who represent lived expertise. (Basically, some representatives from those whom you would conduct research with later in the project.)

The objectives of your kickoff workshop will be to align with this group on what success looks like for the project, the stakeholders, themes you should be focused on during the course of your data collection, and an initial understanding of your key research questions.

In the multilingual learner education project, the articulation of these objectives for you and your team might be the following:

- **What does success look like?** At the end of this program, your team will have an increased understanding of the barriers, challenges, as well as the strengths that middle school multilingual learners bring to the table in the context of their math class experiences.

- **What stakeholders and themes should your team be focused on?** You are focused on elevating student voices by conducting primary research with them and later co-designing with them. You are also focused on understanding the system forces that have an impact on their success, such as tracking, assessments, and pedagogy.

You can also use your kickoff workshop to ensure alignment on your data collection activities, because those in the room are likely to be able to introduce you to other people in the system space. Your workshop will also be the first place to start identifying the demographics of the lived experts (those most affected by the system) whom you will want to conduct primary research interviews with, and engage in later systems workshops. (And if you have lived experts within your kickoff workshop, this is an opportunity to make the whole data collection process more empowering for them.) Essentially, the kickoff is an opportunity to understand your project stakeholders' knowledge and use that to inform your project plan.

The decisions you make in the kickoff workshop help further define your data collection activities: starting out with secondary research and some primary stakeholder interviews, and using those findings to drive your primary research phase of work.

Secondary Research

Returning to the example of your education project, you might first work to gain baseline knowledge on math curricula for middle school students. Reviewing state standards for math, as well as district guidelines (particularly for the school districts that you might engage in your primary research), are good ways of gaining an initial understanding of the space. Other resources might include referring to materials and websites from research and development nonprofit organizations, such as EF+ Math, who have reading resources that they point to (and you could eventually involve in your primary research and interviews during the project).

Reviewing Existing Research

You would then refer to scholarly research on the intersection of multilingualism and math outcomes for middle school students. The research you refer to can have a variety of topics. Some of it can be oriented around speech and language in students' school experience, other research references can center on the intersection of math and language, and still other references can be focused on culturally relevant pedagogy. The objective of reading your way through existing research is to give you an overview and context of salient themes and theories within the system space you are exploring.

If it feels like you are being tasked with trying to boil the ocean, you can seek advice from your project stakeholders, as well as SMEs that you are connected with, to recommend themes, works of researchers, or organizations you can refer to. Think of your secondary research as an expansive exercise; this should feel a bit like drinking from the firehose as you immerse yourself in the subject matter.

Analyzing Existing Data and Statistics

In addition to conducting a literature review, you can seek out publicly available data and statistics that might help inform your understanding of the system space. For education projects, you might refer to state assessment data broken down by state and by student demographics. Returning to your education project example, you could look at a state's assessment data for students in specific programs. For example, in Washington state, there are lots of rich data available to the public about student assessment performance.[2] To understand how multilingual learners performed, you could look for the designation "English Language Learner" and investigate the data that might point to performance gaps (see Figure 4.2).

---

2   Washington Office of Superintendent of Public Instruction, "Washington State Report Card," https://washingtonstatereportcard.ospi.k12.wa.us/

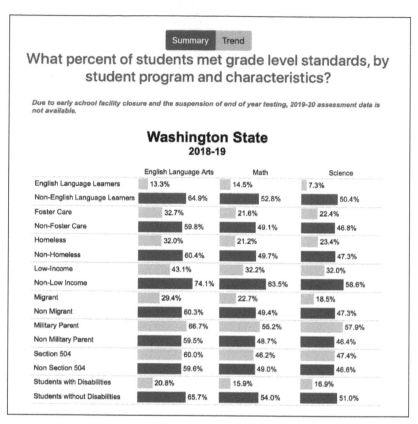

Summary Trend

What percent of students met grade level standards, by student program and characteristics?

Due to early school facility closure and the suspension of end of year testing, 2019-20 assessment data is not available.

Washington State
2018-19

	English Language Arts	Math	Science
English Language Learners	13.3%	14.5%	7.3%
Non-English Language Learners	64.9%	52.8%	50.4%
Foster Care	32.7%	21.6%	22.4%
Non-Foster Care	59.8%	49.1%	46.8%
Homeless	32.0%	21.2%	23.4%
Non-Homeless	60.4%	49.7%	47.3%
Low-Income	43.1%	32.2%	32.0%
Non-Low Income	74.1%	63.5%	58.6%
Migrant	29.4%	22.7%	18.5%
Non Migrant	60.3%	49.4%	47.3%
Military Parent	66.7%	55.2%	57.9%
Non Military Parent	59.5%	48.7%	46.4%
Section 504	60.0%	46.2%	47.4%
Non Section 504	59.6%	49.0%	46.6%
Students with Disabilities	20.8%	15.9%	16.9%
Students without Disabilities	65.7%	54.0%	51.0%

FIGURE 4.2

An example of readily available public data are assessment performances of students. In these statistics, you can clearly see the standards gap between English Language Learners and other students. This is a good starting place to start identifying why this gap exists from a systems perspective.

Statistical data is not only available for education. You can find information on public spending, census data, and socioeconomic demographics by region, crime rates, and property data, among other topics. These data can be found on state, federal, and international organization websites. In addition, research institutions such as Pew Research Center have information on demographic, political, economic, and cultural trends that could be useful for building context about the subject space.

Primary Research

As you are gaining contextual understanding through secondary research, you will start conducting primary research through stakeholder interviews, and building and planning your field research with system stakeholders.

For your education project example, think of the following types of stakeholders as those you will want to learn from—through varying primary research methods—throughout the course of your data collection.

- **Subject matter experts who can articulate their point of view on the system:** These could be academic researchers who have studied math education in primary and secondary school, think tanks, and policy firms. These are folks whose work is oriented around learning about, defining, and analyzing the system space.

- **Practitioners who are system stakeholders themselves:** These could be administrators from school districts or representatives from government entities, such as a state's department of education and other policymakers.

- **Designers of products and services that have an impact on the system:** These are people such as curriculum providers, educational software and content developers, assessment developers and providers, and developers of learning management systems.

- **System stakeholders who are greatly affected by the system:** These are lived experts, often similar to whom you might think of in a typical design research project as end users and end beneficiaries. The question to ask yourself is: Who are the people most affected in the system, but who wield the least power? In the case of the education project example, this might be multilingual learners, their families, and their teachers as well.

This mix of stakeholders builds your understanding of the system at different levels. For example, if you are interviewing children who are multilingual learners and are students in the system, then they will come to the table with a view that is based on their lived experience. If you are interviewing academic researchers, they are more likely to contribute by sharing their perspective on the overarching system. Both perspectives are valuable, and if you are a design researcher, you will likely be comfortable with lived experts, and the idea of engaging multiple levels of system and SME stakeholders may be new to you. This is okay because you can employ similar skills as a researcher—leading with empathy and inquiry, listening and following up, observing—to both types of primary research.

Interviews with Subject Matter Experts

While you are building your baseline understanding through secondary research, you should also be conducting interviews with subject matter experts. These are stakeholders who contribute to your overall understanding of the system space. You want to interview five to six of these SMEs who have varied perspectives, and who will inform your subsequent approach to research with lived-expert system stakeholders. To determine the types of SMEs you should interview, ask yourself these questions:

- **Who brings a critical lens to the problem space?** For example, in the education project example, you might want an expert who has conducted research that has a critical point of view on the school system as it exists today, on how multilingual learners are tracked, or on the policy that's currently in place.

- **Who is currently supportive of the status quo?** Are there researchers who perhaps think very little needs to change in the current system? In the example, you might want to think about researchers who bring an opposite lens to those who are highly critical of the system and its outcomes.

- **Who has experience creating solutions within the system?** It benefits your understanding of the system to interview those who actually have to navigate system decision-making to design and develop. In education, this could include curriculum developers and content providers, as well as high-level school administrators such as a math director in a large school district. It's important to include people in community organizations who are working to address current systemic problems who have clear and consistent context.

- **Who has a quantitative understanding of the system space?** You may want to conduct interviews with analysts who have a broad understanding of, say, the market landscape of products that serve the education market, and who understand trends in the education space when it comes to policy.

Keep in mind that these interviews are meant to be a start, and that you will have an opportunity to further understand the system through your additional forms of primary research, including later stakeholder interviews. The previous questions will also apply to those whom you will engage with further along in your project as you enter your analysis and synthesis phases.

It's possible that those who participate in your key stakeholder interviews will also be ideal candidates for engaging again when you embark on your post-research analysis and synthesis. It's wise to communicate that information to SMEs at the interview stage in order to set expectations if you plan on collaborating with them later.

NOTE A NOTE ON HONORARIA FOR STAKEHOLDERS

In terms of conducting your interviews, you will want to reach out to SMEs, practitioners, and system stakeholders with the context of your project. I usually schedule 30 minutes to one hour for each interview, as SMEs are often busy and are frequently asked for their contribution. I also ensure that all participants are paid appropriately for their time. Although it varies from domain to domain, I usually think of providing honoraria to participants that is in the hourly ballpark of what researchers and strategists on my team might earn. This reflects how much I value their contribution as my work would not be possible without their insight.

Creating a Research Protocol for Engaging with System Stakeholders

Once you have a good landscape view of the system space through your SME interviews, you will shape your formal research with system stakeholders, the lived experts who are affected by the system. This involves creating a research protocol. Your research protocol consists of:

- Key research questions
- Recruiting strategy and research participant demographics
- Research plan and schedule
- Discussion guides for interviews
- Other materials for your research activities

Key Research Questions

Research questions are not the questions you'll ask during an interview, rather they are the questions that you'll need to have answered when you conclude your research. Good research questions will help you determine your research methods. As Erika Hall stated, "Only after you have identified your research questions can you select the best way to answer the question. A lot of people get this wrong and pick the research activity first."[3]

Your questions for your research in which you are uncovering context about the lived experiences of system stakeholders will be focused on the information they can share with you. Their input will be coming from their perspective, so you'll want to focus on that. For example, it likely does not benefit you or your student lived experts to ask them about educational policy. What they can speak to authentically are their own experiences in the classroom, school, and their own community. For your example research into the math experiences of middle school multilingual learners, some research questions might be:

- What are the challenges that multilingual learners face in their math classes?
- What strengths do multilingual learners bring to their classes?
- What kind of decision-making in and outside of the classroom affects multilingual learners' success in math?
- What kind of barriers or challenges do multilingual learners face in their school environments?
- How do the relationships between teachers, administrators, and students affect student performance?
- Are there school or classroom environments in which multilingual students are especially thriving or, on the other side of the coin, struggling?

These research questions will then guide your creation of your system stakeholder recruitment and your research protocol.

---

3   Erika Hall, "Research Questions Are Not Interview Questions," Medium, January 19, 2019.

Recruiting Strategy and Research Participant Demographics

It is critical that you engage with system stakeholders through approaches such as interviews or, ideally, co-design methods. The first step in this process is connecting with them.

My research teams often do a mix of recruiting of system stakeholders both formally and informally. We might use a participant recruitment agency such as Fieldwork, but also use informal recruitment mechanisms such as reaching out to organizations with whom we might be connected. This can be as simple as providing people in those organizations with Google forms that have the details of the research, which they can then share with potential candidates who might fall into our target demographic categories. For example, if we wanted to interview multilingual learners, we might reach out to after-school programs as well as teachers within our network who specialize in teaching students who are English Language Learner–designated.

While you are recruiting, you should be creating your interview discussion guides, as well as the materials that you will use in your interactions with system stakeholders.

Research Plan and Schedule

The research plan is an articulation of the structure of your research activities. For example, in many of my projects, my team has multiple touchpoints with system stakeholders. We will often ask them to engage in cultural activities (a version of what is commonly referred to as *cultural probes*), conduct a 90-minute or two-hour interview, and then follow up with a focus group activity in which they can reflect on the research with us, as well as inform our output. For example, if we were planning to interview students, we would organize our research with them in the following way:

- **One week before interviews:** Send through the cultural activities so your system stakeholders have time to work on them in advance of the interview. This will include guidance on how to submit the outputs from their activities, as well as setting expectations for the interview itself.

- **Stakeholder interview:** This is the two-hour interview that we would conduct with the system stakeholder. We would bring any materials and activities with us, or if the interview is virtual, provide those materials in advance.

CULTURAL MODERATION AND REPRESENTATION IN YOUR DATA COLLECTION

Ideally, you will conduct research and work in system spaces with which you and your team members are familiar. Again, this is a crucial reason to have diversity on your teams. For example, if you are working in complex problem spaces in which a desired outcome is increased equity, you should have representation on your team from communities who are affected by these decisions.

It's possible you might find yourself needing to work on understanding systems within which you and your team lack familiarity with the communities affected. If so, you should first try to include representation on your team; in other cases, you should at least include a cultural moderator. This is someone who has shared lived experiences with your research participants, comes from a shared demographic or racial background, and has familiarity in the domain you are examining. For example, if you are conducting research with multilingual learners and their families, it is advisable to have a member of your team who has experience with having been a multilingual learner themselves, or include someone who works with or teaches multilingual students and has a similar demographic background as the students you'll be interviewing. This approach gives you additional context, helps include perspectives that your team might not have themselves, and prioritizes increased equity in your research process.

- **Post-research discussion group:** This is a group session in which our system stakeholders would come together in a facilitated setting to reflect on the interviews we've conducted, and allow for additional feedback and engagement in our data collection.

For all of these activities, you would articulate the roles for each of your team members in your research plan. For example, every interview should have a moderator and a note-taker. (A note-taker can either be in the session, or can take notes during a later recording.)

Discussion Guides for Interviews

A discussion guide is your written script for conducting interviews (see Figure 4.3). A good thing to remember is that it's not meant to be a word-for-word script; it's called a *guide* because it's intended to loosely guide your discussion. You can use it to orient yourself, as well as ensure that your timing for sections, themes you want to touch on, and activities stays fairly on-schedule. You will also want to leave room for follow-up questions, and to follow conversational paths that could lead to interesting insights.

Discussion Guide for In-Home Visits

Introduction and Warm-up

Introduction (10 minutes)

- Hello, thank you so much for taking time to speak with us today. (Introduce everyone present.)
- Our conversation today should take about 3 to 4 hours. If you need to pause or stop at any point, please let us know.
- *Have participant review and sign the NDA form.*
- Our team is working on a project that examines how we might improve the banking experience for people like you.
- We want to get to know you and learn about your weekly routine and life. We will be asking some questions, but there are no right or wrong answers. You're the expert today, we are looking to learn from you!
- We may have to ask you for clarifying details about a topic we're less familiar with.
- Is it okay to audio record our conversation today and take photos? This is mainly for our own note-taking purposes. *(If so, start the recording.)*
- Great - let's get started!

FIGURE 4.3
A good discussion guide should be scannable, and include timing on the different sections and activities. It should also be in a format that is printable and easy to reference.

Other Materials for Your Research Activities

As mentioned in "Research Plan and Schedule," you could plan for and include projective techniques in your research. This includes pre-interview activities such as cultural probes, or journaling, or in-interview activities such as mapping exercises. You would need to create the materials for these activities so you can share them with your system stakeholders in advance. After your materials, schedule, and recruiting are prepared, you're ready to get out in the field and start talking to system stakeholders.

Conducting Your System Stakeholder Interviews

If you can visit system stakeholders in their school, work, or home environment, this gives you an opportunity to observe their activities and interactions, in addition to asking them questions. Even if you must conduct your activities virtually, you can gain contextual insight about your participants' perspectives through pre-interview activities and creative exercises you have stakeholders do or that you can facilitate with them (see Figure 4.4).

FIGURE 4.4

In one education project in which my team sought to understand students' experience in English Language Arts, we had students create memes that reflected their feelings about their classes and the content used in class. This approach gave a fun opening to discuss their frustrations and joys when it came to their classroom experiences. It's just one way to meet research participants where they are, in order to help promote your dialogue with them.

When you are in your interviews, there are a few tips that uncover information in a meaningful way.

- Follow a thread (even if it's not in the guide).
- Ask open-ended questions: "Why"? "How?" "Tell me about...."
- Don't ask yes/no questions.
- Get people to tell stories: find the story; prompt for it.

When you've completed each interview, it's wise to spend a few minutes debriefing with your team to start capturing your key takeaways.

MAKING YOUR RESEARCH MORE INCLUSIVE

In her book *Mismatch: How Inclusion Shapes Design*, Kat Holmes describes "learn from diversity" as one of the key principles of inclusive design.[4] For stakeholder research, this means taking into consideration the diversity of those who are affected by the system. For your example of research into the experience of multilingual learners, you are part of the way there because you are focused on stakeholders who are usually marginalized, and aren't typically centered in research. You will want to conduct research—with stakeholders such as students and their families—to stay focused on those who might be most affected by the system but hold little power in terms of decision-making.

Going beyond just selecting who you will be conducting research with, your research process and team should reflect the diversity of your research participants. Design research teams often do not reflect the racial, gender, or socioeconomic diversity of research participants, particularly in research that is focused on marginalized groups.

In instances where I'm interviewing those who are from vulnerable or marginalized groups, or those who have different cultural backgrounds, I make sure that my research team includes a cultural moderator, or a researcher reflective of a similar background to those we will be interviewing. (See the sidebar entitled "Cultural Moderation and Representation in Your Data Collection.")

For example, when I've been tasked with conducting research in other countries, I make sure that my team includes a researcher or moderator who is local in order to: 1) help our system stakeholders feel more comfortable, and 2) help interpret cultural nuances that might be lost on me and other researchers. It's hubris for design researchers to think that they can go into situations without biases that will affect their ability to gain insight that's not clouded by their unconscious judgment. Bias, of course, will exist, but self-awareness and minimizing said biases by working with researchers and moderators who have diverse perspectives will help make your research more meaningful.

---

4   Kat Holmes, *Mismatch: How Inclusion Shapes Design* (The MIT Press, 2018).

Subject Matter Expert (SME) Workshop

When you've completed your research with system stakeholders, it's a good idea to take the data back to your decision-makers, as well as subject matter experts whose input and perspective you value as part of continuing to build your system understanding. Think of it as an opportunity to collaborate in order to triangulate the different forms of data you've collected thus far, from project stakeholders, SMEs, practitioners, and lived experts (system stakeholders).

Ideally, you would invite a combination of these stakeholders, particularly those who are practiced at considering the system from perspectives beyond their own experiences. The objective of the workshop is two-fold: to continue to examine the status quo from an ecosystem, as well as from an empathic point of view when it comes to system stakeholders, and to consider potential interventions or opportunity areas for addressing problems. Although you are still in the act of understanding and mapping the status quo, having an initial idea of how SMEs, project stakeholders, and system stakeholders might view problem solving is informative at this point in the process.

You will want to plan your workshop to involve multiple stakeholders, making it accessible to those who might not be familiar with design-thinking frameworks or design research, and work to make it a meaningful knowledge sharing and collaborative activity.

Workshop Structure

Your workshop can be a couple of hours or up to a full day, depending on how much collaboration and how many participants you would like to engage. It's important to be considerate of participants' availability and time commitments, so try to minimize the time commitment and plan carefully to design an engaging experience. I typically break the workshop into two parts: understanding the status quo and identifying opportunity areas. This helps move the workshop from analysis to generative ideation.

In terms of understanding the status quo, you can collaborate on a view of the ecosystem and its stakeholders by bringing in insights from your various interviews. Insights from your interviews with system stakeholders especially help SMEs and project stakeholders view the system from the perspective of a system stakeholder who

1) does not hold a lot of decision-making power, and 2) is deeply affected by how the system currently works. You can provide workshop breakout groups with quotes, outputs, and takeaways from your interviews. With this, you can conduct a simple systems analysis by thinking about the different levels of stakeholders in the system, centering the student for whom the system of education has great impact (good and bad). (See Figure 4.5.)

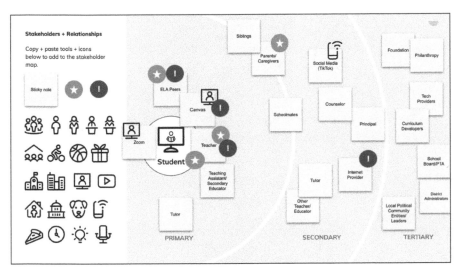

FIGURE 4.5
A systems map that indicates stakeholders and relationships gives you additional context as you continue your systems mapping after the workshop. This is a direct and accessible way to learn quickly from diverse stakeholders, as well as a creative way for them to collaborate.

For identifying key opportunity areas, you can use design thinking techniques that can help participants think about possible interventions in the system. Often with design thinking, you can use "how might we" prompts to spur ideation. In your workshop, try to come equipped with prompts for thinking about interventions that your workshop participants can focus on in their breakout groups. These opportunity-focused exercises enable you to understand their perspective when it comes to the kinds of interventions or solutions that your stakeholders view as essential to more desirable outcomes (see Figures 4.6 and 4.7).

Opportunity
Ideation

Choose one prompt from the three categories below and copy into the next slide.
Feel free to modify the question to better suit your student's needs.

Content	Teacher Practice	Student Voice
OPTION 1 How might we make content more locally relevant for Candace?	**OPTION 2** How might we promote more courageous conversations about race from Candace's teacher?	**OPTION 3** How might we make technology more inclusive and have Candace feel valued?

FIGURE 4.6

For a workshop that is oriented around making English Language Arts more culturally relevant for students, my team created three prompts for each breakout team to focus on.

Opportunity
Ideation

How
might we....

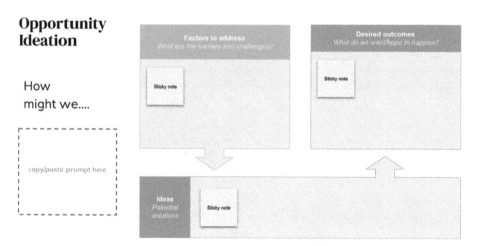

FIGURE 4.7

We provided a canvas for teams to complete their prompts from Figure 4.6. This format creates a structure to drive collaboration about potential solutions and interventions.

You and your team should be able to walk away from your SME workshop with perspectives on the system, combined with ideas, analysis, and ideation. The added benefit of conducting a workshop where you bring many minds together—from academic experts, to practitioners, to solution providers, to policymakers and lived experts—is that you can start socializing your efforts at understanding the space and continue involving them throughout your systems-thinking process.

SYSTEM SPOTTING

THE DOORS ON MY LEFT

When approaching a stop, the Light Rail train in Seattle makes an announcement as it enters the individual stations: "Now entering Beacon Hill Station. Exit through the doors on my right." I've always thought this curious, that the train is represented as a sentient being that has a right and a left. However, I've wondered: in Western culture, how else would you state it? If the announcement said, "Exit through the doors to the west," you can guess the confusion that would ensue, with people lining up on both sides of the train, just taking a guess as to which doors will open to the platform.

For speakers of Guugu Thimithirr, the language of an Aboriginal group of the same name in Queensland, Australia, this type of orientation around cardinal directions (north, south, east, and west) would be perfectly acceptable and well-understood. Unlike most Western languages, Guugu Thimithirr does not have body-relative directions, of which "to my right" is a good example. Rather, a member of that group would say something along the lines of "my sister is southeast of here" instead of "my sister is to your right."

It's a reminder that language shapes the very way cultures think, and also a reminder that as a designer it's important to be cognizant of the kinds of world-view that you bring to the table, even for things that otherwise seem fixed or objective. Everything is dependent upon how you frame things.

Analysis and Synthesis

Now that you have lots of data to work with and you've developed meaningful awareness, understanding, and even a bit of expertise in the system space, you will move into the analysis and synthesis phase of this work, just as you would a design research project. Your analysis and synthesis will be focused on triangulating the various types of data you've collected: through secondary research such as a literature review, and primary research such as project stakeholder interviews, SME interviews, system stakeholder interviews, and your SME workshop. One distinction in a systems-thinking project is that it makes sense to continue engaging many of the stakeholders with whom you've conducted primary research to validate your analysis and co-create with you. There really shouldn't be a "go away and produce something" approach, because, again, you as a designer are here to facilitate and articulate other people's knowledge, whether it is the lived experiences of end beneficiaries or the broad knowledge of SMEs. This engagement, collaboration, and alignment continues as you synthesize your findings into systems maps.

Takeaways

- In a systems-thinking project, your job as a designer is to facilitate other peoples' expertise and knowledge. This approach means involving diverse stakeholders who have a systems lens on the space, as well as conducting research with those who have lived experiences as system stakeholders.

- Secondary research, such as literature review and quantitative data review, is an important way of building foundational knowledge of the systems space.

- A good way of kicking off your primary research is to conduct interviews with subject matter experts (SMEs) to understand and unpack multiple systems-level perspectives.

- Your central primary research activity is to conduct interviews (or other activities) with system stakeholders: people who have lived experiences that are worth understanding. These are folks who are the most affected by the system, and likely hold very little power in how the system works. These interviews help you gain a picture of the impact of the system, as well as its cascading effects.

- Conducting a SME workshop in which you bring diverse perspectives together to review the primary research data that you've collected and to further collaborate is a good way to wrap up your data collection. This workshop helps to socialize your work and gain additional system knowledge from folks who have a perspective on the status quo, as well as potential solutions, interventions, and desired outcomes.

Shree Lakshmi (SL) Rao is an equity-centered system change Principal Service Designer at Substantial with experience across sectors (tech, philanthropy, global health and government) and a background in interaction design. They are a strong proponent of evolving the design practice to be anti-racist, decolonized, and systems-thinking oriented.

How did you end up in design?

I had a circuitous route to design. I studied electronics engineering in undergrad in India, and I enjoy that kind of technical problem-solving. One of the big things that I took away from my technical degree was seeing how systems work. However, growing up in India, I had difficulty finding direct applicability of these systems to the large, complex societal issues I saw around me.

At the same time, I was engaging in civic activism and theater, specifically children's theater, to make up for what I felt my engineering degree was not giving me. Through this, I saw how people react emotionally to storytelling, and that experiences and stories are a way of having impact. This led me to pursue a degree in interaction design, where I saw parallels between developing immersive experiences for children through sets, lights and storytelling, and technology experiences. In design, I saw a process that I felt could apply to the idea of solving things around me, that closed that gap that I felt in engineering.

However, as my understanding of the design process grew, I started realizing that it maybe isn't as innovative as we all think it is. It's still based on the same kinds of experimentation and scientific and technical inquiry that informs engineering. So there is room for improvement, for designers to think more broadly about their practice.

How has your practice evolved to include systems thinking?

My initial experience was as a traditional user experience designer in commercial tech. However, I had been working on platforms that involved working a lot with data, with teams attempting to understand human behavior on a global scale. There's an assumption in what you learn in design school, that you can talk to eight people and define experiences for lots of people. When you're designing an experience for millions, that approach just doesn't make sense.

A few years into big tech, I felt the strong disconnect between what brought me into design in the first place, designing for social impact. I wanted to understand where the gaps in my toolkit were in terms of applying commercial tech design to complex social issues. I shifted my work to global health and immediately recognized that problem-solving is much broader than people using products. You start understanding how, for example, pharmaceutical companies have their own incentives, how people have a myriad of cultural contexts, and how community social norms can shift behaviors around health service utilization. Ultimately, we as designers are also part of the system: we are associated with those who have the opportunity and power to make things happen.

If we focus only on the user, without an awareness of the systems that surround them (and us all), we reinforce existing systems of oppression because of our limited view. So we have to change our approach to recognize not only the system, but also our role in it.

In your work with the Washington State Department of Commerce, you focused on the system that surrounds foster youth. How do you think your approach was more systems-focused than the typical design-thinking project?

I was brought on to support the work to prevent youth homelessness from systems like foster care and the juvenile legal system. System-side stakeholders had already met in working groups that had one or two lived experts. In a traditional design project, designers will gather insights from the stakeholders who are paying for the project (potentially the system) and work uncritically within that system to support improvement of processes. The process would also include pivoting to talk with eight "users" of the system.

I saw the power dynamics of the systems playing out: lived experts are not part of the solution-making in traditional policy processes. I used state level data to better understand who was experiencing housing insecurity at higher rates and researched the historical and current orientations of the system. I not only talked to stakeholders within the systems but also those who were critical of them. I mapped the power dynamics, how the systems worked, and how they interacted with each other.

By understanding the system and its impact, I was able to shift away from the traditional design research process. It made me reconsider: who am I investigating? Am I investigating these young people, or am I investigating the system? Considering what is wrong with the system as a starting point and taking a trauma-informed lens was important.

So rather than conducting interviews that focus on what's wrong with young people who are most affected by the system, I collaborated with lived experts to design youth working sessions that were centered on healing, learning, and visioning. We intentionally included youth who were most impacted by the systems and had the least access to power: youth of color, rural youth, and LGBTQ2. We made the sessions accessible around the state and ensured that they had resources for mental health. During the sessions, we unpacked the systems together because they're invisible. Many youth didn't know that they were involved in multiple systems. We got feedback from multiple young people who appreciated that we didn't do interviews. It was good that the experience instead was an opportunity to be in community with each other and learn together.

We collected what young people said and wrote it into a policy document that was shared with the state legislature, and young people are still involved in the process. The work also revealed how the state needed to invest in more preventative work because the systems were failing to reduce the issues that were causing young people to be involved in the system in the first place. This would not have been as evident without looking at all the intersecting systems.

What are some ways that practitioners can shift their work as you did and incorporate a systems lens?

It's not sexy, but they should do secondary research. See what's out there already. What does the research say, for example, about adolescent development? Utilize what's out there to build upon, rather than starting from scratch. Likewise, work to understand historical context; that helps you recognize how power shows up in the system.

Also, build relationships rather than being extractive in your design research. Connect with lived experts with partnership rather than showing up in your power to take from the lived experts.

Lastly, drink water and rest because the work is never done.

CHAPTER 5

Synthesis and Mapping Stakeholders

You've now done the work of conducting secondary research, interviewing system stakeholders, and conducting participatory workshops with experts, which is a huge accomplishment and the foundation for meaningful insights. The next step in the process is to make sense of all these data by synthesizing them. *Synthesis* is the act of sense-making. According to design research expert Jon Kolko, it is an attempt to "organize, manipulate, prune, and filter gathered data into a cohesive structure for information building."[1] It's critical to recognize that what you've collected thus far is data, which is what information is made of, but it's not yet actual information. Information is organized, categorized, and analyzed data—it's contextually relevant and structured into insights. This is where the rubber hits the road in the design research process: turning data into useful information.

The Synthesis Process

Many designers find the synthesis process to be fairly opaque and difficult. One thing that helps with the "where do I begin?" feeling (or frustration) of the synthesis process is the use of theoretical frameworks that help you categorize the data. Different forms of mapping can be used for both analysis and presentation: the same frameworks that you use for sense-making can be used to present your research output.

Categories of mapping frameworks that you can use in a systems-thinking project include stakeholder mapping, causal loop mapping, root cause mapping, and linear mapping.

- **Stakeholder maps:** For understanding system stakeholders, stakeholder mapping is an effective way to analyze your data and frame your research insights. In systems thinking, you are interested in analyzing interconnectedness and causality. While you can think explicitly about causality by way of events and causal loop mapping, for stakeholder mapping, understanding relationships is key.

---

1   Jon Kolko, "Information Architecture and Design Strategy: The Importance of Synthesis during the Process of Design," *Proceedings of the Industrial Designers Society of America Conference*, 2007.

- **Causal loop maps:** A key focus of systems thinking is understanding causality. Causal loop mapping is a visual way to represent chains and degrees of cause and effect. It is an important form of analysis because it forces designers away from the notion that they are designing for a linear series of events. Instead, you are examining what, within a system, has the most impact from a problem (and incentives) perspective. Everything has multiple degrees of impact and understanding the cause and effect within the status quo of the system helps you determine where to intervene. In a typical user-centered design project, you might map a linear user journey or indicate pain points in your target user's experience. By using causal loop mapping to analyze a problem space, you can do the following:

  - Understand how events currently play out and gain perspective on cause and effect.

  - Uncover problems at many different levels, not just the personal level for a user, but across organizations, and at various levels of hierarchy.

  - Recognize patterns that help you understand the root cause for the most prominent problems within a system.

- **Root cause maps:** Uncovering the root cause of a problem space is an important aspect of systems thinking. The iceberg diagram is a mapping technique popularized by Peter Senge in *The Fifth Discipline*. It helps systems thinkers look at events (the visible tip of the iceberg) and identify what is below the water (root cause). It's a simple way to align on the root cause quickly and effectively. Another common framework for mapping the root cause is the "fishbone" diagram, also known as the *Ishikawa diagram*.

- **Linear maps.** An alternative to causal loop mapping is showing a chain of events. You can think of this type of framework as a form of "if this happens, then that happens." It helps stakeholders consider what leads to certain outcomes, both desirable and undesirable.

To put it simply, a good systems map reinforces the three aspects of effective systems thinking: causality, connectedness, and wholeness. You'll learn about stakeholder mapping in this chapter. See Chapter 6, "Mapping Forces" for causal loop, root cause, and linear mapping techniques for your analysis and synthesis.

THE SHIP THAT GOT STUCK

In March 2021, a mega-container ship called the *Ever Given* wedged itself in the Suez Canal (see Figure 5.1). It entered the canal at too high a speed, and with a nearly magical combination of factors that added up to bad luck, it ended up sideways, blocking the entire canal. In the subsequent six days, crews failed to free it from its position. As a result, 10% (yes, 10%!) of all global shipping came to a standstill, with economies losing billions of dollars per day.

Why did one stuck ship have such a devastating effect on the global economy?

The story began with the introduction of container ships in the 1950s. Most shipping at that time took place with traditional ships, with their goods—and their varied shapes and sizes—being painstakingly offloaded at global ports by lots of sheer manpower. There simply wasn't a system in place for containers to be widely used—for example, the system didn't have ships built for containers, special cranes for containers, and railways in which containers could be directly transported.

During the Vietnam war, everything changed when it became clear to the U.S. government that shipping containers were a more expedient way to move supplies between California and the ports of Vietnam. In turn, this need pushed the necessary standardization that has now made the shipping container ubiquitous in global trading. As a result, the global economy was more readily connected—making technical products (such as computers and iPhones), clothing, toys, etc. much cheaper and more readily available. It's also one reason that much of the U.S. manufacturing industry dried up due to cheaper competition overseas, and consequently, many countries in Asia became far more prosperous.

Shipping containers are a good example for showing the pros, cons, and multiple angles to every system. As Alexis Madrigal put it in his podcast *Containers*, "If you want to understand how the world of commerce works, there's no better microcosm than the system that moves containers around the globe."[2]

One result of global connectivity that occurred with shipping containers is the concept of "just-in-time manufacturing." Journalist Peter S. Goodman said, "Rather than waste money stockpiling extra goods in warehouses, companies can depend on the magic of the internet and the global shipping industry to summon what they need as they need it."[3]

---

2 Alexis C. Madrigal, "Episode 1: Welcome to Global Capitalism," Medium, April 6, 2017.

3 Peter S. Goodman, "In Suez Canal, Stuck Ship Is a Warning About Excessive Globalization," *New York Times*, March 26, 2021.

Even though the *Ever Given* was freed after a harrowing six days during which the global economy hemorrhaged, it still serves as a powerful reminder of how interconnected our global systems are, and how society needs to rethink its ability to be more resilient in the face of unpredictable change, whether it involves a pandemic or a giant ship stuck sideways in a canal.

FIGURE 5.1

The *Ever Given*, which is the length of about two city blocks and was packed with everything from fresh produce to IKEA furniture, is shown lodged in its position in which it spent six days blocking the Suez Canal.

Prompts to consider:

- What kinds of things exist in your daily experiences that point to a larger connected system?
- When you have a package delivered, for example, what kinds of pros and cons are related to that convenience?
- How could the global systems that we see become more sustainable?

Stakeholder Mapping

Formal systems thinking practices usually focus on mapping system forces. This approach typically involves causal loop diagrams, stock-flow diagrams, and other mapping exercises that emphasize the relationship between events and forces.

Within the design practice, there is a fundamental focus on people: who they are, how they behave, and what they do. Because of this focus on understanding people first, a logical and more intuitive starting point for design practitioners is to map relationships among people. There are some good existing frameworks that serve as that starting point.

The Ecological Framework

In the 1980s, psychologist Uri Bronfenbrenner developed a theoretical framework called the *Ecological Framework for Human Development*. Although initially it was intended to be used to understand the system around a child's psychological development, it has been adapted over time by various organizations that address what are called *wicked problems:* i.e., social issues in realms such as healthcare, education, and policy.

It's a powerful core framework that indicates five levels of context in which a human's development occurs: individual, microsystem, mesosystem, exosystem, and macrosystem. Thinking about how context radiates outward into larger and more connected structures is a great introduction to systems theory (see Figure 5.2). The key to this framework is the acknowledgment that, although activity stems from individual behavior, there are multiple layers of collective behavior that result in a system that affects individuals. This abstract view of the context in which an individual sits (in Bronfenbrenner's case, it is a child) has a benefit: "Instead of a narrow focus on the private lives and troubles of people seen as isolated individuals, we look also at the social context within which those troubles occur and to which they are inevitably bound."[4]

---

4   Michael Rothery, "Critical Ecological Systems Theory," in *Theoretical Perspectives for Direct Social Work Practice: A Generalist-Eclectic Approach*, ed. Nick Coady and Peter Lehmann (Springer, 2016).

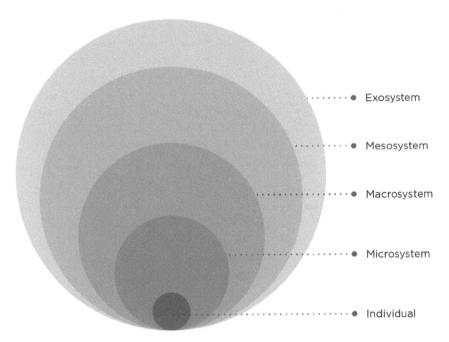

FIGURE 5.2

Bronfenbrenner's Ecological Framework for Human Development has five layers of entities (people, institutions, etc.) that surround an individual.

This model has been modified for different purposes. For example, UNICEF, with its work in global education, has developed a version to drive analysis of problems and potential problem-solving approaches within that space, and it categorizes four levels of educational context:

- **Individual/interpersonal:** Knowledge, attitudes, and practices among children, adolescents, and families that affect educational decisions and actions.

- **Community:** Social beliefs and norms, gender norms, social and economic conditions and resources, knowledge and attitudes about education among community members, sense of empowerment, and collective efficacy that affect educational choices, decisions, and practices.

- **Institutional:** Institutional conditions of the education system that affect inclusion and quality, including educational media.

- **Policy/system:** Policies and governance elements of educational systems that facilitate or discourage inclusive and quality education, as well as positive decisions about education among individuals and families.

In order to engage in stakeholder mapping, you don't necessarily need to use the five layers of Bronfenbrenner's framework. You can simplify it, for example, to focus on just two or three layers of direct and indirect relationships. The best way to think about it is that you are putting a human in the center: a human who serves as a good representation of a core system stakeholder, essentially those who are most affected by the system. You can then use the layers within your map to analyze the layers of stakeholders who swirl around them and affect their experiences, context, and outcomes.

If you return to the example from the previous chapter of your imaginary research project focused on middle school multilingual learners, you can take stock of the different players in your research and organize them into those who are most affected (students and their families), those who have direct influence on students' situations (educators, school administrators, community organizations), those who have indirect relationships with those individuals (local government entities, curriculum developers, district administrators), and those who have abstract, societal impact beyond even those indirect relationships (media, think tanks, researchers, education policymakers).

The key thing to focus on are the relationships among different stakeholders, particularly when it comes to power. Here are some useful prompts as you consider the relationships within a system:

- Who holds power in this relationship?
- Are there misperceptions among system stakeholders?
- Who are the decision-makers in this dynamic?
- Are there relationships that need to be strengthened?
- Are there entities that dominate the varied relationships?
- Are there power dynamics that are harmful? Are there power dynamics that are helpful?

The key to this type of stakeholder analysis is to think about the individuals who might sit at the center of your stakeholder map and the stakeholders who would be in the tiers that radiate outward. You might discover that, within the status quo, there is a disconnect between who the system is centered on versus who it should be centered on.

For example, designer and strategist SL Rao, who conducted research with youth who had been in Washington state's foster system, pointed out that you might think that those at the center of the system, or, in other words, most prioritized in the system, would be the youth themselves. However, when they conducted their research and analysis, they found that the system really functioned around the social workers, because the system was most incentivized to revolve around their work. (You can read more about SL's work in the interview at the end of Chapter 4, "Collecting Your Data.") Similar perspectives exist in many user-centered research projects. For example, researchers in the educational software space often gain feedback from administrators (who are often also the buyers of the software) and possibly teachers. Rarely do they conduct research directly with students, who might not be end users, but are greatly affected by the software nonetheless.

To mitigate this disconnect between what the system is and what it should be, your focus is on building your stakeholder map with those whom you conclude should be at the center of the map and then analyzing the relationships that surround them.

Layers of Relationships

The beauty of stakeholder mapping is that you do not need to be dogmatic about the layers. You can use Bronfenbrenner's five-layered model (individual, microsystem, macrosystem, mesosystem, exosystem), or the UNICEF model, or you can simply map primary, secondary, and tertiary relationships.

Just as Bronfenbrenner's center of the ecological map is the child, in your imagined education project, the center would be the multilingual learner student. Your map is made up of concentric circles, with as many layers as you plan to map (Figure 5.3).

You can then identify stakeholders who fall into each category. For the education project example, you might consider the following prompts:

- **Primary stakeholders:** These could be other students, family members, teachers. Who else has a direct relationship with the student?
- **Secondary stakeholders:** Who are the decision-makers who have direct influence on primary stakeholders? Who are others in the community who have relationships with primary stakeholders?
- **Tertiary stakeholders:** Who drives the system that has an impact on primary and secondary stakeholders? Who influences the broader landscape that affects your primary stakeholders?

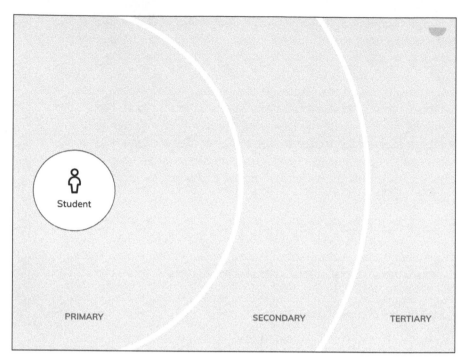

FIGURE 5.3

In this project, the student is the individual at the core of the stakeholder map. The stakeholders in each of the concentric layers are identified in relation to the student. During your analysis, you can do this exercise in a tool such as Miro, or even on a whiteboard.

The multilayered framework is a good way to categorize the hierarchies and layers of system stakeholders. After you've identified stakeholders, you can go on to represent strong and weak relationships with solid (strong) and dotted (weak) lines or emphasize power dynamics through visual emphasis. Figure 5.4 shows an example of stakeholder mapping analysis in progress. This stakeholder map shows a student's relationship with their surrounding math education ecosystem. It's the beginning of analysis based on research insights from secondary research and primary research with students, and it was a tool used in a workshop with subject matter experts to surface their feedback and input.

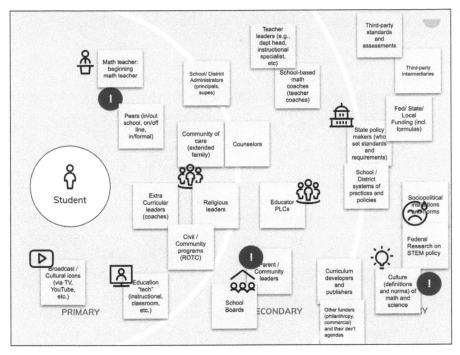

FIGURE 5.4
Stakeholder mapping analysis using Google Slides shows how you can
rapidly understand hierarchy and stakeholder relationships.

The most important aspect of stakeholder analysis that you can communicate to your audience is the power relationships between system
stakeholders. Often, in user-centered design, designers consider only
the relationship between the product they're designing and the end
user. Even with complex products, such as enterprise software, for
example, this purview extends only to different layers of product
users. The biggest distinction when you take a systems-thinking lens
is that an end user is likely to be only one player in the system, and is
quite possibly not even the most important one. The power you want
to understand sits between people and organizations or entities, not
between a product and a user.

Understanding Bounded Rationality

Hundreds of years of economic theory have yielded a specific archetype: homo economicus. You may know this archetype. He—because it's always a "he"— is the person who makes perfectly rational decisions with perfect and complete information. Although it describes an infallible human, it is, in itself, a flawed concept. As Richard Thaler and Cass Sunstein described *homo economicus* in *Nudge: Improving Decisions About Health, Wealth, and Happiness*, "If you look at economics textbooks, you will learn that homo economicus can think like Albert Einstein, store as much memory as IBM 's Big Blue, and exercise the willpower of Mahatma Gandhi. Really. But the folks that we know are not like that. Real people have trouble with long division if they don't have a calculator, sometimes forget their spouse's birthday, and have a hangover on New Year's Day. They are not homo economicus; they are homo sapiens."[5]

That humans are imperfect decision-makers is an important concept in systems thinking. In *Thinking in Systems*, Donella Meadows described this concept as *bounded rationality*, a term first coined by economist Herbert Simon: people are "bound" by what they know, as well as their limitations as humans. These limitations include their biases, experiences, and backgrounds. Meadows shared some examples of bounded rationality: "Tourists flock to places like Waikiki or Zermatt and then complain that those places have been ruined by all the tourists. Farmers produce surpluses of wheat, butter, or cheese, and prices plummet... Corporations collectively make investment decisions that cause business-cycle downturns." Even when humans have broader information, they still trip up in ways that serve short-term interests rather than long-term goals.

You yourself have knowledge defined by bounded rationality. In addition, conducting research that is focused on just one type of stakeholder contributes to a narrow understanding, even if that stakeholder is one who is most affected by the system. Designers might want to focus on, say an end user for purposes of empathy, but too much focus on this type of stakeholder does not give you a view on decisions made by other stakeholders. Systems analysis is a way of expanding your purview. As Meadows further explained, "From a wider perspective, information flows, goals, incentives, and

---

5   Richard H. Thaler and Cass R. Sunstein, *Nudge: Improving Decisions About Health, Wealth, and Happiness* (Penguin Group US, 2008).

disincentives can be restructured so that separate, bounded, rational actions do add up to results that everyone desires."[6]

One way of understanding the limitations of people's decision-making is to map them as stakeholders and connect their relationships, and as you saw in the previous map, the extent to which they are degrees away from each other. The following example shows how one team mapped stakeholder relationships in a project focused on home health services for elderly patients.

Example: Mapping Home Health Services

Imagine that you are seeking to understand how to expand a health service geared toward providing at-home care for home-bound elderly patients. Understanding this system, and finding opportunities for expansion and potentially additional funding, was the task of a student team, composed of Mike Cameron, Maren Muñoz, Kyle Vaughan, and Kat Ward at the Design Leadership program at Johns Hopkins University and Maryland Institute College of Art. The team worked with gerontologists at the Johns Hopkins Home-based Medicine Program (JHOME) to conduct primary research into the home healthcare program's impact, its relationships with patients and other stakeholders, and tangential services and stakeholders. The program is critical for providing preventive care for elderly patients and keeping them out of the emergency room for basic health services. The team mapped these relationships in a high-level stakeholder map (see Figure 5.5).

They sought to understand not just the customer experience and the relationships connected to the customer, but also those on the service side, as well as the financial side of the system.

The stakeholder map bears a similarity to the earlier framework in which a designer maps primary, secondary, and tertiary relationships. Kat Ward, a design strategist on the project explained: "We looked at the different layers of interaction in relation to the customer/patient. First, who are interacting directly with patients on a day-to-day basis? Caregivers, Meals on Wheels, and other services. Then, who is the next tier out from that inner cell? They might be city services, such as mail carriers, or health services, such as emergency care. As we then looked at the tertiary level, we were able to group

---

6   Donella Meadows, *Thinking in Systems* (Chelsea Green Publishing, 2008).

into categories of these organizations that create, fund, and support various services." As design students, the team found this analysis beneficial. According to Ward, "Considering and mapping the system of stakeholders helped expand our imagination beyond what we were seeing on the surface with the patient. These individuals, their world has quite a few limitations because they are often homebound. Although it was incredibly important for us to understand their perspective, thinking a few degrees out helped us see other potential points of intervention that might not be obvious if we just focused on the patient experience." The analysis helped the team expand their own bounded rationality and see beyond their limited knowledge.

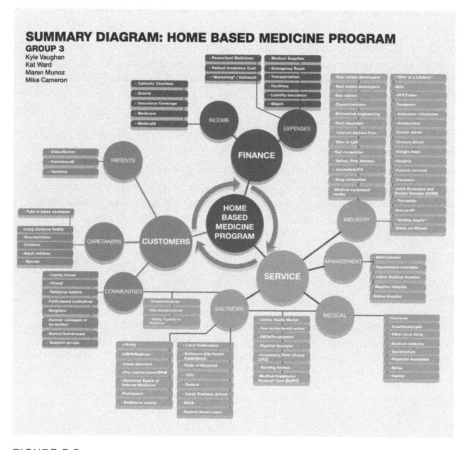

FIGURE 5.5

The design team working with JHOME recognized that it was beneficial to categorize and catalog as many different stakeholders as possible.

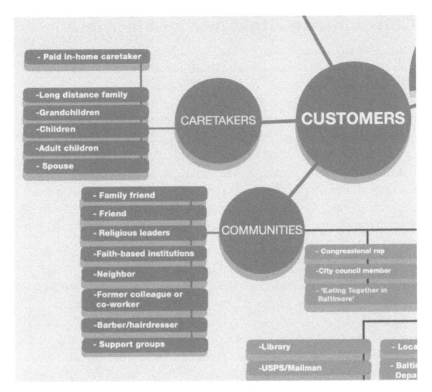

FIGURE 5.6
In this detail of the stakeholder map, you can see the different entities that fall under the "Customer" category.

The act of categorically mapping the stakeholders and their relationship to the JHOME program—not just the patients—gave decision-makers a more complete view of the variety of entities involved (see Figure 6.5). This approach allowed those involved to consider a variety of possible interventions, ranging from partnering with Meals on Wheels for communication and applications for the JHOME service, to expanded forms of funding. And, in the end, the program's focus on preventive care is a long-term healthcare system intervention in and of itself: it is far less expensive than reactive and emergency care, and it meets patients where they are.

Comparative Stakeholder Mapping

Another form of stakeholder mapping is to create an ecosystem map that compares individuals or entities at the center, articulating the difference between their experiences. For example, in your education project, you might want to create a map that shows the varying experiences of multilingual learners: How might the experience of public school versus private school affect multilingual learners? How might the experience of being in a large district with lots of students who are learning English as a second language differ from being the only student trying to learn English? This approach, of course, depends on your key research questions. Do you need to understand the differences between students in different environments?

For example, my team once worked on a project in which we had to understand the various types of hospitals and how those hospitals had an impact on the experience of surgery in a South Asian country's healthcare system. We took data from multiple forms of research (primary and secondary) and boiled the categories down to three distinct types of hospitals: large public hospitals, small private hospitals, and private chain hospitals. The variation of an ecological map that we used had layers that showed the layers of environments: the patient at the center, the operating theater, and the hospital. This framework helped us understand the distinctions between the patient experience, the types of stakeholders in each environment, and the levels of expertise, cost constraints, and bureaucracy (see Figures 5.7 and 5.8).

This type of analysis helps you and your project stakeholders understand system stakeholder relationships and compare diverse experiences within the system. Even if the area in which your project stakeholders can have influence is specific—for example, if you are focused on potential interventions within public institutions—it's still worthwhile to understand comparative environments and experiences to inform your thinking and decision-making.

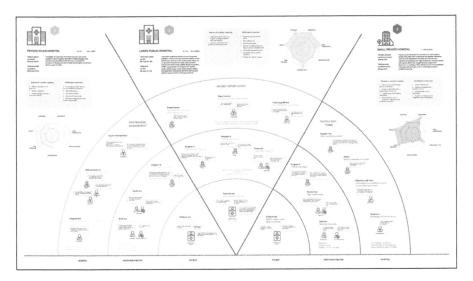

FIGURE 5.7
The stakeholder map for the hospital system included details about stakeholders, environments, and financial and political drivers. You can use a form of
the ecological framework to compare different experiences and environments.

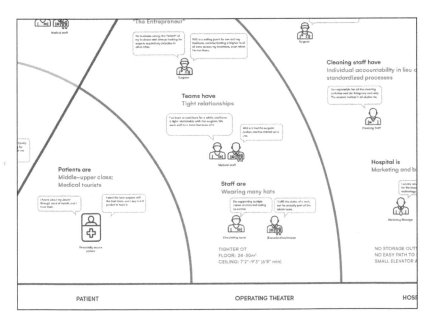

FIGURE 5.8
In a detail of the hospital ecosystem map, you can see the relationships
between patients and those who work in the operating theater: their
motivations and their perceptions.

WHAT'S IN A NAME?

Have you ever thought about where your last name came from? For most of history, many of our ancestors didn't have last names at all.

The fact that many of us have surnames to begin with is the sign of a widespread system instituted by Renaissance-era European states. Many—and you could argue, most—traditional societies have not had a system of permanent surnames. As James C. Scott noted in *Seeing Like a State*, "Among some peoples, it is not uncommon for individuals to have different names during different stages of life (infancy, childhood, adulthood) and in some cases after death; added to these are names used for joking, rituals, and mourning, and names used for interactions with same-sex friends or with in-laws." In other words, in certain cultures, names themselves are contextual. These ways of knowing who-was-who were easy to manage in societies where official authority was local.

To avoid confusion born of shifting names, as well as overly common names (think about if every other person in a town was named John, for example), modern states—those formed in the last 500 years or so—imposed formalized surname systems primarily as a measure of control and for collecting taxes. This process was imposed quickly—and met with resistance in many places—during European colonial rule.

When I was in college, I remember a friend telling me I was lucky to have my last name, Cababa. "Your name is indigenous," he said. "Mine was given by colonizers." We are both Filipino-American, and he was referring to his Spanish-origin surname.

He's not entirely wrong. In 1849, the Spanish governor of the Philippines, Narciso Claveria y Zaldua, ordered by decree that Filipinos (who had, by that time, been under Spanish colonial rule for more than 200 years) take Spanish surnames. The names were available in the *Catálogo Alfabético de Apellidos* (*Alphabetical Catalog of Surnames*), a book that was given to local officials to use for assigning names (see Figure 5.9).

Local officials went on to assign names to families within their townships, sometimes given names that started with only one letter of the alphabet. The ultimate goal was "a complete legible list of subjects and taxpayers," which would ease the administrative burden and be a source of continued revenue for the Spanish state. In addition, it was intended to provide a variety of names. However, it did not include commonly adopted Spanish surnames at the time, particularly "de los Santos" and "de la Cruz", because too many people had already adopted those names, and they wanted to avoid "confusion."

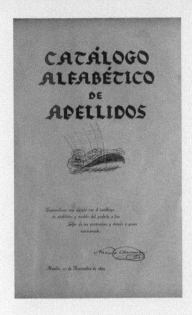

FIGURE 5.9
In 1849, the *Catálogo* was the singular source for the Spanish-origin surnames of millions of Filipinos today.

Unsurprisingly, Governor Claveria's goals fell short for several reasons. Some municipalities ignored the decree altogether, while in other locales, officials failed to connect previous names with new surnames, thereby losing track of people's tax and property history. In addition, the very existence of indigenous names such as Dimayuga, Agpoon, and Macapagal can be read as examples of resistance against the *Catálogo*. However, the fact that there are millions of Filipinos around the world today with surnames like Perez, Ramos, and Garcia serves as a reminder of the colonialist change that was foisted upon their ancestors.

As for my name, I remain unsure about whether it's technically included in the *Catálogo*. There isn't a listing for "Cababa" but there is an entry for "Caba," followed by "Cababan," so it's possible that mine is just an adjustment to one of those terms made somewhere along the way. However, I'd like to think that, just maybe, that difference of a couple of letters was a tiny form of rebellion by my ancestors.

Prompts to consider:
- Are there any remnants of historical colonialism that you see in your day-to-day life?
- Like surnames, what kinds of foundational systems do we take for granted that likely have deliberate institutional decisions behind them?

Takeaways

- Stakeholder maps can be used as a form of analysis and a synthesis output. You can use them to think through the relationships between system stakeholders and communicate your findings to your project stakeholders.

- Variations of Bronfenbrenner's ecological framework are a simple way to show relationships, actions, and impact of various stakeholders at different levels. Putting key system stakeholders (those who are most affected by the system) at the center of your ecological framework is a good starting point.

- Mapping relationships is a good way to start your systems analysis because it allows you to understand power dynamics between different system stakeholders.

Dr. Pierce Otlhogile-Gordon is an innovation catalyst, researcher, facilitator, and evaluator, impassioned by the space between transformation and liberation.

As the Director of the Equity Innovation studio at Think Rubix, a Black-led social innovation consultancy, Dr. Gordon serves as a shepherd for Equity Innovation to shape our collective future.

You describe your work as building the space between transformation and liberation. What does that involve?

For my PhD, I was trained in innovation practice, evaluation capacity building, and international development. The trans-disciplinary fields I decided to focus on involved equity issues.

"Innovation practice" describes the activities that have become, across industries, a valuable set of skills oriented toward building new and useful things. I'm focused on that alongside building power with, and for, historically marginalized communities. These don't always intersect, so in my practice, I make them intersect. I view that as my space. In terms of methods and mindsets. I collect and analyze different forms of strategic analysis methods, and facilitate spaces where people can use these methods to investigate and build things toward the future. I use approaches such as participatory timelines, systems maps, qualitative methods, and deep ethnography. I appreciate and recommend, for example, the POEMS framework as a useful asset for looking for opportunities and obstacles that might affect anything you are trying to create in the world.

What are some ways in which designing for equity and systems thinking intersect?

A lot of people talk about systems without really understanding what systems actually are. Take a term like *systemic racism*. Or related terms like *systemic inequality* or *systemic sexism*. People know that using this term is a way of understanding oppression, but that's it. Traditionally, people might mean there are historical advantages that have existed at the personal level, that makes any manifestation of power inequitably distributed. People understand that this keeps some people in the center, and some people at the margins. That's important, but not the whole story.

Systems as a practice, as a field, as a methodology, represents a collection of actors who engage with each other in unique ways that build a larger unit that functions differently than the sum of its parts. For example, the human body is a system that operates differently than the body's organs.

The American economy is another example, which is a system where the supply and demand connect through systems of trade.

Systemic oppression connects the two. We must understand that regardless of how people, organizations, and institutions interact with each other, the larger body of engagement can predictably lead to interactions that cause inequality, when smaller stakeholders don't have to do the same. If you are to address any forms of systemic oppression, you need to think at multiple scopes: how you're affecting your main area of influence, but also how those effects radiate across the universe of influence.

I think designers often struggle with ideas that involve thinking about people—who they are designing for, at the individual level. How do you create avenues for designers to think about and design for systemic change?

Designers, by approaching single, curated, useful creative problems think about blank slates. They go deep, influenced by design's implementation of ethnography. They consider cultures and context of those deep stories and use that as the fuel to create something new and useful... for that context.

On the other hand, systems thinking is designed to focus on relationships within system actors. You zoom out rather than zoom in. Doing systems thinking well means scaling out: looking past single events toward consistent patterns that reflect a cycle the system aims to sustain, to find what makes a system operate—the behaviors between actors, their underlying assumptions of a system, and more.

Both design thinking and systems thinking are tools. They are different and can be wielded together, but most people don't know how.

If you're in the design-thinking world and you're trying to understand systems thinking, a useful way to introduce the ideas is for you to think about the cycles that exist in your life and in your world. For example, a designer might be interested in the day of the life of a virtual worker and try to empathize with their experience being trapped in their house. For a different perspective, you can also study the things a virtual worker consistently experiences: how their sleeping and eating cycles before and after the pandemic have changed. Systems both capture and are made by humans, so seeing them is the first step to changing them.

What are some potential issues that remain even if design practitioners integrate systems thinking?

Systems thinking is not a panacea for systemic inequality. For example, if you have assumptions built into your beliefs, your way of thinking, then even if you are doing rigorous systems analysis, you could still come to the wrong conclusions. If you are viewing a system through the lens of your own experience or belief, you could end up with a misdiagnosis.

Secondly, the field requires levels of abstraction that average people—normally—don't know or care enough about to learn how it can be valuable to their own lives. It takes time to do systems practice correctly, and if done well, it explains relationships between multiple stakeholders, and sometimes describes patterns across generations. Learning it takes time, and few people from marginalized identities are familiar with the practice at the outset. It's the job of the systems thinker to communicate the outcomes in a way that potential changemakers can understand and act upon.

Finally, knowing systems thinking doesn't mean you instantly understand the culture and knowledge of social change issues. Designers and systems thinkers should also learn from people who practice social change at many scopes, like activists and organizers, policymakers, and communities affected by crises. All social change issues are based in power: how it's been accumulated throughout history, how it's equitably distributed, and how people use it for their own aims. Design, and systems practice, can be an intellectual connector between those insights and a better future.

Lastly, what should designers always keep in mind as they look to engage in systems thinking?

Designers have to recognize they aren't good at everything, and the skill sets that expert systems thinkers have created and utilized are important and necessary. For example, formal systems thinking integrates qualitative and quantitative methods very elegantly, as every system that you are trying to build has a story, and the system underlying those stories is measured using quantitative values. Working with practiced systems thinkers, who can balance the two sides of the methods, takes practice.

Second, how can designers do this work better? They need to educate themselves. This field has a history, a base of knowledge, and a community that you can benefit from. Learn from formal systems thinkers and where they've applied the method to learn about its pros and cons, and how they've done that work.

Finally, designers must be humble. Designers often tend to be methodological colonizers. They engage in ideas around "building a new beautiful future" without learning about where the ideas came from and there are a lot of problems with that.

But what can designers bring to systems thinking? Designers are also really good at valuable intellectual communication. Design thinking is a field that a lot of people know about now, but systems thinkers haven't been able to communicate widely the value of their field. It's mostly remained behind academic silos. Combining these practices and having designers working with systems thinkers and being able to communicate the value of systems thinking can help this approach grow.

CHAPTER 6

Mapping Forces

In 1854 London, a terrifying cholera epidemic broke out. Public health officials believed that the epidemic was caused by a "miasma" or foul odors that traveled through the air and caused disease. We now know, of course, that cholera is a waterborne disease. But when John Snow, a doctor at that time, tried to convince authorities of this, he was basically ignored by London's General Board of Health.

The Soho area of London had a concentrated number of cholera victims. Along with a priest named Henry Whitehead, Snow conducted interviews with victims' families, piecing together the relationship between where they lived and their proximity to water sources, and mapping both of these things. He found that a commonality among them was access to the Broad Street pump, and he deduced that cesspools beneath the buildings in Soho (a common, unsanitary practice at the time) had contaminated the well from which the pump drew water. He convinced the city to remove the handle from the pump, thereby (literally) stopping the flow of contaminated water into the community.

Counter to Snow's efforts, public health officials' dedication to the miasma theory caused them to make decisions that catastrophically increased the spread of cholera. One such decision was flushing sewer systems into the Thames, thereby further contaminating drinking water sources. Drawing from these different data points helped Snow make his case, and key to his case that cholera spread via water, was his visual analysis via his map. As Steven Johnson described it in his book *The Ghost Map* about the 1854 cholera outbreak: "Part of what made Snow's map groundbreaking was the fact that it wedded state-of-the-art information design to a scientifically valid theory of cholera's transmission. It was not the mapmaking technique that mattered; it was the underlying science that the map revealed."[1]

Snow's activities in the public health space were a good example of thinking in systems: building connections between policy decisions and outcomes, understanding the different forces that contribute to those outcomes, and having a good on-the-ground understanding of stakeholders and how their decisions affect outcomes. This kind of cause-and-effect analysis has great similarities to, within systems thinking, building an understanding of system forces *and* mapping them. Like Snow, you can use maps to illuminate problems, diagnose them, and find points of potential intervention.

---

1 Steven Johnson, *The Ghost Map* (Penguin Publishing Group, 2007).

Forces and Events

Now that you understand the stakeholders within your system, the next step is to understand the forces and events within a system.

Forces are the conditions and drivers that make a system the way it is. Forces can include people, trends, events, norms, beliefs, phenomena, institutions, laws, and policies, and can create positive as well as negative outcomes.[2]

A subset of forces is *events*. The best way to analyze events is to think about causality and how events are connected. You'll ask yourself: What causes impact in this system? How do problems potentially reinforce themselves? How are all of these problems connected?

The best way to visually represent events is by creating causal loops and combining them into a map. A causal loop diagram has a core causal loop that is a representation of a root cause. The root cause loop radiates out into the other causal loops, which is why these concepts are referred to as *radiating effects* or *cascading effects*.

Creating a Causal Loop Map

The level of detail and complexity of a causal loop map depends on how broad you need to go with your analysis. A key consideration is your altitude in terms of your analysis, as well as your altitude in terms of considering what are typically described as *solutions* (or, within systems thinking, what you would describe as *points of intervention* or *leverage points*).

Take your imagined education project. Return to your key research questions:

- What challenges do multilingual learners face in math classes?
- What kind of decision-making in and outside of the classroom affects multilingual learners' success in math?
- What kinds of barriers or challenges do multilingual learners face in their school environments?
- How do the relationships between teachers, administrators, and students affect student performance?
- Are there school or classroom environments in which multilingual students are especially thriving or struggling?

---

2   The Omidyar Group, *Systems Practice*. Please take a look: https://docs.kumu.io/content/Workbook-012617.pdf

In this case, it would make sense to orient your initial causal loops on the impact on individual students in the system. Your data from your data collection phase will help you determine where the patterns and forces are that tell a story about cause and effect.

For a causal loop map, you might create three loops, or you might create three dozen. The purpose of creating causal loops is to understand the forces at play and how those forces affect stakeholders within the system. From a team or project level, this map-building is about developing a shared understanding about cause and effect, and being able to identify where there are harmful incentives, behaviors, and radiating effects in a system. This shared understanding allows you and your team to determine where action needs to be taken, so you can subsequently use design methods to consider how to solve problems, intervene in vicious cycles, and reinforce virtuous cycles as leverage points.

Again, the key is understanding that the way systems work is not a beginning-to-end journey, but that they operate in a circular fashion, and that cause and effect feed each other in a system. And the foundational element of your understanding is a causal loop.

Components of the Causal Loop

The building block of a systems map is the causal loop. The causal loop has three components: nodes, direction, and values attached to the node (plus or minus). (See Figure 6.1.)

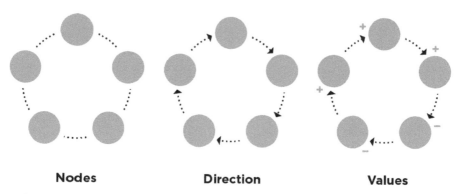

Nodes   **Direction**   **Values**

FIGURE 6.1

There are three key components of a causal loop: the nodes, which indicate the events, the direction, which indicates how they are related, and the values, which show whether events are increasing or decreasing.

A notable aspect of causal loops is that they are closed circles, which means that cause and effect are connected, and are circular, rather than linear. This approach helps you to understand that every action—in fact, every solution—can likely be the cause of a problem. In systems thinking, this concept is referred to as *feedback*. Considering feedback is what makes systems thinking unique from the typical user-centered design process: designers often think about a problem, design a solution, and assume that the solution is enough. Problem solved! However, with anything complex that may affect people or events that you haven't foreseen, you can put money on the solution causing potential problems. To paraphrase Peter Senge: yesterday's solutions are today's problems. Causal loops force you to think about how solutions and problems can be one and the same.

Types of Causal Loops

There are two types of causal loops: reinforcing feedback loops and balancing feedback loops. Reinforcing feedback loops can be virtuous or vicious, and they can represent growth or deterioration. A virtuous feedback loop represents healthy growth, growth that likely leads to improved outcomes. A vicious feedback loop does the opposite: it shows deterioration, or unhealthy, unsustainable growth that will lead to poor outcomes. As David Peter Stroh wrote in *Systems Thinking for Social Change*, reinforcing feedback "explains the development of both engines of growth or flywheels as well as spiraling deterioration."[3]

Balancing feedback loops is the opposite of reinforcing feedback loops. They are a representation of equilibrium, of a series of events that are self-regulating. A common example of a balancing loop is a working thermostat. Let's say your desired room temperature is a comfy 72° F (22° C). When the temperature dips below 72, the heat kicks on. Once 72 degrees is reached, the heat turns off. The temperature is regulated by the balance of hot and cool air (see Figure 6.2).

---

3   David Peter Stroh, *Systems Thinking for Social Change: A Practical Guide to Solving Complex Problems, Avoiding Unintended Consequences, and Achieving Lasting Results* (Chelsea Green Publishing, 2015).

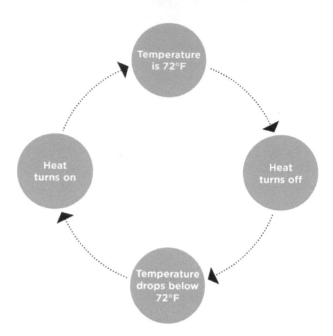

FIGURE 6.2
Ever wonder how
your thermostat
works? It's a simple
reinforcing loop!

As you examine the status quo of a system, perhaps representing a complex problem, it's likely that many or all of your causal loops, rather than balancing feedback like this thermostat example, will represent reinforcing feedback. That's fine, because your causal loop map should capture both the positive and negative impacts, but does not necessarily need to be exhaustive in order to understand where things are particularly broken or require intervention. If a system were working and balancing itself, it's likely that it wouldn't require a great deal of systems analysis or subsequent design thinking to consider interventions.

Now that you have an understanding of the types of causal loops, you can use examples that are evident in the news to practice building them. Here's an example of a reinforcing causal loop. In September 2020, several months into the COVID-19 pandemic, a curious series of events occurred. U.S. states that had been experiencing increases in COVID cases started easing their lockdown restrictions. (These events were months before COVID vaccines were introduced.) In Wisconsin, for example, just as coronavirus cases were rising in September and October of 2020, the state lifted lockdown measures, and mask mandates were being challenged in court.[4] According to data from initial studies,[5] as well as models from the Institute for Health Metrics and Evaluation,[6] the easing of lockdown restrictions correlated with increased cases of, and deaths from, COVID-19.

If you were to think about this series of events as a causal loop, you would map how one event leads to the next, with each event represented as a node. The crucial consideration is figuring out how these events might either reinforce an "unbalanced" outcome, or whether the events themselves, when looped together, balance themselves out, creating equilibrium. In the case of COVID-19 and lockdown restrictions, the events were not balancing themselves out. In fact, the increase of cases had other cascading effects in the system, such as overwhelmed hospitals, so it was very likely a reinforcing loop (see Figure 6.3).

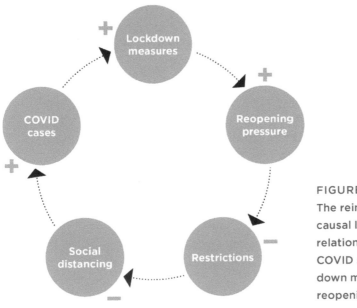

FIGURE 6.3
The reinforcing causal loop shows the relationship between COVID spread, lockdown measures, and reopening pressure.

4   German Lopez, "How Pandemic Fatigue and Polarization Led to Wisconsin's Massive COVID-19 Outbreak," Vox, October 23, 2020.

5   Abdulkadir Atalan, "Is the Lockdown Important to Prevent the COVID-19 Pandemic? Effects on Psychology, Environment, and Economy-Perspective," *Annals of Medicine and Surgery*, August 2020.

6   IHME (Institute for Health Metrics and Evaluation), COVID-19 Projections.

To represent events in a node, a helpful approach is to remember to state the event neutrally, without representing increases or decreases. In this example, if the causal loop starts with COVID cases going up, you would not write "Increase in COVID cases," rather you would represent the node as "COVID cases" or "COVID spread," and indicate the value as a + or - attached to the node. Keeping the nodes neutral allows you to consider—especially as you might eventually use your causal loops to define potential points of intervention—how this particular node could potentially represent a decrease rather than an increase. This approach keeps the nodes flexible.

There are a few ways that this example makes for an interesting causal loop. It has expected nodes, such as a decrease in social distancing leading to an increase in COVID spread. It also represents behavioral events, particularly the node that addresses an increase in "reopening pressure." Many causal loops have nodes that, as a designer, you might recognize as potential areas for design thinking: how might you reduce reopening pressure? This node also makes it clear that there is often a human behavioral component that amplifies an unbalanced reinforcing feedback loop.

This loop serves as an example of a closed feedback loop. Closed loops are a constant reminder that events can be both input and output: that problems are not a passive condition. Everything you do, as individuals, communities, or institutions, creates circumstances that lead to something else, and these actions have an impact on the problems that you mentally consider to be a starting point. Once you've engaged in creating causal loops to think about why problems occur, you'll see causal loops everywhere.

Creating Breadth with Causal Loops and Putting Loops Together

After you've created a series of causal loops, you can identify ways in which they might fit together. Even though you now have an idea of how to create a causal loop, it might still feel daunting to figure out where to begin when it comes to creating a wide range of them in order to form the building blocks of a causal loop diagram. Good frameworks and prompts can help you tackle this in a structured fashion.

When it comes time to create a variety of causal loops, a useful framework to draw from is a simplified variation of the Ecological Framework that is used for stakeholder mapping. In user-centered design, you are often analyzing the behaviors and impact of a product or service on an individual. In systems thinking, you are analyzing the impact of a system on a wider range of stakeholders: you want to understand the impact on the individual, on communities, and on society (see Figure 6.4).

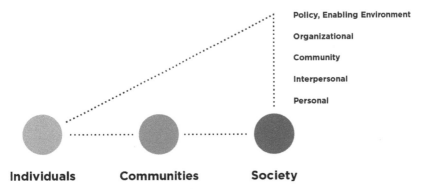

Policy, Enabling Environment

Organizational

Community

Interpersonal

Personal

Individuals   Communities   Society

FIGURE 6.4

A good starting point for building causal loops: who are the people involved in the events that shape your causal loops? What are the ways in which they are affected? Are they affected personally, interpersonally, from a community level, from an organizational level, or from a policy level?

In your education project example, you might use these categories to develop a series of prompts to drive how your team generates ideas for causal loops.

Individual impact:

- What kind of impact do facets of the U.S. education system have on multilingual learners?

- How does the way math is taught to multilingual learners affect relationships between teachers and students?

- How does the way math is taught affect multilingual learners' success or failure?

Community impact:

- How does the way that education is structured affect communities in which multilingual learners live? How does it affect others within those communities?

- What are culturally distinct ways that multilingual learners and their families and communities are affected by the education system?

Societal impact:

- How does funding affect the multilingual learner experience?
- How does multilingual education affect institutions? How does it affect communities at scale?
- How do broad policies such as education policy and immigration policy affect students?

These questions may seem fairly broad, but taking them one at a time, they serve as a good starting point for building causal loops. You don't need to worry too much about the overlap between the categories. There's no need to be dogmatic about whether something falls into the "individual" or "community" category, as each of these categories naturally overlap. You may view societal issues, such as how assessments are conducted broadly in public schools, through the lens of how that might impact an individual student. If that works for you as a way of connecting the dots on issues, that's great. The point is to push yourself to think broadly beyond just an end user or individual, and to consider people, communities, and institutions at scale.

Deep Structure, Root Cause, and the Goal of a System

As a designer, you've probably created synthesis artifacts such as user journey maps. These journeys are typically represented in a linear fashion. For example, a user discovers a photo service through marketing efforts, signs up for the service, onboards in order to learn how to use the service, and starts using it. A system is quite different from that linear process. For example, wouldn't a system that represents the facets of homelessness have a goal of minimizing or eradicating homelessness? However, the magic of systems mapping reveals that, often, when you start examining cause and effect, you find that your desired outcomes (eradicating homelessness) are not reflected in how a system actually behaves (increases homelessness, or has incentives that makes homelessness intractable). What you find out is that well-intentioned but short-sighted decisions, such as greater investment in the overnight shelter system, can actually have unintended consequences that are counterproductive to society's long-term goals. Thus, understanding a system's goals is important to understanding where to intervene.

In Omidyar Group's *Systems Practice* guide, the core causal loop of a systems map is described as "the deep structure." The goals of a system are often represented here, as well as the root causes of the system's problems that then radiate outward.

You'll find, as you build your systems map, that the themes within the deep structure will emerge. Often, the goals are represented in what you can describe as *root cause*: it's the source of the problems that radiate outward. Although it might sound weird that goals and cause can be the same thing, it's important to recognize that systems are circular in nature: cause and effect can be the same thing. It's a bit like a river: if the main river is the deep structure, it is fed by tributaries and sources upstream, but it also has downstream effects, like a river delta fanning out again (see Figure 6.5).

FIGURE 6.5
The Meta River in Colombia is a good metaphor for how a system works: there are tributaries that feed the river, and the river itself feeds other rivers. You can think of the main river as the deep structure of a system.

The causal loops you've created that represent themes at the individual, community, and societal levels all feed the deep structure and derive from it. They are both source and delta.

Finding a deep structure in your systems map gives you and your stakeholders a good starting point for considering where to intervene in system problems. If you were to only examine one discrete area of a system, you might not extend the efforts of your problem-solving to the most effective area. Think of it this way: the deep structure is the diagnosis of the disease, and the radiating effects are the symptoms. Your causal loops that show individual, community, and societal events are the radiating effects, or the symptoms. You can now point these patterns to the "center" of your systems map: the loop that likely connects themes from the causal loops that you created.

Identifying Themes for the Deep Structure

At this point in the process, you've created a series of causal loops capturing the system's impact on individuals, communities, and society. You'll notice that certain nodes may repeat themselves, and that themes will start emerging based on this repetition.

When defining the deep structure of your systems map, it's essential to ensure that it is grounded in evidence, just like the rest of your causal loops, and it tells the core story about the system you are analyzing. Here are questions you can ask yourself to zero in on what the deep structure might be—for example, the core story of your system's goals and root cause.

- **Who:** Who holds the most power within a system, and what kind of impact does their power have?
- **What:** What key themes repeat themselves over and over?
- **Why:** What are the core incentives that drive key decisions by those who hold the most power?

For example, in Michael Goodwin's excellent visual economics book, *Economix*, he includes a section in which he explains the postwar development of suburbs in the United States. A combination of subsidies, such as mortgage tax breaks and free highways, lured the middle class to the suburbs. In order to attract the middle class (and their tax base), cities engaged in highway construction and car accommodation, such as parking to ease their car-centric lifestyle. Goodwin represented the resulting central issue (what could be represented as the deep structure of a shift in the transportation system) in a causal loop (Figure 6.6).

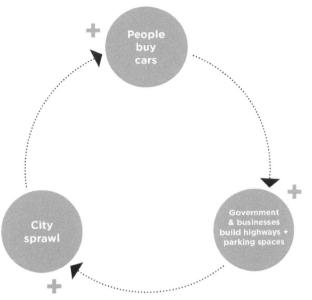

FIGURE 6.6
This causal loop can be the deep structure. It would likely have other causal loops radiating from each of its nodes. For example, "city sprawl" could radiate outward into how suburban spaces are subsidized, or how public transportation is reduced.

Stemming from this deep structure are cascading effects, such as privatization of transportation and subsequent reduced investment in public transportation, increases in fossil fuel usage, and discriminatory housing practices. If you were working within this space, this deep structure would give you lots of themes to work with to investigate potential system interventions.

An example of a causal loop map that involves dozens of loops is researcher Philippe Vandenbroeck's systems-thinking project focused on understanding what drives the institutions of symphony orchestras, their relevance (or irrelevance) and success. His causal loop map was an analysis of what drives orchestral excellence. He identified the central variable as "artistic quality" with a relationship to four other factors: "the public's interest in attending concerts, the societal support for classical music, the orchestra musicians' job satisfaction, and the quality of the artistic and business management."[7] He then built his causal loop diagram around this key theme and the related four factors (see Figures 6.7 and 6.8). This analysis gave him and other stakeholders multiple avenues to consider potential interventions, which is the power of identifying and mapping the deep structure of a system.

---

7   Philippe Vandenbroeck, "Systems Mapping Excellence: How Symphony Orchestras Can Fight a Crisis of Legitimacy," Medium, July 27, 2021.

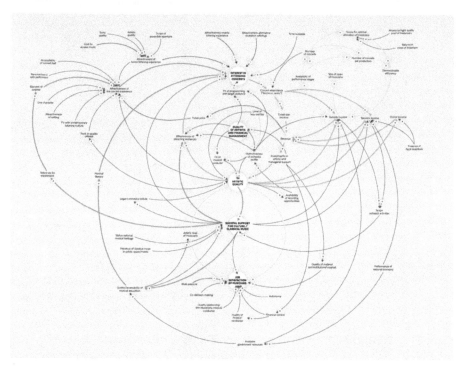

FIGURE 6.7

Large causal loop diagrams, like this one created by researcher Philippe Vandenbroeck, may be difficult to read, but are useful in demonstrating the deep structure, or key forces, that are both affected by, and have an effect on, other forces.

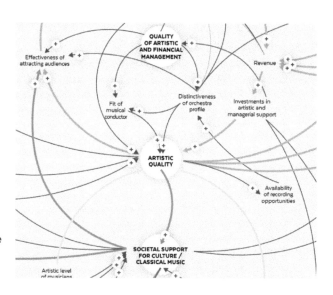

FIGURE 6.8

In this detail of the previous figure, the focus is on some of the central concepts, such as artistic quality.

Identifying System Archetypes

Picture the crank on a bike. As you pedal, the crank turns. As the crank turns, the chain moves and propels the wheel forward. If you have a derailleur, you can adjust the rate at which the bike moves forward.

The deep structure is the crank. It's the center of a radiating set of events, each of which wouldn't happen without the crank turning. Like a system, the cyclist has a goal: to move in a certain direction. The cyclist's goal and the motion set forward by using the crank are in alignment. With a system, if you were the cyclist, you might have certain societal outcomes in mind that might not align with a system's goals, especially if that system had a lot of problems. It would be like the cyclist wanting to move the bike forward, but when she started pedaling, the bike moves backward. Or sideways! In a way, sideways makes even more sense in this overwrought metaphor because system goals can be just as mystifying.

A helpful mechanism for understanding system goals is the categorization of systems into systems archetypes. These categories are specific ways in which systems work to achieve certain goals.

The urban sprawl example from Goodwin's book exemplifies the Success to the Successful archetype. In *Thinking in Systems*, Donella Meadows describes a Success to the Successful archetype in the following way: "If the winners of a competition are systematically rewarded with the means to win again, a reinforcing feedback loop is created by which, if it is allowed to proceed uninhibited, the winners eventually take all, while the losers are eliminated." There's a good example of this concept in halfcourt pickup basketball called *make it, take it*. Basically, if you make a shot, you get to keep possession. If the other team has terrible defense, or if you happen to be on a pickup team with Kevin Durant, you could just steamroll the other team. Being rewarded with more success after you succeed is a good example of the Success to the Successful archetype.

Meadows, as well as Stroh and Senge, identifies several other system archetypes that are worth noting (see Table 6.1). The benefit of understanding system archetypes is that it helps you understand, from a high level, the core problems of a system. If the incentives are perverse, or those who are systematically rewarded continue to gain at the expense of others whom you would expect the system to serve, then it's worth categorizing your system to be able to eventually address that core, archetypical dynamic.

TABLE 6.1 VARIOUS SYSTEM ARCHETYPES.

System Archetype	Description
Balancing Process with Delay	Stakeholders (individuals, groups, or organizations) adjust their behavior to respond to a delay. "Overreacting" is a theme.
Limits to Success	Success or growth ends up being constrained by limits that need to be overcome in order to sustain success.
Shifting the Burden	Quick fixes that inadvertently end up being used long-term. Also sometimes described as *addiction*, it refers to solutions that often only treat a symptom.
Fixes That Fail	Short-term solutions for long-term problems.
Eroding Goals	A system in which long-term performance levels fall.
Escalation	Aggressive behavior begets aggressive behavior.
Success to the Successful	Winner takes all. Success begets further opportunities for success, thereby starving other entities.
Tragedy of the Commons	Everyone takes advantage of a resource that doesn't belong to anyone. The resource eventually depletes or erodes.
Rule Beating	People try to "game" the system: engaging in perverse behavior that gives the appearance of abiding by rules, but actually distorts the system. It means following the *letter* of the law, but not the *spirit* of the law.

---

8   Peter Senge, *The Fifth Discipline* (Penguin Random House, 2006).

Example	Intervention Possibilities
When you adjust the temperature in a shower, there is a delay in the hot water, so when it finally arrives, the water is too hot. You might then "overcorrect" the other way.	Be careful of overcorrection. In a sluggish system, aggressiveness produces instability. Either be patient or make the system more responsive.[8]
A company's widgets are popular, thereby stoking increased demand. The company does not invest in hiring more workers to meet demand, so they fall behind.	Find ways to remove or weaken the source of limitation.
Applying pesticides to a monoculture crop so more of the monoculture can be grown, thereby creating a dependency on the pesticide. Drinking coffee to gain energy, but the caffeine disrupts sleep, thereby creating a dependence on coffee to maintain energy.	Shift investment toward long-term change rather than short-term relief.
A company engages in cutting down on maintenance, thereby increasing the problem of eventual breakdowns, which are even more costly.	Stay focused on the long-term goal, striving for outcomes rather than short-term relief.
Deteriorating customer service: when performance slips, the goals then slip.	Hold the vision. Keep performance standards related to best performance rather than worst performance.
An arms race. Advertising that gets more and more brash to keep people's attention (think Times Square).	Find ways for the competing sides to both (or all) win, perhaps even taking reverse action.
The rich get richer, while the poor get poorer.	Institute policies that level the playing field by removing advantages for those benefiting most, or increasing advantages for those benefiting least. Decrease competition for the same limited resources.
A national park becomes so popular that its natural beauty is compromised. Shared company resources, such as a shared salesforce, that experiences too much demand because each division wants more and more of that resource.	Educate users of the common resource on the issue of its scarcity. Regulate access to the resource.
The Cobra Effect: where people bred cobras to turn them in for a bounty. A law intended to fight congestion by limiting the number of cars on the road by tracking license plates. People buy more cars to get more license plates so they can continue to drive anyway.	Devise ways for people to use their creativity to work toward the spirit of the goals and toward the desired or intended outcomes, not against them.

What's helpful about identifying a system archetype for your system is that it connects patterns within the system with the results of how the system is operating. If you return to the transportation causal loop from Michael Goodwin's book, you could depict it in a way that it reflects the Success to the Successful archetype (see Figure 6.9).

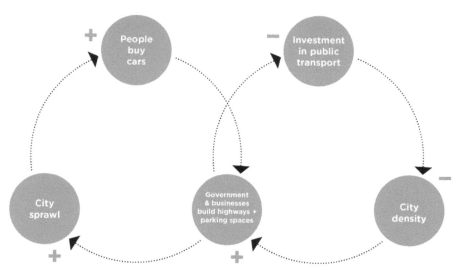

FIGURE 6.9

Adding detail about not just the reinforcing loop driven by car purchases, but also expanding on what is not being invested in as well, tells a more complete story that fits the Success to the Successful system archetype.

Of course, this system could have other incentive patterns that fit other system archetypes. (The archetype Fixes That Fail comes to mind when considering the growth imperatives for urban sprawl.) Because the point of systems mapping is not only understanding what exists, but identifying potential points of intervention, being cognizant of potential system archetypes helps get you started on recognizing the patterns of the system's "design": particularly its incentives and outcomes.

Other Types of Systems Maps

Causal loop diagramming is an effective way to understand system forces, but there are other frameworks that work just as well in conveying forces, as well as root cause and system dynamics. The iceberg model, fishbone diagram, and the bathtub analogy are frequently used in formal systems thinking to express the story of a system: its causes and its effects.

Mapping a System Iceberg

The iceberg model is a framework used to analyze the connection between events and the forces that affect it. The model, which was created in 1976 by anthropologist Edward T. Hall, expresses the idea that there are aspects of culture that are visible, but most of what affects culture is hidden below the surface (see Figure 6.10). It has since been used by systems thinkers like Peter Senge to articulate systems perspectives. In Chapter 2, "A Systems-Thinking Mindset," you read about an iceberg model that identified the events as George Floyd's murder and the resulting riots. Underneath the surface were diverse systemic forces, such as mass incarceration and a racist justice system. Although it did not have the layers of the framework here, it is a good high-level example of the kinds of themes that an iceberg model can help unpack.

IMAGE: NBC/GETTY

FIGURE 6.10
Using the iceberg model might not give you the perspective of the iceberg, but it should help uncover new perspectives.

The iceberg model has four layers: events, patterns and trends, structure, and mental models (see Figure 6.11).

- **Events:** This top layer is the layer of the iceberg that is visible. It's usually the things that people are most aware of within a system, such as an event that people are reacting to. It could be the series of events that lead your analysis: it's often a symptom of what needs to be changed.

- **Patterns and Trends:** This layer below events is meant to articulate the things that have been happening over time. It can refer to patterns of behavior or trends within an organization, or trends within the system that you are analyzing.

- **Structure:** This layer refers to formalized structure that contributes to causing the patterns and events. It could be institutions, rules, laws, and policies.

- **Mental Models:** This layer articulates the beliefs, mindsets, and cultural assumptions that inform the system's formalized structures, which in turn affect the patterns and trends.

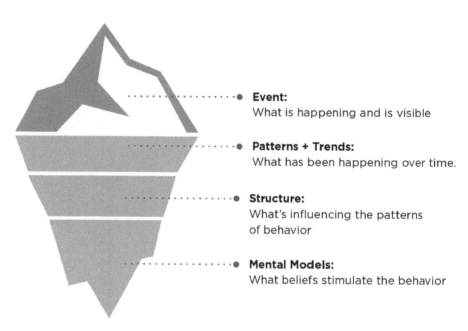

Event:
What is happening and is visible

Patterns + Trends:
What has been happening over time.

Structure:
What's influencing the patterns of behavior

Mental Models:
What beliefs stimulate the behavior

FIGURE 6.11
The iceberg model is a good way to articulate different categories of system forces, such as behaviors, institutional and formalized structure, and mindsets.

Ecochallenge.org has a simple example that shows what an iceberg model might look like if you used it to show the different layers of forces at play when you as an individual might catch a cold (see Figure 6.12).

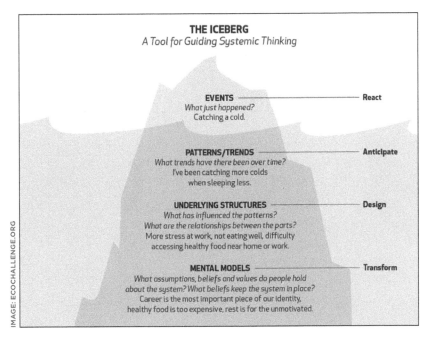

FIGURE 6.12
You might not use an iceberg to analyze what happens when you catch a cold, but you could absolutely use it to analyze personal or social events, career decisions, organizational problems, and other areas where you'd like to understand the root cause better.

The iceberg model is a versatile tool that can be used to analyze the underlying system for lots of potential prompts, not just wicked problems. You could absolutely use it to analyze personal or social events, career decisions, organizational problems, and other areas where it's beneficial to better understand the root cause of events. I've used it in my practice to analyze organizational issues such as employee attrition, as well as applying it to broad problem spaces such as schools and how they use assessments. It's particularly useful to consider how to be more thoughtful and think long-term and holistically about issues that are surfacing without just being reactive to the events themselves.

To engage your team and other stakeholders in using the iceberg model for synthesis, you can start with the following prompts.

Events: What is happening and is visible?

- What is happening that people are noticing and talking about?
- What are you and others reacting to?

Patterns and Trends: What has been happening over time?

- What are recurring things that have been happening?
- Are there things that people perceive are happening over time?

Structure: What are the institutional structures as well as norms that affect patterns?

- What are the rules, norms, policies, guidelines, power structures, distribution of resources, or informal ways of work that have been tacitly or explicitly institutionalized?

Mental Models: What is the thinking that creates the structures that manifest themselves in the patterns of events?

- What are people's deeply held assumptions and beliefs that ultimately drive behavior?
- What are the attitudes, beliefs, morals, expectations, values, or culture that allow structures to continue functioning as they are?
- What are some culturally held beliefs that are inherent in driving people's mindsets?

The model can be used in combination with research insights to help stakeholders align on the big themes within the problem space. (See Figure 6.13 for a workshop example.) Where does it make sense to think about interventions? Once synthesized, you can bring a polished version into the next phase of your work to drive discussion about opportunity spaces within the system.

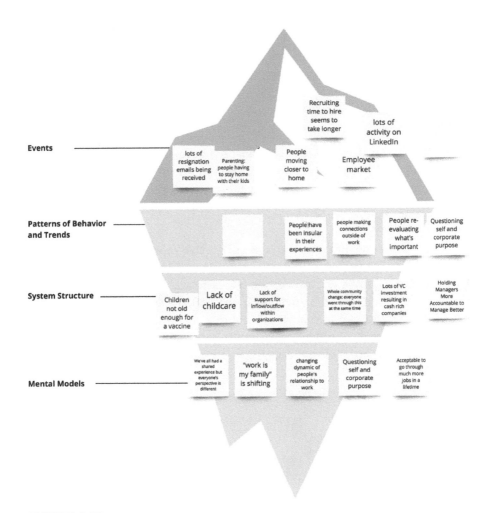

FIGURE 6.13

This iceberg model was an analysis of "The Great Resignation" of 2021. Using Miro, the team was able to take events, trends, structures, and mental models to conduct analysis and understand the system better.

Fishbone Diagram

In 1972, Dr. Kaoru Ishikawa, a quality control statistician, published *Guide to Quality Control*. Within it was a framework that would come to be known as the *fishbone diagram*, a visual way of understanding the root cause of quality control issues.

This framework would go on to have wider-ranging impact, eventually being used for root-cause analysis beyond manufacturing and quality control. It's a useful tool for systems thinking in that it helps you analyze cause and effect in a linear fashion, so it's accessible to those for whom models like causal loop diagrams might present a challenge.

In a fishbone diagram, the bones of the fish represent causes, and the head of the fish represents the resulting problem, or the effect. In the original quality control version, the factors representing causes were categorized into 6Ms: manpower, method, machine, material, mother nature, and measurement (see Figure 6.14). Within each of those factors, there would be secondary factors that would provide a more detailed picture of root causes.

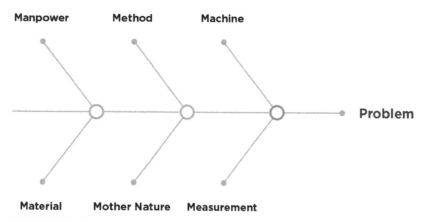

FIGURE 6.14

The original Ishikawa diagram had six categories related to manufacturing quality topics.

When using the fishbone diagram for analyzing cause and effect for different domains, you can define the factors most relevant for your analysis. You don't even need six different factors; you could have as few or as many as you need for sensemaking.

For instance, writer Daniel Markovitz used the example of using a fishbone diagram to analyze why morale was low within an organization. He organized the factors into five categories rather than six: work environment, technology, psychology, communication, and norms, and listed the secondary factors under each category.[9] (See Figure 6.15.)

What are the causes of low morale?

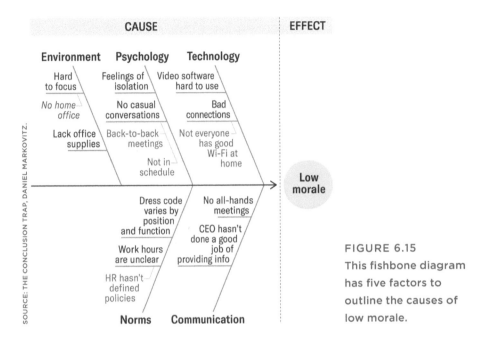

FIGURE 6.15
This fishbone diagram has five factors to outline the causes of low morale.

The "five whys" method is a good way to determine your factors for a fishbone diagram. This is exactly as it sounds: you basically need to ask "Why?" at least five times to uncover root cause. So in the case of the example above, you might ask: "Why is morale low in the organization?" An answer might be, "People feel isolated." You would then go on and ask, "Why do people feel isolated?" Again, an answer might be, "Because they no longer see their colleagues casually," or "Virtual interactions are socially unsatisfying." You would then continue to inquire until you've asked "Why?" at least five times. This method is good for freely identifying causes, which can then lead you to figuring out your "Factors" categories for your fishbone diagram.

---

9   Daniel Markovitz, "How to Avoid Rushing to Solutions When Problem-Solving," *Harvard Business Review*, November 27, 2020.

Like the iceberg model, the fishbone diagram is an accessible way to engage stakeholders in conversation about cause and effect, which is an excellent starting point for identifying opportunities for change.

Stock and Flow Diagrams: The Bathtub Analogy

A famous example of a model that captures the systems-thinking mindset is the bathtub analogy. It has been used to describe everything from housing stock to carbon output. The foundational idea is that within a system, there are stocks and flows. Stocks are things that can be increased or depleted, whereas flows are things that affect the increase or depletion of stocks. If you think literally about how a bathtub works, you can think of the water flowing from the faucet as a stock, and the faucet and drain as flows. The idea is that a balanced system should maintain the water level in the bathtub, so it neither overflows, nor drains completely.

For example, imagine that you are conducting analysis on attrition within your organization. You could potentially create a causal loop that shows how you are losing more employees than you are gaining. A stock-flow diagram gives you a more nuanced picture by breaking entities into stocks and flows. So, for example, employees in your organization would be stocks. Flows would be the speed of hiring, as well as attrition and other "flows" like layoffs and firings. According to Daniel Aronson at The Systems Thinker site, a good way to determine whether something is a stock or a flow is to ask yourself what would happen in the system if time stopped. Stocks would continue to exist, but flows, because they are actions, would disappear. In your organizational example, employees would continue to exist, but hirings and firings would cease.

A popular example of a stock-flow diagram is "The Carbon Bathtub" by MIT's John Sterman, published in *National Geographic* in 2009. It depicts factors that drive the increases in carbon in our atmosphere and shows why we collectively need not only to slow the addition of carbon, but we also need to increase the "draining" of carbon (see Figure 6.16).

The benefit of stock-flow diagrams is that, unlike causal loops alone, you can distinguish between stocks (the entities that are affected) versus flows (the entities that do the affecting). Even if you don't need this level of nuance, as you see with The Carbon Bathtub, you can tell an understandable high-level story about the system and convey important themes to your stakeholders.

The Carbon Bathtub – Infographic

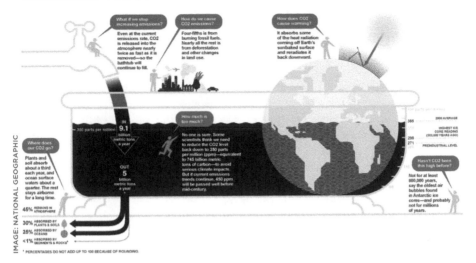

IMAGE: NATIONAL GEOGRAPHIC

FIGURE 6.16

The Carbon Bathtub is a model from 2009 that shows how the influx of carbon (9.1 billion metric tons per year) is much greater than the absorption or outflow (5 billion metric tons per year). It also shows what factors play a role in the imbalance.

SYSTEM SPOTTING

C-SECTIONS, CALCULATORS, AND RACISM

The U.S. has a striking childbirth statistic: almost a third of births are through cesarean section. Once a woman has had a C-section, her success rate of being able to have a vaginal birth (usually called VBAC, which stands for vaginal birth after cesarean) is reduced, with the understanding that different factors contribute to an individual's risk. I was surprised to hear that, since 2007, a VBAC calculator, developed by Maternal-Fetal Medicine Units (MFMU) Network, includes race as a factor along with other factors such as age, weight, and history of C-sections. If a woman is identified in the calculator as Black or Hispanic, her predictive score for being able to have a successful VBAC would drop drastically.

continues

The investigative journalism podcast *Reveal* spoke with Darshali Vyas, a resident at Massachusetts General Hospital, who, in 2019, wrote a research paper that challenged the use of race in the calculator.[10] The paper included a series of sobering statistics: Black women are three to four times more likely to die from pregnancy-related causes than white women, and are more than twice as likely to die because of childbirth. "Decreasing the number of unnecessary cesarean sections is important to reducing racial inequities in maternal health outcomes," Vyas wrote. With a calculator that gave Black and Hispanic women lower predictive scores, many women in those racial categories were being advised against VBAC, which increases risk by definition because C-sections are far riskier (see Figure 6.17).

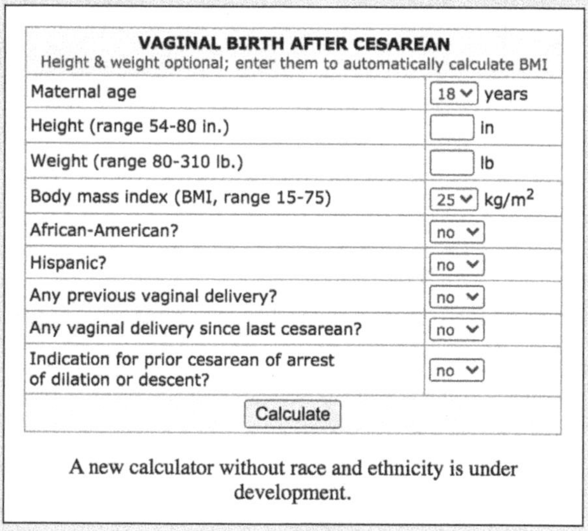

FIGURE 6.17

The VBAC calculator only includes a race category for African American and Hispanic (both of which are incredibly diverse racial categories).

VAGINAL BIRTH AFTER CESAREAN
Height & weight optional; enter them to automatically calculate BMI

Maternal age	18 ⌄ years
Height (range 54-80 in.)	in
Weight (range 80-310 lb.)	lb
Body mass index (BMI, range 15-75)	25 ⌄ kg/m^2
African-American?	no ⌄
Hispanic?	no ⌄
Any previous vaginal delivery?	no ⌄
Any vaginal delivery since last cesarean?	no ⌄
Indication for prior cesarean of arrest of dilation or descent?	no ⌄

Calculate

A new calculator without race and ethnicity is under development.

10 Darshali A. Vyas et al., "Challenging the User of Race in the Vaginal Birth After Cesarean Section Calculator," *Women's Health Issues*, April 12, 2019.

So why was race included in the calculator to begin with? Those who designed the tool based the criteria on observational data that concluded that "Women who achieved successful VBAC were more likely to be Caucasian, married, privately insured ... and to have BMI less than 30 when compared with those failing a trial of labor." The problem is that, even if that observational data held true, creating a predictive tool based on that historical data *proves to perpetuate the very patterns of racial inequities* because doctors use the tool to steer women based on its results. And what that means is that Black and Hispanic women are being steered away from VBAC, which has desirable maternal health benefits.

Vyas pointed out why historical racism (such as the racist assumption that Black and Hispanic women have different pelvic structures) and use of race in predictive tools is so dangerous: the category of race is historically and socially constructed rather than natural. "[R]ace is included as a proxy for other variables that reflect the effect of *racism* on health: factors like income, educational level, or access to care ... If these factors comprise the true connection, then we have failed to acknowledge these critical upstream factors by conflating them with race. These impacts should be uncovered and addressed, rather than being hidden and legitimized by the algorithm."

The MFMU network has since reworked their calculator to eliminate race as a factor, which will hopefully contribute to continued change in trying to achieve more equitable outcomes in healthcare.

The story of the VBAC calculator is a good example of an intervention having its own repercussions. Stakeholders solving problems and making decisions in systems can often have adverse effects, or perpetuate the status quo in undesirable ways. It's a cautionary tale about being cognizant of the relationship between history and the present, and how that affects one's ability to create change.

Prompts to consider:

- How might data inadvertently be used to perpetuate existing harmful behaviors?
- How might your intervention be used in ways that you did not intend?
- What might a causal loop look like for an intervention like the VBAC Calculator?

Takeaways

- Creating a causal loop map helps you articulate system forces in the form of cause and effect. You can use layers from the ecological framework (individual, community, society) to identify forces at various levels in the system.

- Within a causal loop map, you want to identify a deep structure, a core loop at the heart of your map. The deep structure is often representative of events or relationships that indicate the root cause.

- Systems archetypes are patterns in system incentives and behaviors. Archetypes such as Success to the Successful, Shifting the Burden, and Tragedy of the Commons help identify core system behavior.

- Iceberg models are good for identifying what's "below the surface" in a system. Events—which are visible—are usually the result or symptom of patterns, structures, and mental models. Fishbone diagrams are also a good way to uncover root cause.

- Stock-flow diagrams, often referred to as the *bathtub analogy* create nuanced pictures of systems by differentiating stocks (entities that are affected by flows) and flows (entities and actions that affect the flow of stocks).

Boon Yew Chew is a Principal UX designer at Elsevier, where he works on products and services for scholarly communications. He formerly served on the board of the Interaction Design Association (IxDA) and is a local leader for IxDA London.

How do you think design and systems thinking intersect?

In design, we talk about systems, but not so much about systems thinking: design and systems thinking are quite different communities of practice. There's not much cross-pollination between the practices, and not many people hang out across the communities.

I see some blending of methods being shared and used by some systems-thinking practitioners—from domains like design thinking, service design, complexity theory, and organizational change. I think that's quite tricky to do when there are so many different methods, perspectives, and practices.

That being said, within the community spaces I'm active in (mostly the IxDA), I try to share what I'm learning, and I encourage others as well in the community to open up their learning journeys.

What kinds of systems-thinking methods and tools do you engage in your work?

People can get caught up in thinking that there's a specific way to engage in systems thinking. First and foremost, I'm always trying to be mindful about what I can let go of versus what I should hold onto when it comes to methods. And I prioritize the ability to explain my analysis to my colleagues in a way that makes sense to them.

For example, I don't really create causal loop diagrams on a daily basis. If I do use a technique like causal loop diagramming, it's to model out systems to make sense of stuff. But I often hesitate because I work with people who can struggle with things like causal loop diagrams: it takes a lot of effort to explain and understand it. It's a huge mindset shift to go from a conventional, linear, logical approach to a more dialectic, synthetic, cyclical way of problem-solving. Essentially, I need to speak the same language as my colleagues so we can build a shared understanding. To adapt to that need, I engage in activities like creating journey maps, which have been widely accepted and understood, comparative analysis, and other end-to-end mapping frameworks that can give people a shared baseline. I can see that incorporated therein is a systems view, but it might be visible to me, but less visible to other people. But as long as we can both understand the implications and outcomes of something systemic, I consider that a win.

It's important to establish and reference various artifacts that can act as baselines for people to familiarize themselves with aspects of a system, but from the perspective they can understand. So, if we were to consider products and services as a system, we might start building up a baseline with common things like user journeys and flows, user needs and contexts, metrics like NPS scores, but then later add more artifacts that help people appreciate systems-y things about the product, services, organizations, and things they're already familiar with.

Even when I attempt to develop some kind of system intervention, I try to do it in ways that stakeholders can understand. For example, one intervention I've been working on is a set of high-level principles from which we can work backward. The goal of this intervention from a systems perspective is to establish common ground about the health of a system—in this case, the experience our customers have with our services. The key to all of these activities is to develop a common language, using common tools used in more known and established practices like service design but applying them with a systems perspective.

What kind of perspective do you think is important in your work as a designer and systems thinker?

I think part of how I think about problem-solving is to go long-term, like several years, and go broad, end-to-end, which is, again, a service design way of thinking.

Sometimes the mechanics of things like causal loop diagramming feels like it leaves out important factors like human behavior. Those diagrams are good for hard variables that make feedback loops persistent, and that don't change very often. But it's difficult when that tool is used to represent things like people's opinions. This is where the "soft" types of systems practice become important: understanding people, organizations, contexts, worldviews, and behaviors.

I try to look at my work through five different lenses: services (e.g., from service design), value chains (inspired by things like Wardley Mapping), futures (from futures thinking), people, and finally, systems. Not always in that order.

One of the issues with systems thinking for designers is the large amount of abstraction that gets applied to problems and situations. Systems practice has always leveraged abstraction to model and make sense of complex situations. The danger of this is that it removes the embodied context, for example, people's lived experiences, actual contexts in the real, physical world.

In design practice, even if designers can and often do work with abstractions, such as with journey mapping or sketching or diagramming, they still must return to that embodied context—the actual experience they're designing for! Designers start in the embodied space to understand it, sense it, then eventually build solutions with that in mind, and the solutions go out into the world and people interact with them. I can see more acceptance of this abstracted way of working or thinking in some areas of design like information architecture, where design work concerns itself on the structure (invisible and visible) of things, while other design work like interaction design more directly focuses on the embodied space—using experience and real-world contexts as design materials.

What do you think is needed to further bring systems thinking into designers' practice?

Systems thinking as a community of practice is complex. It has grown out of several different historical developments, has many different tools, heroes, practices, and so on. All of it is valid and useful, but it's definitely harder to teach than, say, product design.

Designers can learn a lot by reading systems-thinking literature, meeting and getting to know practitioners, and attending their events. We can then bring what we've learned back to our own communities and share stories. That type of approach has helped a lot in my own journey.

I would also suggest learning some of the most common methods. Even if you're not sure about how you might use them, it doesn't hurt to learn causal loop diagramming. Soft systems methodology is also an interesting method for designers. I'm a fan of Peter Checkland's rich pictures tool, which is an inspiring and fun way to convey people's perspectives of complex situations through drawings and visuals. There are also things like the Vanguard method, which is useful for service design, and the Viable Systems Model, which is an interesting and helpful way of thinking about organizations as systems. All of these things can help your analysis in ways that help expand your ability to think in systems.

Creating a Theory of Change

When I was little, one of my favorite movies was *Peewee's Big Adventure*. And one of my favorite scenes from that movie was Peewee's breakfast machine. Peewee wakes up in the morning, goes downstairs, and lights a candle. As he goes about getting ready for... work? School? Who knows!... The candle burns a string, setting off a series of contraptions, including jointed dinosaur skeletons and an Abe Lincoln statue, which crack eggs, squeeze oranges for orange juice, pour dog food for Peewee's tiny dog, and make pancakes, all while Pee-Wee does important things like taping up his face with Scotch tape. (It's a weird movie. You should definitely watch it if you haven't seen it!) In the end, he has a perfect Grand Slam-ish breakfast, over which he pours Mr. T cereal and eats three bites (see Figure 7.1).

The breakfast machine is a classic Rube Goldberg machine, named after a twentieth century cartoonist who drew elaborate contraptions in which a chain of complicated machines performed a simple task, such as putting stamps on envelopes. Rube Goldberg machines were a good example of chain reactions, a series of events that led to a single end.

FIGURE 7.1
Peewee Herman's breakfast machine did it all!

You might be wondering what Peewee's breakfast machine has to do with systems thinking. I imagine it to be an example of how complex mechanisms can contribute to outcomes that you are seeking.

In Peewee's case, it was creating the perfect breakfast and feeding his dog Speck; in your case, it's figuring out how to map multiple, potential interventions to the preferable outcomes you are seeking. In Peewee's Rube Goldberg machine, there were inputs (such as a drinking bird toy), activities (the drinking bird toy cracking eggs), and outputs (a plate of breakfast with curiously perfect sunny-side-up eggs). And not only was there a full plate of breakfast, but Speck had already been fed as well, and the machine also made orange juice. Multiple outputs!

Likewise, inputs, activities, and outputs are how you will think about the series of events that will lead to desired outcomes. At this stage of the process, you should be able to identify the outcomes that you want to happen and use what you've learned about the existing system to identify ways of creating change. It's an opportunity to think about the future. And, again, this is where mapping comes in handy.

In Chapter 3, "Systems Thinking and Design Thinking," you were introduced to the human-centered design process and how it might intersect with systems thinking (see Figure 7.2).

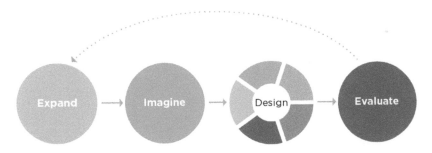

FIGURE 7.2
The circle labeled "Design" represents the five parts of the design-thinking process: gaining understanding (*empathize* and *define*) and taking action by designing (*ideate, prototype, test*). The *expand, imagine,* and *evaluate* phases are how systems thinking can intersect with the design process.

The *expand* phase of the process is represented in the work you've done to understand and map the status quo. This phase included your work of doing research, collaborating with stakeholders, and mapping system stakeholders and system forces. Now you will enter a phase in which you imagine interventions, approaches, and possibilities for the problems that you identified in the *expand* phase.

Identifying Interventions

An important aspect of integrating systems thinking into the traditional human-centered design process is acknowledging multifinality. This means that when you intervene in system problems, multiple types of interventions and leverage points will have to be considered. Each of these points of intervention should contribute to the broader outcomes that you are seeking. If you look at Figure 7.3, you can see a representation of multifinality in the process: you can imagine several types of system interventions, and then use the human-centered design process to potentially pursue several of them. Of course, there are some interventions that will fall outside of the scope of the HCD process (policy interventions are a good example), but you can still include them as you imagine what needs to be done in order to lead to the outcomes that are desirable.

So how do you identify interventions within the systems that you've analyzed? Analyzing the causal loop maps and stakeholder maps that you've created in your previous phase of work is one way, and you can combine that with design-thinking methods to brainstorm and ideate on potential interventions—with your stakeholders—within the existing system.

NOTE WHAT IS AN INTERVENTION?

You might be wondering about the use of *intervention* rather than *solution*, or even more specific terms like *product*. I resist using the term *solution* because it implies finality: that there's a linear connection between a problem that's been identified and a singular way to solve it. It's a reminder that today's problems come from yesterday's solutions.

The term *intervention*, on the other hand, implies a grounding in context, an acknowledgment that it could involve multiple avenues to create systemic change, and an understanding that continued support may be needed. An intervention could describe programs or initiatives that potentially make up a multipronged approach to changing the system.

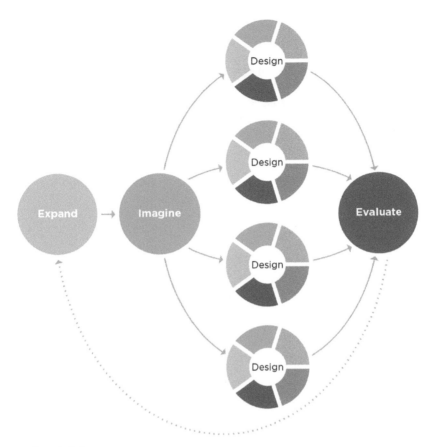

FIGURE 7.3

The *expand*, *imagine*, and *evaluate* circles are how you integrate systems thinking into a human-centered design process. The multiple paths leading to and from the design circles show that there are multiple forms of intervention and problem-solving.

Finding Opportunity Areas and "How Might We...?"

In a recent project, my research team conducted a systems-thinking project in which we sought to understand the landscape and role of Algebra 1 in K–12 education, particularly for students from historically under-resourced communities. In the final report for the project, the team summarized the system this way: "Algebra 1 [is a] critical milestone in adolescent academic achievement. However, this current reality of mathematics, laden with internalized negative beliefs, behaviors, patterns, and values, is not for lack of student assets or efforts, but rather something much weightier and systemic."

The analysis revealed multiple levels of problems within the existing system. It surfaced everything from educational policy that led to assessments being misused to track students, content being overly focused on rote memorization of mathematical algorithms rather than conceptual understanding, and a lack of support for students as they struggled with math.

These problems could be represented by an iceberg diagram (see Figure 7.4), which captured several of these issues.

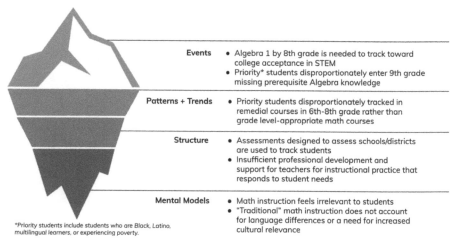

FIGURE 7.4

A high-level iceberg diagram that shows key themes can help define where to focus when you and your stakeholders are starting to identify opportunity areas.

Now that the team had a good high-level understanding of the problem space, we engaged stakeholders—subject matter experts, district decision-makers, teachers—to identify potential areas of intervention. This is a critical step in figuring out where to problem-solve within a system: involving a diverse set of people who play different roles in the existing system. Combining their expertise with your creativity, perspective, and facilitation as a design thinker drives a generative energy that enables you to consider multiple levels of system intervention.

HOW TO PRIORITIZE EQUITY IN THE DESIGN AND SYSTEMS-THINKING PROCESS

Justifiable criticism has been directed at the "How might we?" (HMW) prompts method. It's often used to reinforce traditional power structures, might be based on erroneous assumptions, and could oversimplify wicked problems into absurd questions like "How might we solve racism?" As strategist Tricia Wang, co-founder of Sudden Compass, stated, "I've seen HMW used to hide biases and assumptions. Worse, I've seen it exacerbate the lack of diversity on design teams and within corporations at large. The "we" in HMW refers to the people in the room, not to the users, customers, or populations for whom teams are designing their products and services."[1]

HMW has been applied in exactly these insidious ways, used by teams that are privileged, lack diversity, and have unfounded biases and assumptions about those for whom they are designing. These approaches confirm Wang's criticism. However, "How might we?" prompts have a place, particularly when the right people are in the room, especially those who are most affected by the system. For example, in projects focused on education, you will want to hold participatory design sessions with students—especially those who are marginalized in the current system—to be part of imagining and ideating. This approach turns "How might we?" from a prompt that assumes that the "we" in question are the privileged and powerful, and instead turns it into an empowering question for those who are often ignored by the system.

---

1   Tricia Wang, "Design Thinking's Most Popular Strategy Is BS," *Fast Company*, June 28, 2021.

In the case of the project focused on students' experiences with Algebra, diverse forms of interventions surfaced through workshops in which stakeholders were encouraged to think about various types of opportunities for correcting existing problems within the system. In facilitating the workshops, the team focused on framing the conversations using "How might we?" prompts. This was a good way to shift the mindset of workshop participants from understanding the problem space into a generative mode of thinking focused on how to move forward. "How might we?" is a prompt that is often used in design thinking.

According to IDEO.org's Design Kit, "We use the *How Might We* format because it suggests that a solution is possible and because they offer you the chance to answer them in a variety of ways. A properly framed How Might We doesn't suggest a particular solution, but gives you the perfect frame for innovative thinking."[2] The key to using this method effectively is to ensure that those who are most affected by the system are part of workshops or ideation sessions. It's a corrective measure to make sure that your stakeholders are diverse and that your approach is inclusive.

The key to creating the right level of prompts is to base your opportunity ideation on your detailed understanding of the existing system. It does not make sense to use a prompt like "How might we solve Algebra?" because this question is not drawn from any issues that you understand are within the system. At the opposite end of the spectrum, you would not prompt with "How might we create an app that solves the problem with Algebra?" because it leaves no room for your stakeholders to think about the space in an open way: a solution in this case is far too predetermined. It's possible that the way to address challenges in the system might have nothing to do with a digital product. A good way to facilitate opportunity ideation is to use a framework that accounts for multiple points of intervention. The STEEP framework is one such mechanism.

The STEEP Framework

When you are involving diverse stakeholders, a framework can be helpful for prompting ideation. The STEEP framework is typically used by businesses to scan the landscape for external factors that may affect business decisions (see Figure 7.5).

In the context of determining interventions within a system, this framework is useful for encouraging people to think broadly about potential interventions for change, without limiting your idea generation to only what those in the room can accomplish. Unlike the typical business context in which this framework can be used to understand how you as a *business* might be affected by the factors within the framework, rather, the factors are used as categories for which you (and your stakeholders) can consider how *you* will affect

---

2   IDEO Design Kit, "Methods: How Might We?," designkit.org/methods/3.

the system. To drive this move into thinking about interventions, design-thinking methods (such as ideation) can be used to facilitate the broadening of perspectives, and for all stakeholders to think beyond their immediate realm of expertise.

Socio-Cultural	**Technological**	**Environmental**	**Economic**	**Political**
Social forces such as demographics, culture, trending lifestyle habits	Material innovations, process innovations, digital technologies	Waste reduction, recycling, sustainability initiatives	Cost of living increases, market prices of commodities, exchange rates, etc.	Attitudes and approaches from political participants

FIGURE 7.5

As you think about interventions, you can broaden your thinking by considering categories that are both beyond design and also encompass design.

STEEP has five categories:

- **Socio-Cultural:** Social forces such as demographics, culture, and trending lifestyle habits
- **Technological:** Material innovations, process innovations, and digital technologies
- **Environmental:** Waste reduction, recycling, and sustainability initiatives
- **Economic:** Cost-of-living increases, market prices of commodities, exchange rates, etc.
- **Political:** Attitudes and approaches from political participants

There are overlaps between these categories, but the main purpose is to extend how you and your stakeholders think about problem-solving.

Take an example that was introduced in Chapter 2, "A Systems-Thinking Mindset," Mirjam de Bruijn's Twenty project. She considered how to reduce the carbon footprint of household and beauty products such as shampoo. Because these products are 80 to 95 percent water, she decided that one form of intervention would be to ship the products without water, thereby reducing the carbon footprint caused by shipping.

Imagine that you are working to figure out how to further reduce the carbon footprint of shipping such products. You would bring together multiple stakeholders from the system to think about potential opportunity areas. If you were to use the STEEP framework, you could use a series of prompts to drive the ideation. You would focus on both understanding the landscape, as well as how you might use the categories to intervene in the problems in the existing system.

- **Socio-Cultural:**

  Landscape: What are some trends when it comes to consumer attitudes and behaviors that align with care or consideration of environmental impact? What might align with the outcomes you are seeking?

  Interventions: How could you help consumers engage in behaviors that are mindful of environmental implications?

- **Technological:**

  Landscape: Are there any emerging technologies that would help reduce the environmental impact of shipping?

  Interventions: How could material advances further reduce carbon output?

- **Environmental:**

  Landscape: What kinds of sustainability initiatives related to product shipping might you engage in?

  Interventions: Are there processes that could reduce waste in production, transport, or disposal?

- **Economic:**

  Landscape: Are there macro-economic trends, such as supply chain changes, government regulation, or investing that could facilitate positive outcomes?

  Interventions: How could you find ways to be sensitive to how economic trends affect people and communities?

- **Political:**

  Landscape: Are there existing political barriers that would prevent your business from making progress?

  Interventions: How could you engage in political momentum that is in support of reducing environmental impact? What kind of regulation or policy would be helpful?

If you were to extend your thinking into these spaces, you could think about how political policies, such as reductions or bans on single-use plastic, might also lower carbon output. You might also find that more retailers engaging in zero-packaging solutions could further reduce the environmental impact of household and beauty products, and also capitalize on consumers' growing concern about the amount of plastic waste produced through these products. You could also consider who is being incentivized by the current wasteful system and correct for it, such as holding companies responsible for the amount of waste generated by their products, and instead, incentivize different behavior.

You can structure your ideation by using themes accompanied by the STEEP categories. For example, use the themes that emerged from your status quo systems maps and create a canvas for each theme with the STEEP categories and their descriptions (see Figure 7.6). Encourage your team and stakeholders to generate ideas for interventions in each category. The prompts should allow them to think broadly beyond their own expertise, rather than overindexing on categories that they understand best.

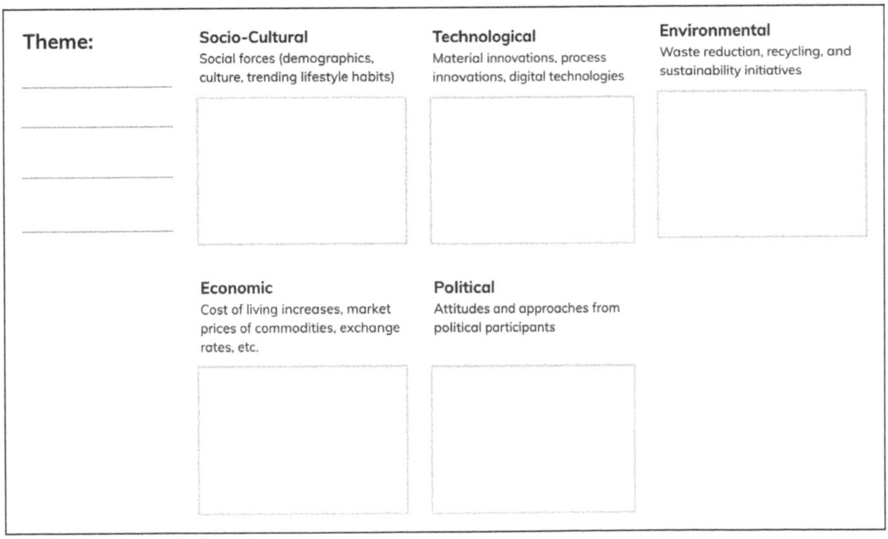

Theme:	Socio-Cultural	Technological	Environmental
	Social forces (demographics, culture, trending lifestyle habits)	Material innovations, process innovations, digital technologies	Waste reduction, recycling, and sustainability initiatives
	Economic	Political	
	Cost of living increases, market prices of commodities, exchange rates, etc.	Attitudes and approaches from political participants	

FIGURE 7.6
Stakeholders can work together to generate ideas for potential interventions in each of the STEEP categories.

After you've generated ideas for interventions using this framework, you can map your interventions to figure out how to get from point A to point B.

Another source for ideating on potential interventions is by returning to the Ecological Framework introduced in Chapter 5, "Synthesis and Mapping Stakeholders." How could you intervene when it comes to the following categories? Again, imagining that you are working on an education project, your themes could be oriented around the following categories.

- **Individual/Interpersonal:** Knowledge, attitudes, and practices among children, adolescents, and families that affect educational decisions and actions.

- **Community:** Social beliefs and norms, gender norms, social and economic conditions and resources, knowledge and attitudes about education among community members, sense of empowerment and collective efficacy that affect educational choices, decisions, and practices.

- **Institutional:** Institutional conditions of the education system that affect inclusion and quality, including educational media.

- **Policy/System:** Policies and governance elements of educational systems that facilitate or discourage inclusive and quality education, as well as positive decisions about education among individuals and families.

Defining a Theory of Change

In the white paper, *The Strategy Lifecycle: A Guide*, the Bill & Melinda Gates Foundation outlined its strategic decision-making process, with the explicit objective that their "investments must be highly strategic and focused on impact." What they mean by "impact" is that they can create the most positive change possible, for the biggest number of people, through the investments that they make. As Bill Gates once elaborated, when describing the foundation's dedication to malaria eradication: "Once we've committed to malaria eradication, we're not going to abandon that. Sadly, there's very few fields where you can save millions of lives for small sums of money."[3]

---

3   Molly Wood and Stephanie Hughes, "Bill Gates: "Our Values Do Change What Gets Funded in This Economy," NPR Marketplace, September 15, 2020.

As a designer, your work should also be focused primarily on impact. What is the impact that you want your work to achieve and how do you work backward from that?

One method for connecting action to impact is to create a theory-of-change map. Social impact consultant Isabel Vogel described theory of change as "an outcomes-based approach which applies critical thinking to the design, implementation and evaluation of initiatives and programmes intended to support change in their contexts."[4] She went on to describe two views of the term *theory of change*. First, it's viewed as a tool that can be used to map the logical sequence of an initiative from inputs to outcomes. Second, it's considered "a deeper reflective process and dialogue amongst colleagues and stakeholders, reflecting on the values, worldviews and philosophies of change that make more explicit people's underlying assumptions of how and why change might happen as an outcome of the initiative."

How you might approach creating a theory of change for your initiatives involves both views: that it works as a tool *and* a process. You should continue to collaborate with stakeholders involved in analyzing the status quo. And, just like your systems mapping of the status quo, it involves not just analysis, but also mapping. A map is a good way to capture, align, and communicate a shared understanding of how you and your stakeholders assume that change will happen. USAID'S Learning Lab described theory-of-change activities as "the thinking behind how a particular intervention will bring about results."[5] It's a way of breaking down the steps of what needs to be done in order to carry through the intervention, as well as the layers of outcomes and impact that will happen as a result of those actions.

Based on the work that you've done thus far to understand the status quo, you have a range of assumptions that are grounded in this holistic view of the systems space. However, when it comes to how you might solve problems, you're only at the point of having hypotheses, of having ideated on and identified potential interventions that will shake up the system space that you've mapped. How do you now figure out how these interventions, these changes, will play out? This is where your theory-of-change framework comes in handy.

---

4   Isabel Vogel, "Review of the Use of 'Theory of Change' in International Development." UK Department of International Development, April 2012.

5   https://usaidlearninglab.org/lab-notes/what-thing-called-theory-change

Vogel described the elements that a theory of change should include as the following:

- **Context:** The current state of the problem that the project is seeking to influence and other actors able to influence change

- **Long-term change:** What the project or initiative seeks to support and for whose benefit

- **Process/sequence of change:** The process that should theoretically lead to the desired long-term outcome

- **Assumptions:** What stakeholders assume about how these changes might happen, as a check on whether the steps articulated are appropriate for influencing change

- **Diagram and narrative summary:** The map that articulates the outcomes of the discussion

If you reflect on these elements, you'll find that much of the work that you've done to understand the status quo, the current landscape, and causality up to this point constitutes the "context" piece. As you work toward defining the types of initiatives, interventions, and solutions that would drive change toward desirable outcomes, you will articulate further context.

As a designer, you can view the creation of maps (the diagram) and storytelling (the narrative summary) as a distillation of the other elements: long-term change, process or sequence of change, and assumptions. These are the things that are best captured in a theory of change.

There are multiple forms of theory-of-change frameworks. Let's look at two models that enable you to determine the best altitude for the types of conversations and decision-making that you'll be engaged in. What they have in common is that they should help you create clarity and alignment with your stakeholders about what will lead to the impact that you are trying to achieve.

Mapping Initiatives and Interventions

Now that you and your stakeholders have a good idea of possible interventions, and you are prepared to create a theory of change, you can map them in a few different ways. Creating an outcomes map is a straightforward way to align your group of project stakeholders. You can then move on to a more detailed theory-of-change framework in order to better articulate what needs to happen to execute on your potential intervention. The objective of working through how to get from problem to intervention to outcomes and eventually impact is to start being able to identify where you, as a designer, can use design thinking to intervene, and where you, as a designer, can facilitate, clarify, and align stakeholders to make change happen.

A key tenet of systems thinking is that the design process will not solve all systems problems. Other forms of expertise are needed, such as those of policymakers, research experts, lived experts, system stakeholders, and others. However, design methods of mapping, workshopping, and creative ideation can facilitate other people's expertise and ideas in a way that leads to alignment and action, just as it has throughout your systems analysis.

As you map the interventions you're considering, you should be primarily focused on what happens at the end of a chain of events: the outcomes you are trying to achieve. This means that if you do something (create an output), then something else (an outcome) will happen as a result.

The two frameworks that I typically use—Outcomes Mapping and Input to Impact—have different purposes, going from clarification and alignment to detailed articulation (see Figure 7.7).

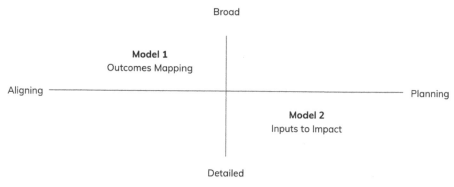

FIGURE 7.7

The subsequent frameworks have different objectives but a shared purpose: to align your stakeholders on the action that needs to be taken in order to create change.

Throughout the process, you might employ different theory-of-change frameworks to elicit responses from your stakeholders, ranging from broad alignment to detailed planning. In addition, you can use a series of frameworks in succession to get more granular in your discussions and decision-making. A structured way to think about each of the frameworks is to understand the following:

- **When to Use:** Are you trying to answer "What should we do?," "Why should we do it?" or, more specifically, "How should we do it?" The granularity you are seeking determines which framework you might want to use.

- **Objective:** Are you trying to get buy-in from key stakeholders, are you trying to involve new stakeholders whose input is sorely needed, or are you working with a core team to articulate a plan?

- **Components:** What are the key categories that make up the framework?

To illustrate the various frameworks, imagine that you have been working with various stakeholders in education to address the increases in childhood obesity and childhood diabetes in your region. You will first conduct research with various system stakeholders, lived experts, and field experts. You will then synthe-size what you've learned through systems mapping of the current space. Finally, you will re-engage your stakeholders to identify multiple potential interventions, creating initiatives to address the problems within the system. Imagine one of those initiatives is to start vegetable gardening programs in partnership with a local school district. You now can engage in running workshops that will help your stakeholders gain clarity and a shared understanding of how to carry through on this initiative.

Framework 1: Outcomes Mapping

In the typical product design and development process, you follow a logical process of setting goals and creating specifications and requirements that lead to that goal. In digital design, you don't necessarily consider what might happen outside of the context of the use of your product, as the direct benefit of use is what you are most focused on.

In systems thinking, what you are going to do, and how you are going to do it, is not the first consideration. Rather, you start with outcomes and impact, and map things backward.

You've used the STEEP framework to identify potential interventions, so now's a good time to map some of those potential interventions so that you can explicitly map the connections between the challenges you are trying to address and the outcomes you want to achieve.

- **When to Use:** You have worked with your stakeholders to iden-tify potential interventions and initiatives. Now you are looking to facilitate a discussion that helps your group explicitly connect those potential initiatives with outcomes, as well as the barriers and challenges you are trying to solve.

- **Objective:** This framework can be used as a check to make sure that your group hasn't lost sight of the outcomes you are trying to achieve, as well as the problems you are trying to address. Often during the ideation process, people can go pretty far in different directions. There may be some folks who are focused on blue sky solutions, while others might limit their thinking to what can be accomplished. This framework helps connect the dots for either approach and ensures that you focus on outcomes.

- **Components:** (See Figure 7.8.)
  - **Outcomes/Impact:** What do we (the societal "we") want to happen? How would situations improve for the key system stakeholders?
  - **Potential Solutions/Interventions:** What are some ways that change can happen in order to lead to the desired outcomes?
  - **Current Problems and Barriers:** What are some of the key issues in the current system? What is happening that is currently leading to poor outcomes? What might prevent change from happening?

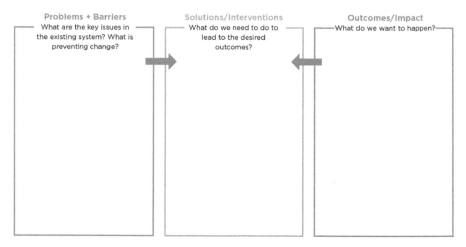

Problems + Barriers
What are the key issues in the existing system? What is preventing change?

Solutions/Interventions
What do we need to do to lead to the desired outcomes?

Outcomes/Impact
What do we want to happen?

FIGURE 7.8

When mapping outcomes you can think about it as first working backward, from outcomes/impact to solutions/interventions, but you can also think about how to solve existing problems and barriers.

Using an Outcomes Map

For this simplified form of Outcomes Mapping, outcomes and impact can fall into the same category. The goal is to be generative: to capture all of the things that you want to happen after your purported actions. As David Peter Stroh noted in *Systems Thinking for Social Change*, "Developing a shared picture of what people want as well as of reality at a deep level enables stakeholders to experience their responsibility for the whole system instead of just their role. It produces a state of alignment where people freely commit, 'I'll get my part done, and I'll make sure we all get the whole thing done.'"[6]

---

6   David Peter Stroh, *Systems Thinking for Social Change*, p. 74.

So imagine you are back to the school gardening program example. If you were to do an Outcomes Mapping exercise, you would start by identifying a series of outcomes. In a systems-thinking project, you would have started with a system-oriented problem space. For example, perhaps your project stakeholders have been trying to understand the causes and problems related to childhood obesity, inequitable access to fresh produce, and links between nutrition and other child health outcomes. Assuming that you've done the work, you can consider ideal outcomes and impact.

Some ideal outcomes might be:

- Improved access to fresh produce for students from under-resourced schools and low-income communities.

- Increased consumption of fresh fruit and vegetables by students from those settings.

- Improved health outcomes (decreased childhood obesity, decreased childhood Type-2 diabetes).

You would capture outcomes and impacts such as these in the Outcomes column in your outcomes map, as well as the problems that you've come to understand through your previous (imagined) systems analysis. Your map would look something like Figure 7.9.

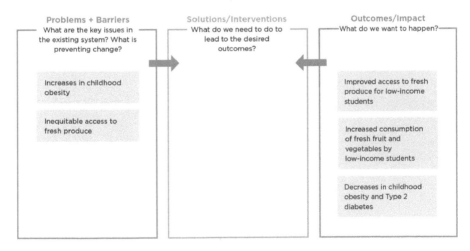

FIGURE 7.9
Start by filling out outcomes, as well as the problems/barriers that you've identified in your previous systems analysis.

Despite this simplified example, you can still see the connection between outcomes and identified problems, i.e., "inequitable access to fresh produce." In terms of desirable outcomes, the focus is on students from low-income families as a response to those existing inequities, even if the status-quo analysis was broader than a focus on these specific students.

In addition, you might point to the third outcome on your canvas as something you might later separate as an "impact." The difference between outcomes and impact is that the identified outcomes should lead to the impact, but impact might be harder to connect directly with your intervention efforts. For example, there could also be a regulatory policy that added a tax to sugary drinks (which is an intervention that has been instituted in some local governments). In addition to your potential interventions, this policy could also contribute to a decrease in childhood diabetes, which could make it difficult to link your intervention to that particular impact. On the other hand, "increased consumption of fresh fruit and vegetables by low-income students" could be more readily linked to your (assumed) garden-based intervention.

Lastly, you would fill out the middle column with the most promising interventions identified through your ideation sessions. Once you've mapped potential interventions, your canvas could look like Figure 7.10.

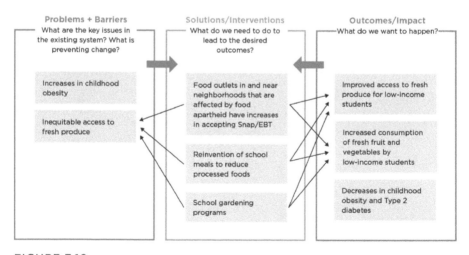

FIGURE 7.10

There would typically be dozens of ideas in each of these categories, particularly your idea generation for solutions/interventions. However, you can see the potential connections to the desired outcomes that you identified.

You might notice that none of the arrows connect to the problem of "increases in childhood obesity" or the outcome of "decreases in childhood obesity and Type 2 diabetes." The reason is that those are a degree away from what has been proposed as potential interventions. The inequitable access to fresh produce could play a role in the increases in childhood diabetes. (Actually, this has been supported by studies that show the connection between a lack of healthy food access and the connection to childhood nutrition-based health problems.) The hypothesis here is that if you solve for the inequitable access to fresh food, then it should lead to outcomes that will contribute to the eventual impact of a decrease in childhood obesity and other health problems. This will emerge in more detailed forms of theory-of-change mapping, such as the subsequent Input to Impact framework.

SYSTEM SPOTTING

TEEN DRINKING AND AFTER-SCHOOL PROGRAMS

In the 1990s, Iceland had one of the worst rates of teen substance abuse. In 1998, 42 percent of children between the ages of 15 and 16 reported having gotten drunk at least once in the past month. By 2016, that number was down to five percent.[7] In a world in which many forms of substance abuse are increasing, how did Iceland turn around its teen substance abuse problem?

Researchers surveyed students to understand better why teenagers were engaging in drinking and other drugs, and they found a correlation between the amount of time they spent in organized activities, spending time with parents, and being indoors in the evening, and reduced rates of substance use.

continues

---

7   *Mosaic Science* had an excellent story on the Youth in Iceland program, titled, "Iceland Knows How to Stop Teen Substance Abuse but the Rest of the World Isn't Listening" by Emma Young, *Mosaic Science* (podcast), January 17, 2017.

Researchers Jón Sigfússon and Inga Dóra Sigfúsdóttir used these insights to propose a multipronged set of interventions that's been described as both radical and evidence-based, focused primarily on preventive measures. The Icelandic government implemented multiple strategies, including night-time curfews for teens and programs aimed at parents to emphasize the importance of the quantity—not just the quality—of time that they spent with their kids. Most extensively, the government heavily funded afternoon and evening organized activities such as sports, music, and dance to keep kids busy and off the streets. In essence, rather than a focus on strategies like drug education, which typically focuses on decreasing drug use and has minimal impact, they focused on *increasing* teen well-being, by offering lifestyle alternatives to the use of drugs and alcohol.

In addition, the researchers have continued to conduct surveys, so the data on shifting behaviors continues to be up-to-date.

Hundreds of other communities, from state to municipal levels, are trying "the Iceland model" as they seek to emulate Iceland's outcomes. Of course, the unique contexts of different communities often need to adjust the model to reflect their local needs, and many have to consider other systemic issues, such as inconsistent, or short-term types of funding for programs that would make these types of wraparound initiatives challenging. However, it is promising that rather than focusing on "just say no to drugs" campaigns, and other forms of direct education, government entities are instead examining root causes and are focusing on kids' well-being as an avenue for change.

Prompts to consider:
- As you think about potential interventions in the system, are there preventive measures that could lead to positive outcomes?
- What are some different categories of intervention that you haven't yet considered? (Think about the STEEP framework.)
- What kinds of stakeholders need to be involved to see different types of initiatives through?

Framework 2: From Input to Impact

One of the most established theory-of-change frameworks is a logic model that was established by the United Way in 1996. It is focused on articulating how a program influences change that results in specific outcomes. I've called this model *From Input to Impact* to differentiate it from the many different theory-of-change frameworks that exist.

- **When to Use:** Now that you have a series of potential initiatives, you can start mapping them individually. This framework is good for mapping single initiatives in a more detailed way than the outcomes map. Who needs to be involved? What kinds of activities need to take place, what do those activities produce, and how do they connect to outcomes? This framework is useful for bringing together stakeholders who will either execute the initiative or be affected by the initiative's activities and outcomes.

- **Objective:** The purpose of this mapping activity is to better understand the process of an initiative so that you can start pinpointing what would need to happen to put the plan into motion.

- **Components:** The typical components that are articulated in this particular framework are Inputs, Activities, Outputs, Outcomes, and Impact (see Figure 7.11). You can divide these components into two main categories: your planned work, which captures the things that the program and its participants must do, and your intended results, which capture what should happen if what you've planned is successful.

Your planned work (the sphere of control): These are the actions that an organization takes in order to lead to certain outcomes and impact.

- **Inputs:** These are the resources that you'll need to engage in the activities that you will embark on: for example, people, physical, or environmental resources, or information going into your project.

- **Activities:** These are what you will be doing to produce your intervention (or a type of solution). It's how you will use your inputs to do something new.

- **Outputs:** These are what you deliver, the product of your work, and the things that you produce that should, in theory, lead to the outcomes and impacts that you expect and predict. It could be products, services, and other responses to problems, as well as measurable results from your activities. For example, how many people has your initiative served, such as how many students are enrolled in a program.

Your intended results (the sphere of influence and sphere of interest):

- **Outcomes:** These are the results of your outputs. Outcomes are what happen beyond your direct actions or control, and they should articulate the benefits to those for whom you are designing.

- **Impact:** This is the broader and lasting effect and, ideally, benefits—to organizations, systems, communities—of the outcomes.[8]

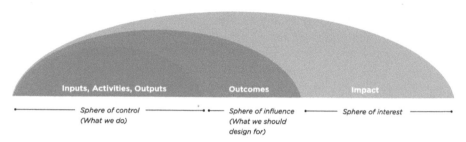

FIGURE 7.11

A good way to think figuratively about a theory of change is what you have control over, what you can influence, and what you are interested in happening as a result.

To arrive at an articulation of these components, it's useful to map interventions end-to-end. Really, what you are specifically articulating is the series of assumptions that lead to a desired result.

Using the Input to Impact Framework

Like all of these frameworks, this one works really well when turned into a canvas (either physical on paper, or digital via tools like Miro or MURAL) and used in a workshop setting with your diverse stakeholders (see Figure 7.12).

Let's return to the school gardening program initiative. Like the Outcomes Mapping framework, here, too, you would start with the outcomes you want to happen. Take the two "connected" outcomes from the previous outcomes map (see Figure 7.13).

---

8   https://blogs.lse.ac.uk/impactofsocialsciences/2014/10/27/
     impact-vs-outcome-harding/

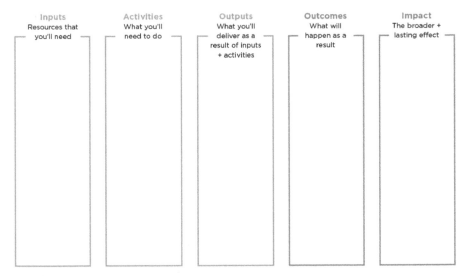

Inputs	Activities	Outputs	Outcomes	Impact
Resources that you'll need	What you'll need to do	What you'll deliver as a result of inputs + activities	What will happen as a result	The broader + lasting effect

FIGURE 7.12

Everything can be turned into a canvas for adding sticky notes!

Outcomes/Impact
What do we want to happen?

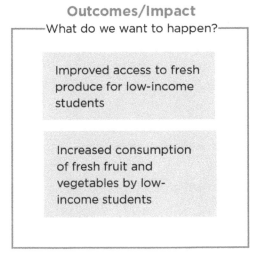

Improved access to fresh produce for low-income students

Increased consumption of fresh fruit and vegetables by low-income students

FIGURE 7.13

Here are outcomes identified in the previous exercise.

You can use these as a starting point for capturing and articulating outcomes. As you work on the other components, it's likely that more outcomes will be identified and can be further added to the canvas. Developing a shared idea of outcomes is critical to your organization or stakeholders' ability to carry through on the initiative. You don't want the outcomes to become diluted based on what's feasible, even if the initiative doesn't necessarily connect directly or is a few degrees away from the desired outcome.

While in the previous canvas the item in the solution/intervention column was "school gardening programs," here, your entire sphere of control and its three categories is a more detailed description of that particular intervention. Because you are now detailing how to take action, it makes sense for the terminology to shift from "intervention" to "initiative."

It's practical to work through the three columns with prompts and afterward to connect the items in the columns. Some prompts for these columns could include:

- **Inputs:**
  - What kinds of staff or facilities will be needed for this initiative?
  - What kind of budget, funding, or other financial resources will this initiative require?
  - Are there partnerships that will be critical to establish for this initiative?
- **Activities:**
  - What do you and your stakeholders need to do to get this initiative going?
  - What do you and your stakeholders need to do to maintain the initiative?
  - What do other stakeholders need to do?
  - What kinds of activities will your program participants engage in?
  - What do program participants engage in to achieve the desired outcomes?
- **Outputs:**
  - What should the immediate results of your activities be?
  - How should you measure the immediate goals of the initiative? (For example, it will serve X number of students.)

Your canvas might look something like Figure 7.14. This is by no means comprehensive, but it can serve as an example of some of the things that might be included on this canvas.

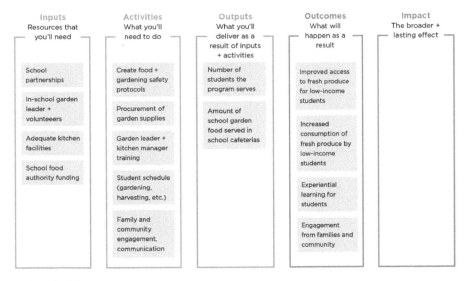

FIGURE 7.14

Your canvas will likely have far more ideas included, but this could be a good starting point for getting an initiative started.

You'll see that additional outcomes have been added. Often, the conversations around the Sphere of Control will lead to more nuances and additional ideas in the outcomes space.

Finally, it's important to align with the broad impact that this initiative—ideally, one of many different initiatives within the system—will lead to (see Figure 7.15).

This framework is effective in surfacing as much as possible, but still at a high level that doesn't require deep-seated technical expertise, for a broad set of stakeholders to start imagining what a program would look like and how it would work. It creates both clarity and a shared understanding that everyone can use going forward as they delve into even greater detail (creating program roadmaps, for example) that will make what's articulated in your theory of change actionable.

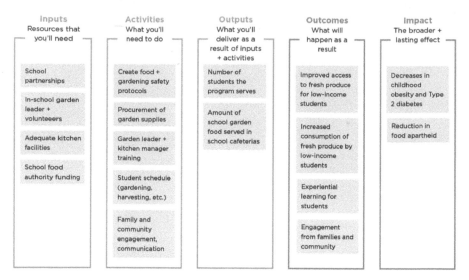

Inputs Resources that you'll need	Activities What you'll need to do	Outputs What you'll deliver as a result of inputs + activities	Outcomes What will happen as a result	Impact The broader + lasting effect
School partnerships	Create food + gardening safety protocols	Number of students the program serves	Improved access to fresh produce for low-income students	Decreases in childhood obesity and Type 2 diabetes
In-school garden leader + volunteeers	Procurement of garden supplies	Amount of school garden food served in school cafeterias	Increased consumption of fresh produce by low-income students	Reduction in food apartheid
Adequate kitchen facilities	Garden leader + kitchen manager training		Experiential learning for students	
School food authority funding	Student schedule (gardening, harvesting, etc.)		Engagement from families and community	
	Family and community engagement, communication			

FIGURE 7.15

The Impact column points to the broader societal outcomes toward which this particular initiative should contribute.

Takeaways

- Moving from your systems analysis of the status quo to generating ideas for interventions once again requires engagement from your organizational and system stakeholders. This means that those people who will be affecting change, as well as those who will be most affected by change, are well-represented throughout the process.

- The STEEP (socio-cultural, technological, economic, environmental, political) framework is good for generating ideas for interventions that address problems within the system. It's also good for understanding potential trends that may affect the system.

- A theory of change is the thinking behind how a particular intervention will bring about results. Developing a theory of change is useful for planning initiatives that will lead to desired outcomes and impact.

- You can use different theory-of-change frameworks to engage your stakeholders in aligning and planning. Outcomes Mapping is a framework for developing broad understanding and alignment, while the Input to Impact framework is good for high-level planning and articulating how an initiative will work.

Dr. Behnosh Najafi, PhD, is the founder and principal of Circular by Design, a consulting agency that supports organizational and business efforts to drive positive growth, resiliency, innovation, and sustainability through the adaptation of circular and regenerative economy principles.

I know a lot of designers interested in sustainability. How did you make this a core focus of your work as a designer?

I have always been interested in working on topics related to sustainability, but it was hard work to understand how I as a design researcher could provide offerings in that space. A focus on the circular economy provided lots of inroads in its focus on more sustainable product and service delivery. I started out as a research psychologist, but I ended up gravitating toward design because I saw it as a natural extension of doing applied research, and it afforded the opportunity to have impact in a more immediate way. A few years ago, I started intentionally seeking design projects that were more in alignment with my values around serving the environment and working on issues related to equity.

How do you think a systems mindset and circular design intersect?

I don't necessarily regard myself as an expert in systems thinking. I think where it's had the most relevance in my practice is the concept of doing no harm. It's really important, for example, to have a holistic view of how you design your business model.

Thinking specifically about harm, there's a lot of greenwashing in consumer goods and services, and companies not really thinking about the full impact of their efforts. An example I often draw upon is boxed water. It's marketed as more sustainable. But often the infrastructure isn't in place to remove the plastic and aluminum that lines the boxes, so the packaging just goes to waste. And even when a recycler can remove the lining, they can't do so on a level that recoups the cost of removing it. You can design things that from the outside seem more sustainable, but in context, they can actually have a negative effect.

A systems view on how all of these things are connected can help you recognize when something might be creating more harm than good.

What are some approaches that you use in your circular design practice?

I've focused recently on using a systems-design lens for modeling circular business design and strategy. What I've found is that when it comes to circular design, most people are thinking only about the materials they use. This is important, but I often help people transition their thinking away from just the use of materials into thinking about things like their business and service model. I'm taking a more expansive view of the business than just the materials they use.

Tools like the Circular Business Canvas[9] support my work with organizations to help take that birds-eye view and focus not only on traditional considerations related to putting together a business plan, but also include aspects of circularity like positive and negative environmental and social externalities.

I also think service design tools like service blueprints can be systems-oriented, particularly because in a similar way they take an overarching view of company systems and the touchpoints needed to deliver a great customer experience.

In addition to tools, are there certain views within systems thinking that resonate with you in your work?

I prefer to think about systems as a set of relationships that hang together like constellations rather than thinking about causal loops. Causal loops support a mechanistic view of how things happen in the world; indeed, we don't always know what the perfect combination of factors together is that create cause-and-effect relationships. In contrast, the constellations metaphor is perfect for designers because through merely identifying the variables that often present themselves together, we can start taking action by tweaking the model here and there in the spirit of experimentation. So we can solve problems not by our perfect knowledge of cause and effect, but rather through trial and error (that, of course, has been initially informed through our understanding of the problem space as well as the perspectives of users).

How can designers activate their interest in the kind of work you do?

Follow your values and what has the most meaning. The easiest, sexiest problems that you use your skills to help solve are not always going to be the ones you feel proudest of. The design problems that you struggle with the most because they are important to you are probably the ones most worth solving, even if you don't have the perfect process or tools right away.

---

9   The Circular Canvas is an element in Circulab's circular economy toolbox. You can find it on Circulab's website: circulab.com//toolbox-circular-economy/.

CHAPTER 8

Anticipating Unintended Consequences

In 1902, French colonial Hanoi had a problem: a rat infestation. The French colonial government, spearheaded by Paul Doumer, the Governor-General of French Indochina (present-day Vietnam), sought to make Hanoi an example of French conquering modernism and civility: wide boulevards, tree-shaded villas, and modern amenities, such as a sewer system. These amenities only applied to the neighborhoods occupied by French Europeans, with the native Vietnamese population, through heavy taxation, literally paying the cost of this colonial luxury.

A key element of this showcase of modernity was the French colonial government's newly installed sewer system. Of course, the sewers served only the Vietnamese city's wealthy French quarter, providing running water and flush toilets to the European occupants.

Unfortunately, and counter to the idea of the sewer system being a shining example of modern sanitation, the 15 kilometers of sewer lines in the tropical climate acted as the perfect rodent breeding ground. In the cool dark sewer, rats were safe from the usual tropical predators, and as a result, the rat population exploded, bringing cases of bubonic plague with it to the fancy French Quarter homes (see Figure 8.1).

FIGURE 8.1

In Michael Vann's historical comic book *The Great Rat Hunt*, he shows the absurdity, humor, and tragedy of the French colonial initiative to rid Hanoi of rats.

The colonial government's creative solution? Hire locals as rat hunters to exterminate the rat population, paying a bounty for every rat exterminated. The effort started in the spring of 1902, and by the summer of that year, the numbers of exterminated rats were staggering: on June 12, according to the colonial archives, 20,114 were killed *in a single day.*

How was it possible there were so many rats? Well, with the bounty being dependent on turning in rat tails, and the French government increasing the bounty per rat to motivate local rat hunters to continue trying to make a dent on a seemingly infinite number of rats, local residents began cutting off only the tails, and allowing the rats to run free to continue to breed. In addition, French authorities realized that individuals had actually started breeding rats to be able to turn them in for the bounty. As researcher Michael Vann explained, "One can only imagine the frustration of the municipal authorities, who realized that their best efforts at *dératisation* had actually increased the rodent population by indirectly encouraging rat-farming."[1]

The "Great Rat Massacre" often serves as an example of what Vann articulates as the unintended consequences overall of French colonial rule: "Frequently, the most celebrated aspects of French colonization directly produced the forces and individuals that overthrew French rule."

Just for fun, here's how the causal loop would look for that tragic (for the French!) colonial decision (see Figure 8.2).

> **NOTE** THE COBRA EFFECT
>
> The Hanoi rat eradication program and its results are typical of a systems-thinking concept called *The Cobra Effect*. The Cobra Effect is so named after yet another example of perverse incentives: in British colonial Delhi, the government put a bounty on cobras, thereby causing an increase in the cobra population once local cobra hunters started breeding cobras in order to make more bounty money. (If you didn't already think colonialism was bad, perhaps these examples, among others, will sway you!)

---

1   Michael G. Vann, *Of Rats, Rice, and Race: The Great Hanoi Rat Massacre, an Episode in French Colonial History* (Michigan State University Press, 2003).

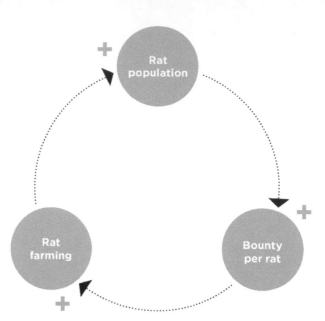

FIGURE 8.2
I never thought I would have the term *rat farming* in a causal loop, but there's a first time for everything.

Perverse incentives and unintended consequences are not, of course, confined to poor colonial-era decision-making. You may have seen examples play out in policy today, or even in decision-making within your own organization. Think about your own key performance indicators: do they potentially punish risk-taking? Do people work toward the metric itself, rather than the outcomes the metrics are meant to accomplish? These decisions within the confines of your organization, and about your products and services, can often be host to a series of cascading effects, some of which are intended, and some of which are not intended at all. In order to better anticipate potential cascading effects, designers need to think about outcomes that are both good and bad. As Ursula K. LeGuin wrote in *A Wizard of Earthsea*, "To light a candle is to cast a shadow." You want to be able to anticipate the shadows you might cast.

Techno-Optimism and the Law of Unintended Consequences

So now that you have a theory of change (or multiple theories of change) for various interventions, you need to be intentional about anticipating unintended consequences. There are lots of examples of organizations that fail to understand the impact of their actions, particularly for those who are not typically part of the development of solutions or interventions. In the technology sector, for example, there are forms of techno-optimism that only recognize the possible benefit of products and services and fail to see the potential harm that these products and services might cause.

This failure is a particular problem with emerging technologies. Technologists frequently struggle with the inability to consider how an exciting new technology might cause harm. The technology is so new that they find it impossible to predict its ramifications. This attitude applies to everything from various forms of machine learning like facial recognition to augmented reality to autonomous vehicles.

Of course, this inability to consider unintended consequences is not limited to technology companies. Corporations, philanthropies, governments, and other public entities also fail to anticipate the potential ramifications of decisions they are convinced will be mostly or entirely beneficial. Much like the French colonial government in Hanoi, they fail to understand the people outside of their own organization, and their hubris gets the best of them.

The inability to foresee potential undesirable effects of decisions happens for a number of reasons. According to sociologist Robert Merton, who in 1936 wrote a paper titled, "The Unanticipated Consequences of Purposive Social Action," there are five main limitations to anticipating unintended consequences:[2]

- Ignorance
- Error
- Imperious immediacy of interest
- Basic values
- Self-defeating predictions

The first limitation is ignorance. When you are designing solutions, you often don't know what you don't know, so most people are guided by their past experiences. This is a reason that so many technology teams, for example, have difficulty considering how things will play out with their solutions post-implementation: often, they lack an understanding of human behavior and sociological conditions.

---

2   Robert K. Merton, "The Unanticipated Consequences of Purposive Social Action," *American Sociological Review* 1, no. 6 (December 1936).

One way to mitigate this is to gain external knowledge. Luckily, this is where systems thinking is especially handy! The process of analyzing a system, integrating the perspectives of many different stakeholders, considering both problems and solutions beyond your expertise, and understanding causal loops are all good ways of lessening your ignorance within a systems space, and therefore, give you greater capability to anticipate potential consequences.

The second limitation is error. Most people engage in a type of logical fallacy that, as Merton stated, is the "too-ready assumption that actions which have in the past led to the desired outcome will continue to do so." This is particularly relevant in changing social environments.

> **NOTE** FALSE ASSUMPTIONS MADE DURING A PANDEMIC
>
> During the worldwide pandemic of 2020–2022, social norms were constantly changing, making it difficult to anticipate individual and collective reactions to these changes. When implementing policies such as mask mandates, government entities and businesses often failed to anticipate the resistance to such mandates, nor did they have a built-in plan for addressing the resistance. The entities implementing these policies made assumptions based on past widespread (compliant) behavior related to public health.

The third limitation is what Merton described as "imperious immediacy of interest." This describes a type of confirmation bias: people who are creating solutions often want something to happen (positive outcomes), so they are resistant to ideas that point to undesirable outcomes. This point describes much of techno-optimism.

Merton wrote the fourth limitation as "basic values." He described it as, "activities oriented toward certain values release processes which so react as to change the very scale of values which precipitated them." An example of this limitation is ride-hailing services. Companies like Lyft were born of values that were oriented around improving modes of transportation, in essence, extending what they as private companies considered to be "public" transportation. However, the increase in ride-hailing services has had a deleterious effect on actual, government-funded public transportation.[3]

---

3 Michael Graehler, Alex Mucci, and Gregory D. Erhardt, "Understanding the Recent Transit Ridership Decline in Major US Cities: Service Cuts or Emerging Modes?" Transportation Research Board Annual Meeting, January 2019.

Lastly, Merton pointed to "self-defeating predictions" as his fifth limitation. (In fact, he coined the more common term "self-fulfilling prophecy" later in his life, which describes the opposite effect.) This refers to predictions that, once made and publicized, end up being proven false because of their paradoxical effect on outcomes. A historical example of this is the "population bomb" predictions of 1968 stemming from Dr. Paul R. Ehrlich's book of the same name, in which Dr. Ehrlich predicted population growth so explosive that it would cause mass starvation. The popularity of this prediction, and the resulting fear, could be perceived as having changed the course of history because society mobilized as a result, preventing the mass starvations that he had predicted.

A WORD ON PERVERSE INCENTIVES (INCENTIVES AND METRICS)

So much of what we think about as unintended consequences tie back to incentives that lead to undesirable outcomes. Think back to the rats in Hanoi. This was a problem born directly of a policy that was meant to result in the opposite outcome.

Many nontheoretical examples of perverse incentives fall into the realm of policy. For example, approaches like generous water subsidies can lead to overuse in places where water should be conserved. Another example involves government subsidies aimed at the fishing industry. Although global fish stocks are depleted or continue to deplete, governments often continue to provide subsidies to local fishing industries in order to maintain jobs and livelihoods. In the long term, both stocks and jobs suffer: "Once fishermen's livelihoods are in danger, governments provide plentiful incentives for them to catch more rather than fewer fish—thus exacerbating the problem from top to bottom." If there aren't enough fish, no amount of jobs in the industry will be able to be maintained.[4]

continues

---

4   OECD, *Perverse Incentives in Biodiversity Loss* (OECD Publishing, 2003).

What can you as a designer do to bring discussion of incentives into your work? Even if you are not working in a space where you have any input into policy, incentives play a role in all your work, particularly in the form of metrics and the goals they are intended to achieve. For example, if you are a product designer, your success at your company might be dependent on how your product performs. And your product performance may be judged by, for example, how many people use it. If your individual and organizational success is dependent on as many users as possible, you and others in your organization may be reluctant to take any action that may slow the number of users, or decrease users, even if it might be better for the long-term health of your usership and product. In *The Tyranny of Metrics*, author Jerry Z. Muller points to this type of simplified metric as "measuring the simple when the desired outcome is complex."[5]

If you are interested in whether incentives and metrics align with your desired outcomes, you can reflect on the following questions:

- How is the success of the product of your work being measured?
- Does the way that success is being measured align with your organization's and stakeholders' desired outcomes?
- Does it align with your desired outcomes for society?
- How are people in your organization incentivized to achieve the measures of success? Do the incentives align with the desired outcomes?
- If success metrics have a clear connection to desirable outcomes, are people likely to cheat the system to achieve their own incentives?

It's important to keep in mind that people are people, and behaviors may align with incentives but not with what is ultimately better across the board. Think back to some of the system archetypes in Chapter 6, "Mapping Forces." For example, in the 1980s and 90s, Vermont's desire to preserve pastoral views by banning billboards sometimes resulted in more extreme expressions of sculptures—huge genies, giant gorillas—that were clearly an attempt to skirt the ban.[6] Further ordinances were required to prevent this type of counterproductive—albeit creative!—behavior, and are a good example of needing further intervention to support the initial intervention in order to achieve the desired outcomes.

---

5   Jerry Z. Muller, *The Tyranny of Metrics* (Princeton University Press, 2018).

6   "Vermont Journal; Billboard Ban? Try a 19-Foot Genie!" *The New York Times*, January 16, 1991.

How Merton's Framework Affects the Designer's Work

As you reflect on your work as a designer and strategist, and how it sits within your organization, it's helpful to consider what kinds of limitations exist that may prevent you and your stakeholders from being able to anticipate and plan for unintended consequences. They may not exactly align with Merton's framework (for example, you are probably not in the business of making massively popular predictions about society at large), but they do have potential overlap with some of his concepts, combined with especially prevalent lenses such as techno-optimism.

Barriers you might face in your work could stem from a variety of sources, including the following:

- A lack of organizational diversity that results in a narrow perspective
- An inclination—and schedule/budget—oriented toward the "happy path"
- A lack of alignment between values and actions

Lack of Diversity and Narrow Perspectives

Think about your most recent team or project. Who were you designing for? What were you designing, and who was doing the designing? As you think about those two groups, think about the representation of people on the team: were the people on your team reflective of those whom you were designing for, particularly from a demographic perspective?

As a former product designer who has been involved in designing products for the global market, I, like many designers, would have to say that no, most teams I've been on have not been reflective of the audiences for whom we were designing. A good example of this type of limitation in an organization is Meta's presence in Myanmar. (Meta is the name of the organization, while Facebook is the name of their most prominent product.) Although Meta is a large enough organization to have a global workforce, as of 2018, they did not have a single employee in Myanmar. (In early 2015, when attacks on the Rohingya were prevalent, there were only two people who were reviewing problematic posts on Facebook who could speak Burmese.[7]) Despite this lack of regional representation, Meta has operated in Myanmar for years, resulting in the Facebook platform playing a fairly disastrous role in the spread of hate speech and misinformation connecting directly to the Rohingya genocide in the country. Part of their inability to respond to the negative activity on their platform was that no one in the organization understood the languages in which Myanmar residents were communicating. How can you catch hate speech if you don't even know what people are saying? Keep in mind as well, that this is a country where 53 million people—more than half of the country's population—used Facebook.

This example is a reminder that representation is important, and it should not be limited to whom you have access to regionally. A good perspective to keep in mind is the idea of "Nothing about us without us," a phrase created by disability activists, and used more broadly to reflect the needs of diverse minoritized groups. The United Nations Development Programme has adopted the phrase, noting that it aligns with their goals: "A world in which all persons can exercise their right to equal participation in decision-making... They know best the barriers that they face and the impact that such barriers have on their lives."[8]

Stakeholders within your team should represent those whom you are designing for and serving, and in fact, you should be designing with diverse stakeholders. Even if people are not members of your immediate organization, engagement with diverse stakeholders is critical throughout your design process. Make sure to gain an understanding of representation from multiple demographic categories, including diversity by region, race and ethnicity, socioeconomic background, ability, age, and language. These aren't the only categories, of course, but they are a starting place as you design your organization to have greater parity with those who will be affected by your decisions.

---

7   Steve Stecklow, "Hatebook: Inside Facebook's Myanmar Operation," Reuters, August 15, 2018.

8   Xu Haoliang, "Nothing About Us Without Us," *UNDP* (blog), December 2, 2021.

The "Happy Path" as a Default

Have you ever worked on a project that's gone over—maybe even way over—on your budget or schedule? (If you've answered "no," perhaps you live in a unique universe or are just incredibly lucky!)

This is just one good example of how we, as humans, tend to have a bias toward the "happy path": the ideal scenario for whatever it is we're doing. The *happy path* is a term used commonly in software development that describes the ideal flow that a user might experience as they are using a product. This can be a strength if, for example, you work to direct users toward the happy path so they become unlikely to experience any of what might constitute the "unhappy path."

However, life is messy, and it is hubris to assume that you can maintain control at every turn, particularly if you are designing for complex systems. One example of a lack of consideration of potentially negative scenarios starts with Uber's autonomous vehicle crash that killed a pedestrian in Tempe, Arizona, in 2018. When the National Transportation Board released a report about the collision, it revealed that Uber's software was not able to recognize pedestrians outside of a crosswalk.[9] So basically, if you were jaywalking,[10] the car at that time had no mechanism to *recognize you as an object.*

Obviously, this is an extreme example of a failure to recognize a fairly common real-life scenario, but this is the type of decision-making that every team needs to consider. How might your team consider "real-world scenarios" that acknowledge peoples' behaviors? How might you better anticipate how people might misuse products or services, or use them in ways they weren't intended?

Values Versus Actions

Another barrier to being able to anticipate unintended consequences is the disconnect between your values and your organization's actions. Practically every organization has a mission statement, and it is useful for you as a facilitator to ask teams about their organization's mission statement and whether it is reflective of their personal values.

---

9   Aarian Marshall, and Alex Davies, "Uber's Self-Driving Car Didn't Know Pedestrians Could Jaywalk," *WIRED,* November 5, 2019.

10 See the "System Spotting: Jaywalking and the Language That Surrounds Us" sidebar (p. 197) about the term "jaywalking" and why I often think twice about using it.

Mission statements can be vague and all-encompassing to the point where it's impossible to disagree with them. Take Meta's mission statement, for example: "Meta's mission is to give people the power to build community and bring the world closer together." This sounds like a mission that might align with your values, so a question that is worth asking is: Do you feel that the company's actions align with the mission?

Amazon's mission statement, which is part of its four guiding principles, is fairly direct: "Amazon is guided by four principles: customer obsession rather than competitor focus, passion for invention, commitment to operational excellence, and long-term thinking. Amazon strives to be Earth's most customer-centric company, Earth's best employer, and Earth's safest place to work." For some employees, this may ring true: Amazon truly delivers on customer experience, and some employees have great career experiences with the company. For others, they might find that the company's actions in response to topics such as environmental impact and unionization of its warehouse workforce are a reminder of the misalignment with the company's principles and mission statement.

A cynical way to view a company's mission is to reduce it to a single purpose: profit. When push comes to shove, in a capitalist world, this is not necessarily an incorrect reading. However, you can demand more of your organization than just profit. For example, Patagonia's mission statement is "We're in business to save our home planet." One of their core values is "Cause no unnecessary harm." As a systems thinker, you might appreciate this statement. Most companies would shy away from presenting "harm" in any form when it comes to their mission and values. But acknowledging that we all cause harm in some form is practical, and also leaves an opening for improvement. It feels authentic and human, and it leads you to understand why Patagonia is perceived as a mission-driven company.

It is possible for employees, customers, and other stakeholders to hold an organization's leadership's feet to the fire when it comes to vision and mission statements. By making these idealistic, world-changing words real, you can also reduce unintended consequences and negative externalities.

JAYWALKING AND THE LANGUAGE THAT SURROUNDS US

The words that we collectively use are often a visible marker of a system. Take the term *jaywalking*. *Jaywalking* refers to the act of crossing a street outside of a crosswalk. Although many people take the seemingly innocuous term at face value, there is a lot of history underlying it. In particular, in the early 20th century, there was a shift in the collective mindset: the onus of safety in city streets ended up falling on the shoulders of pedestrians, rather than on drivers.

In the early 1900s, streets were filled with pedestrians, children playing, people walking, with very little need for safety considerations (see Figure 8.3). As early automobiles became more popular, pedestrian deaths increased due to the speed of this new form of transportation. People were outraged, often referring to motorists as "joy riders" and "speed maniacs."

IMAGE: COURTESY OF PICRYL

FIGURE 8.3

Mulberry Street in New York City at the turn of the twentieth century. No joy riders anywhere!

continues

Cities responded by creating traffic laws that prioritized cars, and ran education campaigns that encouraged people to cross only at crosswalks, thus shaping a new perspective about pedestrians who didn't do so. Peter Norton, who has written extensively about how, in the early 20th century, streets shifted from being prioritized for pedestrians to being prioritized for cars, noted that the term *jaywalking* was an important factor in that shift. A "jay" was a term from the American Midwest, used to describe country bumpkins who were out of place in the city. The term had a lot of baggage, making pedestrians who crossed streets without acknowledging traffic rules look like rubes. "Because jaywalker bore the right connotation of rural backwardness, it was just the tool for this reeducation effort."[11] Education campaigns by the National Automobile Chamber of Commerce (NACC), AAA, and even the Boy Scouts adopted the term. So laws and policies upheld traffic laws that legitimized the illegality of jaywalking, thereby solidifying the position that streets were for cars rather than pedestrians.

It's a reminder that the language and terms we use are important in shaping systems. As Norton noted, "Language is a component in sociotechnical systems, and like other components, it plays a role in the success or failure of the larger system."

Prompts to consider:

- In the system you are focused on, what are some terms that are accepted as the default? How do they shape people's perceptions of the problem space?

- What are terms that can be used to either neutralize or shift perspectives in a different direction? What are some consequences of doing so?

---

11 Peter Norton, "Street Rivals: Jaywalking and the Invention of the Motor Age Street," *Technology and Culture*, April 2007.

Creating Dialogue About Unintended Consequences

So how do you go about anticipating the potential unintended consequences of your work? The best starting point is to create dialogue by using prompts that might be outside of the typical purview of your organizational stakeholders. And the easiest way to do that is by using frameworks and toolkits that prompt those discussions. Lots of proprietary toolkits exist, including a few that I'll make reference to here, but I will stick to tools and frameworks that are publicly available.

The Futures Wheel

The futures wheel is a framework invented in 1971 by Jerome C. Glenn, a graduate student at Antioch University New England (which is a reminder that even students can develop frameworks that resonate far and wide). Glenn wrote that the futures wheel is "a method for identifying and packaging primary, secondary, and tertiary consequences of trends, events, emerging issues, and future possible decisions."[12]

The framework is as simple as it comes, but it often leads to interesting conversations about potential futures, particularly if you involve diverse stakeholders in the exploration. In some ways, it's a bit like a collective mind map comprised of wheels and spokes, but structured around degrees of effect. The five steps for creating a futures wheel are:

1. Identify the change you want to analyze.
2. Identify direct or first-order consequences.
3. Identify indirect or second-order consequences.
4. Analyze and prioritize implications.
5. Identify actions.

Identifying the Change You Want to Analyze

You first need to define the center of your futures wheel. For the purposes of being able to consider potential unintended consequences, you can focus on an intervention or solution that you and your stakeholders are focused on, and for which you may have even developed a theory of change. For this exercise, let's picture an organizational

---

12 JC Glenn, "The Futures Wheel," in *Futures Research Methodology 3.0* (The Millennium Project, 2009), chapter 6.

decision you are making: you are a director who wants to create a remote work environment that will be sustainable and inclusive. During the COVID pandemic, many organizations were forced to accommodate working from home, whether they had flexibility for it or not. And now, many organizations have shifted to either entirely remote organizations or hybrid work. Even with this simple example, you can build a futures wheel.

Identifying Direct and Indirect Consequences

The first thing you need to do is to identify the direct consequences of this decision. Ask yourself:

- What are the effects most likely to happen based on the change?
- What are some positive and negative consequences?

In Figure 8.4, your imaginary team has identified four direct consequences to a decision to move to remote work.

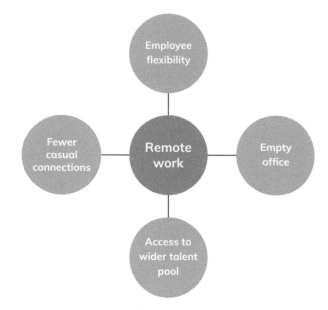

FIGURE 8.4
First-order effects of moving to remote work. How much are you paying for that empty office?!

Using the first-order effects, you can now identify second- and third-order effects that result. For example, "fewer casual connections" result in some employees feeling more isolated (see Figure 8.5). On the other hand, the increased flexibility stemming from remote work will lead to increased autonomy for other employees. One thing to keep in mind is that this exercise isn't meant to steer toward either a positive or negative direction. It should allow you and your team to have open dialogue about any of these directions, and taking a neutral stance as you are doing this exercise leads to increased honesty and directness.

You can connect many of the effects to different layers in the diagram. For example, a first-order effect might directly connect to a third-order effect, and some nodes might connect to multiple nodes.

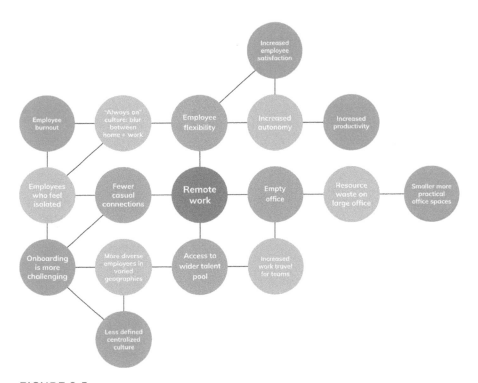

FIGURE 8.5
Second- and third-order effects range from increased workforce diversity to smaller offices. Even though this is a fairly limited topic, you can see how wide-ranging the effects might be.

You can also probe second- or third-order effects by various time-lines. For example, what might happen in a year? What might happen in five or 10 years? These prompts encourage your team to speculate and imagine both short- and long-term impact. Going back to the remote work example, could shifting cultural practices and emerging technologies lead to an overlap of synchronous and asynchronous collaboration and communication? Could you work synchronously with people in multiple time zones without people having to sacrifice a flexible schedule? Applying varied timelines helps open the conversation beyond short-term planning.

Analyzing Implications and Identifying Actions

You now have an understanding that moving to remote work has several implications. The purpose of your futures wheel is to view this type of analysis and figure out where you can potentially take action. Maybe it's being more intentional about creating points of connection for your employees, whether that involves an increased mix of social events, or travel for teams to be able to work together. It could also be more avenues to address employee burnout. The point is to push your team or stakeholders to imagine potential impact beyond your initial decision, and be more effective at understanding its implications.

Prompts That Broaden Perspectives

Aside from picturing the degrees of impact that decisions, interventions, and solutions might have, your team might need prompts to ensure that you are thinking about different categories of consequences, as well as diverse stakeholders. Several tools have been created to help technology teams think about the multitude of ways your solutions might have an impact. The most easily accessible tools, however, can also be the simplest—nothing more than a series of well-organized questions or prompts. A couple of tools that I am most familiar with are the Tarot Cards of Tech and the Ethical Explorer. These toolkits are both good starting points for discussions about unintended consequences and potential harm.

The Tarot Cards of Tech

When I was a design director at Artefact, a design consultancy based in Seattle, part of our focus as consultants was integrating a more explicit focus on outcomes within our design work. As my team ran workshops and led strategic design work with clients, we concluded that our clients often brought the techno-optimistic perspective to the table. What this meant was that imagining and understanding potential positive outcomes was easy for technology and social impact clients, but they found it difficult to picture potential unintended consequences or negative externalities that could result from the solutions they were working on.

This lack of perspective was always unintentional; when teams are working on something that is new, such as an emerging technology that can be used in exciting ways, it's hard to see past the optimistic viewpoint.

The Artefact team created the Tarot Cards of Tech to open the door for those conversations and to encourage teams to think more broadly about how they might have an impact on the world. The cards are organized into twelve "characters" which each represent a category that is often missing in technology development discussions, and they were developed with many of the same questions my team had in mind as we worked on various types of technology products. Each category has a series of prompts that help teams imagine unintended consequences, but also reveal opportunities for creating positive change. Although it's heavily product-focused, it can be used as a way of encouraging discussion around services and other types of interventions as well.

An interesting aspect of these cards and their focus is that they acknowledge that technologists tend to be focused just on their users, and, even more narrowly, a certain type of user that is either familiar to them or harmonious to their idea of the benefits of their product. The cards not only challenge the notion that you as a designer need to think about different kinds of users and anticipate their use, but you also need to think about those you leave out of your ideas of your user base altogether, as well as those who might be unexpectedly affected or harmed by your products.

Some of the card categories include the following (see Figure 8.6):

- **The Big Bad Wolf.** Once a technology product is released into the world, the team that developed the product might discover the effect of "bad actors" on their system. This term usually refers to those people who use products in ways that are not intended and that produce negative outcomes. This category is a good example of expanding your idea about different users of a product, including even those who are undesirable so you can address the problems they may create. Some of the prompts include: "What would predatory and exploitative behavior look like with your product?" and "What product features are most vulnerable to manipulation?"

- **The Radio Star.** This category asks teams to imagine the deleterious effects of their products on people, systems, or things. It's an introduction to the idea of negative externalities. Prompts include: "Who or what disappears if your product is successful?" and "Who loses their job?" Technology teams often think first and foremost about innovation and disruption, and these prompts are a good way to peer directly into the difficult space of potentially permanent change that might not be favorable to some.

- **Mother Nature.** This category is a reminder that one of humanity's biggest stakeholders is not even human. Every product or service has an impact on the environment, and reducing harm to the environment is a crucial consideration for every intervention. Though the prompts are fairly broad, it's a good starting point for teams who haven't taken this perspective in their work. Prompts include: "What feedback would the environment give about your product?" and "What is the most unsustainable behavior your product encourages?"

Practitioners often wonder when prompts like these are best used. They can inform your product strategy as you are first shaping products or services. They can also be used on established products to determine features. Essentially, these types of questions are useful throughout the product development cycle and can help shift a team's mindset about actively anticipating unintended consequences.

FIGURE 8.6

The Big Bad Wolf, the Radio Star, and Mother Nature are some examples of the Tarot Cards of Tech.

When I was working on the Tarot Cards of Tech, one of my colleagues, Dave McColgin, asked about the prompts. "Maybe one of the questions should be: 'What if we did nothing?'" he said.

Though that question did not make it into the toolkit, I've thought about it ever since. For those of you working in technology, this question may seem unfathomable. The industry holds a philosophy of biasing toward action, of changing the world by doing something, and doing something by using the power of the technology that we create.

However, doing something is not always the right action, particularly in the frameworks within which we're expected to act. If, in your work, your only avenue for creating change is through the very technology that you believe is creating harm, then you might want to consider whether actions that you might use to mitigate harm might, in their own way, continue to perpetuate systemic forms of harm. This perspective aligns with the idea of questioning the framing of everything, which is not just a form of critical thinking, but is also a way of engaging in systems thinking.

For example, I often think about a park in Duisburg, Germany that I would visit a few times a year with my kids when we lived across the border in The Netherlands (see Figure 8.7). The Landschaftspark Duisburg-Nord was created in 1991 on the site of an abandoned coal and steel industrial plant. The park is an excellent example of postindustrial park design, as the designers, Latz + Partners, decided not to remove the industrial structures, and intentionally kept them in place as a reminder of the past. They allowed vegetation to grow around it, with nature taking over the most polluted areas, and converted some of the industrial structures into recreational features, such as a former gas tank that is now the world's largest indoor diving center, and concrete bunkers that are now rock climbing walls. It is now a vibrant and inspiring locale, with enormous rusted structures entwined with wild vegetation.[13] Writer Judith Stilgenbauer explained what can be learned from the Landschaftspark design: "Among its lessons are... to give equal weight to social and ecological considerations; to respect the genius loci; and, most importantly, to allow the form of a park to evolve from the past use of a site." The park is not exactly an example of doing nothing, but it makes me consider the parameters in which we work, and how "doing the most" might not always be the best avenue.

---

13 Judith Stilgenbauer, "Landschaftspark Duisburg Nord - Duisburg, Germany [2005 EDRA/*Places* Award—Design]," Places 17, no. 3 (2005).

FIGURE 8.7
My kids walking through the Landschaftspark Duisburg-Nord, near one of the steelworks structures that now has trees growing within it.

In her book *How to Do Nothing*, artist Jenny Odell considers "doing nothing" as a way of reclaiming the space to think about how you might do something. "For me, doing nothing means disengaging from one framework (the attention economy) not only to give myself time to think, but to do something else in another framework."

As a designer, acknowledging your role in the system you are part of perpetuating is an important activity. It might be that doing nothing within your current parameters could be an option for creating change in other ways.

The Ethical Explorer

Another well-designed tool for considering and mitigating unintended consequences is Omidyar Network's Ethical Explorer.

A commonality between the Ethical Explorer and the Tarot Cards of Tech is their playfulness and conceptual accessibility. Product teams can be reluctant to have conversations about harm. I've heard these types of topics described as a *buzzkill*, leading to avoiding them altogether. For teams that aren't used to having these conversations, a playful entry—who doesn't love characters and adventure maps?—is a spoonful of sugar that reminds teams that these topics do not need to be met with dread. Hannah Hoffman, the design strategy lead for the Ethical Explorer, expanded on the need for a friendly framework. "Because of the approachable nature of it, you can pick up a card and say 'Let's have a discussion about this as a group,' rather than an accusatory moment of 'Why didn't we do it this way?'"

The Ethical Explorer is divided into eight technology Risk Zones, meant to elicit dialogue oriented around the cascading effects of technology, and support technologists who "want to create tech that's healthier, safer, fairer, and more inclusive."[14] Each Risk Zone is divided into two sets of prompts: one set that's focused on the current state of your product or organization, and another that's focused on anticipating risk (see Figure 8.8). The categories include:

- Surveillance
- Disinformation
- Exclusion
- Algorithmic Bias
- Addiction
- Data Control
- Bad Actors
- Outsized Power

---

14 Omidyar Network, Ethical Explorer

ALGORITHMIC BIAS

SYSTEMS BREAKING

ALGORITHMIC BIAS

Objective AI is an illusion. As humans, we all have unconscious biases that impact algorithms, potentially causing or amplifying harm through predictive policing, hiring decisions, and more.

Researchers found racial bias in a medical algorithm used across the US to determine which patients require further care. Although the algorithm didn't explicitly include racial data, using information impacted by societal biases created a system consistently favoring white patients over sicker black patients.

Simply diversifying datasets will not fix these issues. Addressing biases requires further understanding of society's inequalities and accounting for them in tech.

How will we promote fairness?

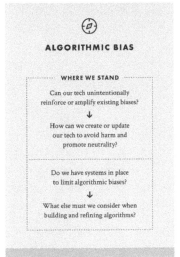

ALGORITHMIC BIAS

WHERE WE STAND

Can our tech unintentionally reinforce or amplify existing biases?

↓

How can we create or update our tech to avoid harm and promote neutrality?

Do we have systems in place to limit algorithmic biases?

↓

What else must we consider when building and refining algorithms?

How will we promote fairness?

ANTICIPATING RISK

How could we monitor whether our product's algorithm benefits or hurts individuals, communities, and societies?

What might we do if we discovered our users have been profiled or discriminated against?

LEADING THE WAY

How can we encourage a diverse and global community of experts on AI to counteract biases?

FIGURE 8.8
The Ethical Explorer Risk Zone of Algorithmic Bias includes a description, prompts about the current state, and questions to encourage discussion about how to anticipate risk.

The brilliant thing about the Risk Zones is that it is easy for any organization to find a category and prompts that are relevant to their work, including those who do not work in a technology-specific organization. Even if you work in healthcare, government, or education, these topics affect all of us because of the way digital technology is used in every sector.

The simplicity of each of these tools means that they are fairly flexible. You can use any of them for starting the conversation (the Tarot Cards of Tech, the Ethical Explorer) and investigating possibilities, and for mapping a broader view of degrees of impact (the futures wheel). Hoffman explained, "The benefit of this toolkit is that there's flexibility in its use. It can fit into any phase of a product development life cycle. You can use it in the discovery phase, and you can also use it in critique to gut check some of the decisions you're making."

She also noted that the toolkit is unique in that it acknowledges the context in which your dialogue about consequences will sit, which is within a company or organization. Included in the toolkit's Field Guide, are tips for making the case for integrating more explicitly ethical mindsets into not just your own work, but also within your leadership and organization. "When we were conducting research for the Ethical Explorer, we noticed that there's been a rise in individual contributors who are demanding this in their workplaces, so it's not just a top-down leadership effort." As a result, they included things like discussion prompts about how to find allies in your organization, so practitioners can make an ethical orientation more of a standard practice rather than just a one-off workshop. In addition, "Being able to ask questions, and having the bravery to do it, helps create a culture where you can ask questions openly in your organization."

The Ethical Explorer also works brilliantly in combination with other tools such as the futures wheel. It puts you and your team in a space of imagining and speculating on outcomes, both positive and negative. This will better serve your decision-making and allow you to imagine the future from a systems perspective.

Takeaways

- Part of fulling thinking about the systemic impact of potential interventions and solutions is to direct energy toward anticipating unintended consequences.

- The futures wheel is a good tool to imagine the first-, second-, and third-degree impact of your decisions.

- It's critical to examine whether your incentives—and those of your organization and stakeholders—align with desirable outcomes.

Dr. Dimeji Onafuwa is a Nigerian-American designer, researcher, artist, and educator with combined experience in UX design and research, transition design, service design, and social design. He has worked in various capacities—from UX consultant to researcher and design leader. He is currently a Principal UX Research Manager at Microsoft.

What would you say are some of the shortcomings of the typical design practice?

The biggest shortcoming is that design itself, as a practice, has been designed to exclude. Even the culture of design is very exclusionary. We build enclosures around the discipline that are particularly oriented toward colonial dominance and modernity. There's an underlying perspective that something is not "design" if it's not modern from a Western context. This has led us to think of design in binary ways, which makes it reductive.

This perspective is how we ended up with UX design. It's very solutions-oriented, and often prioritizes the needs of the business over those of the individual. Every problem needs a solution, and the solutions ultimately are very linear and techno-deterministic as well. We create a feature or app, and we think that the problem is solved.

Through this outlook, design has been made small, as a practice, as a discipline, and as an activity. Design has the capacity to be a lot more than that.

What can designers do to shift their thinking?

I think of my practice as designing at the edges. I leverage the methodologies that shed light on new ways of designing. It's really about thinking about the broader ecosystem, incorporating Elinor Ostrom's theories about collective action.[15] I'm quite political in the work I do, always asking the question of, "How do we change design as a system?"

In order to reorient their practice, I believe designers need to do three things. First, they must act to shift systems. Second, they must think about consequences. And third, they need to amplify the lived experiences of those whose stories we haven't been telling.

---

15 Economist Elinor Ostrom theorized that collective action is a response to what theorist Garrett Hardin called *the tragedy of the commons*: when resources are shared but no one owns them, people will overuse them and no one takes responsibility. Ostrom argued that communal ownership and shared rights could spur protection of shared ecological resources, not just private ownership solutions.

Building on this, I think of you as a designer who is working to design the design practice itself in many ways. How do you go about this?

In my doctoral work, I looked at designers and their forms of problem-solving. There are designers working within the problem, and I think of this as working as a "design commoner." Then there are designers who work as co-facilitators who are trying to understand the problems with others. And then there is the designer as a meta-practitioner, working in the system, but also stepping out of it to examine the effects of the interventions you're proposing, kind of like Donald Schön's theory of acting as reflecting and reflecting on one's actions.[16]

I've focused on the ideas of transition design and of pluriversal design in my work. Pluriversal design reminds me that, for example, in my experience as a Black male in America, that my perspective matters, that my view of the world is also important. The multiplicity of lived experiences that we have is acknowledged and celebrated. There's a saying from the Zapatistas (who were engaged in a liberation struggle in Mexico several decades ago): a world where many worlds fit.

We must not think only in terms of one center, that is the idea that design's center is the Western modern world. Instead, designers can now think about how they can build platforms that allow multiple stories and narratives to be amplified and acknowledged.

I taught a college course on design for the pluriverse, where I challenged students to consider wicked problems, that is, those that are complex and unsolvable—the housing crisis is a good example. Students started working immediately toward a solution, and I emphasized that, "Most of your grade has nothing to do with a solution. In fact, you might not have any solution. You could just share your process, how you reconsidered the process, and how you changed your understanding." And it was quite difficult for some of the students to understand because they've been trained that every design effort has to have a solution. This is the perspective at large. But, what pluriversal design is about is that sometimes as designers we need tools that serve as provocations: not to solve, but to ask questions.

---

16 Donald Schön was a pioneer of the concept of the reflective practice, which is focused on reflecting on one's actions with a critical lens, as well as reflecting while acting.

What advice would you give to designers looking to engage in systems thinking?

I want to emphasize two things. First, that you can effect change wherever it is that you are working. You have to understand that you can work with some of these big ideas even if you are working at the level of intervention, at a small scale. I use the metaphor of designers being gardeners and tending to the garden: you can't control the weather and the crops, but you can tend to the garden. Hold on dearly to that: find like-minded designers and continue to educate yourself.

Second, you need to keep questioning many of the things we've accepted. For example, designers often talk about the hierarchy of needs, which is a problematic framework. Don't just assume that because something is widely accepted, that it shouldn't be questioned. Designers must open themselves up to new theories and extend their knowledge. Expose yourself to new ideas.

In the end, you need to commit to the work. There's a posture of humility and patience that is required to do this kind of work or aspire to it. As Donna Haraway said: Stay with the trouble.

CHAPTER 9

Speculative Design Futures

There's a moment in the 2002 film *Minority Report* that I think about a lot. The movie is set in 2054 and Tom Cruise's character, John Anderton, is walking through a shopping mall. At every turn, the virtual advertisements throughout the environment call out to him. Partway through the movie, he enters a Gap store. At the risk of spoiling a decades-old movie, a subsequent scene shows a virtual greeter calling out to Anderton's newly adopted identity: "Hello Mr. Yakamoto! Welcome to the Gap. How did those assorted tank tops work out for you?" (See Figure 9.1.)

FIGURE 9.1
Gap is still selling khakis in 2054!

There are some funny aspects to this scene that make it so striking. First, the Gap looks exactly the same in 2054 as it did in 2002, the clothes look exactly the same, and it's even still playing Billie Holiday over the speakers. Second, viewing this scene through the lens of the 2020s, those things hold true, and so does the personal advertising. Like me, I'm sure you get tons of personalized ads on social media, as well as through online shopping that feel very much like the Gap greeter. We're also well into an era where facial recognition is being used for everything from payment to security.

I've always read this scene as satire, as a commentary on advertising and commercialism, a reminder that the more things change, the more things stay the same. Even with all of the advances of technology available to us as a society, we still are applying it with a capitalist mindset even in 2054. That the same retailer even exists in this scenario speaks to how entrenched our societal mindset is.

Although this movie falls squarely in the realm of science fiction, this scene has a lot of overlap with themes that are often expressed through speculative design: criticism, speculation, and imagination manifested in objects and other design outputs. Design can be used for other purposes aside from problem-solving.

A former design colleague of mine used to be fond of saying, "Art asks questions. Design provides answers." As a UX designer, I believed this to be true for a very long time. Why indulge in aspects of creativity that feel more like self-expression, or fixated on qualities like beauty, when you should be solving problems?

Needless to say, my perspective has shifted dramatically from that linear form of thinking. I do think that problem-solving is an important use of creativity as well as design skills and methods. (In fact, much of the purpose of systems thinking is finding ways to address issues both broad and narrow.)

However, systems thinking also requires a more expansive mindset, and so much of the necessary mindset involves reframing: reframing problems, reframing what constitutes problem-solving, and reframing the role of design itself. And a big part of that reframing is using the creative methods of the design practice for provocation, for imagining the way things could be (good and bad) and imagining the world in which we find ourselves in the future.

This type of approach has several names: *futuring, critical design, speculative design*. The commonality is that it is a deliberate use of design as provocation: design as a way of asking questions rather than providing answers.

What Is Speculative Design?

In *Speculative Everything*, Anthony Dunne and Fiona Raby's foundational text on speculative design, the authors described speculative design as a way of imagining possible futures and as a form of critique: "There are many possibilities—socially engaged design for raising awareness; satire and critique; inspiration, reflection, highbrow entertainment; aesthetic explorations; speculation about possible futures; and as a catalyst for change."[1]

---

1   Anthony Dunne and Fiona Raby, *Speculative Everything* (MIT Press, 2013).

Back in Chapter 1, "The Shortcomings of User-Centered Design," I shared a (horror) story about *Black Mirror*. *Black Mirror* is a show that explores the future of various types of technologies and their potential repercussions, and is a strong example of speculative thinking. The visions of how technology shapes culture and the impact it has on people both individually and collectively do not paint a rosy picture. However, it is a break from the techno-optimism that the culture of technology creation typically embraces. As you'll see in the forthcoming examples of speculative design, this uncomfortable space of criticality is where much of this practice lives.

Discursive, Critical, and Speculative

There are a few other terms that apply to the type of design that is meant to spur discourse rather than provide utility. Discursive design can be viewed as an umbrella term under which these design practices sit. According to Bruce and Stephanie Tharp, who wrote *Discursive Design: Critical, Speculative, and Alternative Things*, discursive design's primary purpose is encouraging discourse: "While 'good design' is often professed to be unobtrusive, intuitive, invisible and something that does not make the user think too much, discursive design instead actually targets the intellect. The primary goal is to prompt self-reflection, ignite the imagination, and foment contemplation—to deliberately make the user think (deeply)."[2]

Critical design and speculative design describe design practices that fall under the discursive umbrella. What they have in common is that they question the role of design itself: they confront a traditional design philosophy that is rooted in utility.

A way of visually representing where speculative design ideas often sit is the futures cone. A framework that was first introduced by Trevor Hancock and Clement Bezold in 1994,[3] the futures cone is a staple of the foresight strategy practice, which usually focuses on future trends and scenarios in order to help organizations be more resilient in the face of uncertainty, and more deliberate in their planning to respond to changes in the landscape.

---

2   Bruce and Stephanie Tharp, "What Is Discursive Design? Whether You Call It Critical, Fiction or Speculative Design, It's Time for Design to Be a Thought Catalyst," Core77, December 9, 2015.

3   Trevor Hancock and Clement Bezold, "Possible Futures, Preferable Futures," *The Healthcare Forum Journal*, March 1994.

The futures cone diagram is cone shaped because, like a type of multiverse, the future can go in any number of directions starting at the singular point in time that is the present (see Figure 9.2). The length of the cone represents time. The farther out you go, the more uncertain the possibilities, which is why the cone gets wider the longer it gets. Within the cone are four paths:

- **The possible future:** This describes what might happen. It includes possibilities that challenge current technological and scientific capabilities. In addition, the possible future includes both high-probability and low-probability events, such as a financial crisis (high probability) or an asteroid hitting the earth (low probability).

- **The plausible future:** This focuses on what could happen, which is a narrower purview than the "possible" category. Dunne and Raby describe this category as a space for "exploring alternative economic and political futures to ensure an organization will be prepared for and thrive in a number of different futures." A strategic foresight method called *scenario planning* is most focused in this space: identifying future trends and scenarios and considering how to plan to respond to them.

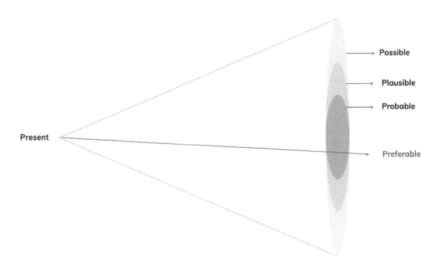

FIGURE 9.2
You can see that within the futures cone that "plausible" and "probable" are nested within what's "possible." "Preferable" can take many shapes. In this case, it fits within what's probable, but it could take place anywhere within the cone.

- **The probable future:** This describes what will likely happen, and it is even narrower than the "plausible" category. Most people view the future as an extension of the present, and this category describes what most think will happen if there aren't huge upheavals. The "probable" future aligns with current trends.
- **The preferable future:** This describes what we want to happen. This is the only category of the futures cone that is prescriptive: it's meant to be a reflection of how you might intentionally steer future events rather than just reacting to, or, predicting them.

It's critical to remember that, in the context of speculative design, the objective of understanding these varying paths is not to predict the future. Rather, it's about speculating on the changes in the societal landscape and imagining how it will affect people. With this in mind, it's important to acknowledge that speculative design does not have to live only in the "preferable" future path. Rather, it should spur debate on what developments are preferable.

As a result, speculative design projects can raise uncomfortable questions about what the future may hold, often residing in spaces that have a dystopian sensibility. A unique aspect of this type of design is that it's a form of debating ideas rather than a form of "solutioning." The same methods that are used to deliver design for commercial products can be used to question commercialism itself.

Traditional Design Versus Speculative Design

The reframing of commercialism is just one aspect of speculative design that stands in contrast to what you can think of as traditional design. Dunne and Raby presented this contrast in what they called an "A/B Manifesto" with "A" representing traditional approaches to design, and "B" representing the space occupied by speculative design. In his paper "The Young Designer's Guide to Speculative and Critical Design,"[4] Leon Karlsen Johannessen created a more structured version of the A/B Manifesto that further articulates the distinctions between traditional design and speculative and critical design (see Table 9.1).

---

4   Leon Karlsen Johannessen, "The Young Designer's Guide to Speculative and Critical Design," Norwegian University of Science and Technology, 2017.

TABLE 9.1 THE DIFFERENCE BETWEEN TRADITIONAL DESIGN AND SPECULATIVE DESIGN.

	Traditional Design	Speculative and Critical Design (SCD)
Attitude	Normative	Critical
Foundation	Information	Speculation
Mindset	Pragmatic: Productive	Idealistic: Dreaming
Purpose	Commercial: Satisfy industry's need to make money	Discursive: Spur debate on the development of society
Goal	Develop solutions: Provide answers by solving problems	Explore ideas: Find problems by asking questions
Intent	Serve a user: In seriousness, provide clarity	Provoke an audience: Use ambiguity to make satire

An extended perception of the A/B Manifesto can envelop the relationship between speculative design and systems thinking. Systems thinking is fundamentally an inquiry-driven process, engages in the reframing of problems, applies a critical lens to the status quo, and seeks to uncover implications. This is why this form of discursive design has a relationship with systems thinking: imagining *what could be* is a form of integrating greater intentionality about what "preferable" means, as well as presenting a way of debating political, ethical, and social implications of technological and societal decisions.

Examples and Forms of Speculative Design

Speculative expressions can take many forms that embody visual, narrative, and temporal expressions. The common thread is that speculative design is the use of design imaginings to paint a vision of the future. Here are some examples of speculative projects that are physical objects, video and temporal storytelling, narrative storytelling, and storyboards and comics.

Physical Objects

Many speculative and critical design projects take the form of physical objects representing a specific idea. They often represent a form that might not necessarily be technologically feasible, but asks "what if?" when it comes to possibility.

One example is Dunne & Raby's *Technological Dreams Series: No. 1, Robots* (2007) (see Figure 9.3). Their objective was to consider the relationships between robots and humans: "What new interdependencies and relationships might emerge in relation to different levels of robot intelligence and capability? These objects are meant to spark a discussion about how we'd like our robots to relate to us: subservient, intimate, dependent, equal?"[5] The "needy robot" for example, depends heavily on its owner to move it around, giving the owner a sense of control.

FIGURE 9.3
A needy robot that needs help from its owner.

Rather than being designed to articulate how robots might solve humans' problems, the robots are designed to make the viewer think about what kinds of relationships they would want to have, or are destined to have, with robots.

---

5 Dunne & Raby, *Technological Dreams Series: No. 1, Robots* (2007), Dunneandraby.co.uk

If you've ever seen, or experienced riding, Japan's Shinkansen, known in English as the *bullet train*, it's easy to marvel at it as a triumph of engineering and design. An interesting fact is that the front of the train was modeled after a kingfisher's beak (see Figure 9.4). A kingfisher, which is a bird that plunges its beak into water to feed on fish and other small aquatic creatures, has a pointed bill that reduces the friction between it and the water when it dives. The Shinkansen design team mimicked the shape of the kingfisher's bill to prevent the train from creating a sonic boom when it went through tunnels.[6]

IMAGE: BOUDHAYAN BARDHAN

FIGURE 9.4
The kingfisher's beak served as inspiration for making the Japanese Shinkansen both faster and quieter.

This is a good example of biomimicry, a term coined by biology writer Janine Benyus. She described biomimicry as "the conscious emulation of life's genius. Innovation inspired by nature."[7] Borrowing from nature not only frees designers from being inspired by other human-created technologies and ideas, but also creates the added benefit of prioritizing aspects of nature that are more sustainable, waste-reductive, and enduring. Designers not only learn from copying nature's form, as in the case of the Shinkansen, but also learn processes and ecosystems. How cycles of birth and death are connected in nature, for example, is very much what we desire from concepts such as circular design, where nothing goes to waste.

continues

---

6   Kurt Kohlstedt, "Biomimicry: How Designers Are Learning from the Natural World," *99% Invisible* (podcast), November 9, 2017.

7   Janine M. Benyus, *Biomimicry: Innovation Inspired by Nature* (Harper Perennial, 2002).

In her book, Benyus articulates nine principles that serve as a foundation for biomimicry:

- Nature runs on sunlight.
- Nature uses only the energy it needs.
- Nature fits form to function.
- Nature recycles everything.
- Nature rewards cooperation.
- Nature banks on diversity.
- Nature demands local expertise.
- Nature curbs excesses from within.
- Nature taps the power of limits.

Guided by these principles, designers can push themselves to think about ways of designing things—forms, processes, and systems—that adhere to them. Biomimicry can also be used as provocation, as seen in many speculative design projects. One example is designer Veronica Ranner's *Biophilia—Organ Crafting* project. In it, she imagined a scenario in which genetically modified silkworms could weave organs such as donor hearts. Part of the intent is to consider the relationship between technology and nature: "The current focus on artificial organ technology lies on 3D printing and machinic production, straight in line with technological determinism. But does dealing with living material not afford a more humane way of production? What options does biotechnological fabrication offer, other than its imminent material qualities?"[8]

There's a humility inherent in biomimicry. It's a reminder that humans don't have all the answers, and that the rest of nature, which has existed in a cycle for 3.8 billion years, has a lot to teach us.

Prompts to consider:

- Are there ways in which your system resembles concepts present in nature?
- How might nature's cycles inspire ideas related to sustainability as you think about problem-solving?

---

8   Veronica Ranner, *Biophilia—Organ Crafting* [Hand-blown glass, RP Zp150, degummed silk, C-type printed photographs] (2011), (available at: www.veronicaranner.com/biophilia-organ-crafting)

Video and Temporal Storytelling

A good example of video-based storytelling is *Uninvited Guests*, a video by Superflux, a studio founded by designer and futurist Anab Jain. In it, an elderly British man goes about his day in his apartment. He's surrounded by "smart" devices that his adult children insist he use: a cane that tracks his steps, utensils that track his food intake, and a bed that tracks his sleep are just a few of the objects he's forced to interact with. To satisfy the goals on the devices, he gives the cane to a teenage neighbor to walk around the block, uses the utensils to push around broccoli while he eats chips and sausage, and piles books on his bed to make it think he's sleeping. These subversive efforts keep both his children and the devices off his back (see Figure 9.5).

FIGURE 9.5
Frames from Superflux's *Uninvited Guests*. Pushing a cane around while you watch TV is one way to make the activity monitor quiet!

The video raises questions about our relationships with technology and each other. Rather than being physically present, the man's children, who mean well, replace their emotional relationship with devices. And neither the man, who feels surveilled by these devices, nor his children, find these relationships satisfying.

One way that this video embodies a speculative design approach is that it presents a fairly mundane day-to-day scenario that is hyperrealistic, but unusual because these futuristic technological expressions are embedded in a way that feels familiar or expected, but still jarring. A commonality in speculative design projects is that it combines both the sensibility of the familiar and unexpected.

Narrative Storytelling

In her book, *Blockchain Chicken Farm*, artist and writer Xiaowei Wang wrote about the technological landscape and its impact on rural China. She focused on neither a purely utopian or dystopian vision of digital technology in the context of Chinese politics and sociology, but rather the impact that technologies such as biometric data, drones, blockchain, and AI have on humans when combined with themes such as farming, policing, and intellectual property. Interspersed between nonfiction reporting from Shenzhen, Beijing, and Silicon Valley, Wang presents speculative fiction scenarios about feeding AI, GMO foods and data storage, and food cultivated on the moon. They are presented in typical and familiar recipe prose, with a food recipe seated between an introduction and the futuristic concept. One such scenario is titled "How to Eat the World":

Ingredients for Filling

butter | 45 g

moon-maize meal | 40 g, may substitute for regular cornmeal

powdered cream | 40 g, may substitute with powdered milk

powdered sugar | 30 g, may add 5 g more for a sweeter filling

eggs | 2 large

After explaining the recipe a bit further, Wang continues:

While moon living hasn't taken off as predicted in the past few years, the popularity of moon-grown foods has soared. As fires, pollution, and climate change worsened, farming on earth produced increasingly low-quality, low-nutrition foods, including some vegetables tainted with cadmium or lead. Automated farming on the moon took off, in response to upper-middle-class consumer demand. For those who can afford it, moon-cultivated foods are not only higher in nutrients but also far healthier. Studies have shown that the average lifespan of someone eating earth-cultivated foods is about fifty years, while those eating moon-cultivated food since birth can live up to a hundred years on average.[9]

Like *Uninvited Guests*, this is a good example of the juxtaposition of the mundane and the fantastical that is captured in good speculative design. It creates a cognitive dissonance for viewers and readers, at once familiar and jarring. Even the ingredients list causes a double-take: is moon-maize meal a thing? The rest of the ingredients seem to be real! Wang also raises socioeconomic issues throughout her speculative narrative, prompting readers to think about the implications of continued inequities in a future world.

Storyboards and Comics

Storyboards and comics, both panel-based illustrated narratives, are often used in traditional design approaches to articulate experiences from a user perspective, and to represent how, for example, service design might affect them. The same methods can play a similar role when used for speculative storytelling. In *Flash Forward: An Illustrated Guide to Possible (and Not So Possible) Tomorrows*, futurologist Rose Eveleth guides the reader through several future themes, each illustrated by a different artist. Included are topics such as animal rights, misinformation, gender fluidity, environmental change, and smart cities (see Figure 9.6).

This type of graphical storytelling is a great format for articulating scenarios without needing to be concerned about feasibility. Like video or written narratives, it enables you to show (not only tell) a sequence of events that are representative of an idea about the future.

---

9   Xiaowei Wang, *Blockchain Chicken Farm and Other Stories of Tech in China's Countryside* (FSG Originals x Logic, 2020).

FIGURE 9.6

Ben Passmore's "Welcome to Tomorrowville" depicts a city where citizens wear smart watches and are tracked throughout their movements in the city. It not only surfaces issues about the dangers of surveillance, but also raises questions about whether the same surveillance technologies can make a city more accessible for some people.

Who Is Engaging in Speculative Design?

A criticism of discursive, critical, and speculative design is that those who are practitioners and thought leaders in its practice are of a limited—and privileged—demographic: racially, geographically, and socioeconomically. The typical thought leader is white, often male, hailing from European and other white-dominant countries, with education and research based in elite institutions. Berlin-based artist Luiza Prado de O. Martins stated that "Speculative and critical design have been, up until now, practiced and theorized largely within the privileged walls of costly universities in developed countries."[10]

So how should a designer, inhabiting a privileged position from a race, gender, and socioeconomic lens, possibly engage in the kind of foundational critical thinking required for speculative design? They must take on an intersectional feminist perspective. The "intersectional" in this term is critical: this perspective does not just mean feminist, but acknowledges other forms of marginalization, particularly race and class. According to Prado de O. Martins, this position stems from two key beliefs: "That taking up an apolitical position means complying with and contributing to the *status quo*, and that oppressions (of gender, race or class, among others) cannot be understood separately." In essence, the work of provocation cannot be truly critical if it does not acknowledge these forms of oppression.

> **NOTE** A PATRIARCHAL EXAMPLE FROM THE PAST
>
> I sometimes think about 20th century movements in art and design, and how, though considered groundbreaking and perspective-shifting, they still often embodied a type of patriarchal hegemony that was so internalized that the designers themselves failed to see it. Consider how women in the Bauhaus school were pushed into design disciplines such as weaving because its male founders held traditionalist views about the shortcomings of women: "Paul Klee and Wassily Kandinsky associated masculinity with genius and creativity, respectively. Gropius—who believed that women lacked the mental capacity to work in three dimensions—held bizarre convictions about certain forms or concepts as being masculine (the color red, the triangle) or feminine (the color blue, the square)."[11]

---

10 Luiza Prado de O. Martins, *Privilege and Oppression: Towards a Feminist Speculative Design* (Universität der Künste Berlin, 2014).

11 Kriston Capps, "The Women of the Bauhaus," Bloomberg, March 15, 2019.

Speculative, critical, and discursive design have the possibility of falling within similar traps when they are practiced by designers with a limited privileged purview. However, acknowledging those limitations, and understanding that so much of the way the world is framed is through the narrow lens of *those with the most power*—particularly white, male, cisgendered, and centered on the Global North—is a starting point. Again, disrupting this lens requires an intersectional feminist perspective. As Arturo Escobar noted, "Feminists from the Global South are particularly attuned to the manifold relational politics and ways of being that correspond to multiple axes of power and oppression."[12]

In Chapter 3, "Systems Thinking and Design Thinking," the theme of interrogating your position as a designer was introduced as an important aspect of engaging in systems thinking. Speculative design embodies a perspective that inherently questions the status quo. But how can you question the status quo without being cognizant about not only your own position, but also how you potentially perpetuate systems of oppression?

You as a designer can respond by, as mentioned earlier, adopting an intersectional feminist perspective. In addition, you must ensure representation of those who are typically marginalized throughout the design process. This includes diverse demographic representation on your own team. For example, my own background is as a child of Filipino immigrants, so I often bring a perspective that acknowledges (and has, experience with) racial oppression, as well as my lived experience outside of (and within) white-dominant culture. Intentional representation should extend to your speculative outputs as well. As Prado de O. Martins states, "If a video or photo series on a future scenario only depicts white, European, middle-class people, what does that say about the future of minorities?"

Interrogating the way the world is framed is also essential. To paraphrase Escobar, thinking new thoughts requires stepping out of Eurocentric experiences and Western social theory altogether, and considering the diversity of perspectives, frameworks, and experiences of "worlds of struggle." This means questioning positionality (for example, from a global standpoint, are you in a privileged position that fundamentally narrows your point of view?) and assumptions about what is fundamentally objective.

---

12 Arturo Escobar, *Designs for the Pluriverse: Radical Interdependence, Autonomy, and the Making of Worlds* (Duke University Press, 2018).

Speculative design is about questioning how things are framed and imagining scenarios based on those questions. To reinforce Dunne and Raby, "All good critical design offers an alternative to how things are." Current systems of oppression and how they may affect the future need to be part of the discourse.

The Benefits of Imagining

You may be wondering what kinds of practical applications these types of projects may have. In "Discursive Design Basics: Mode and Audience"[13] Bruce and Stephanie Tharp described discursive design products as having four different forms of utility (Figure 9.7).

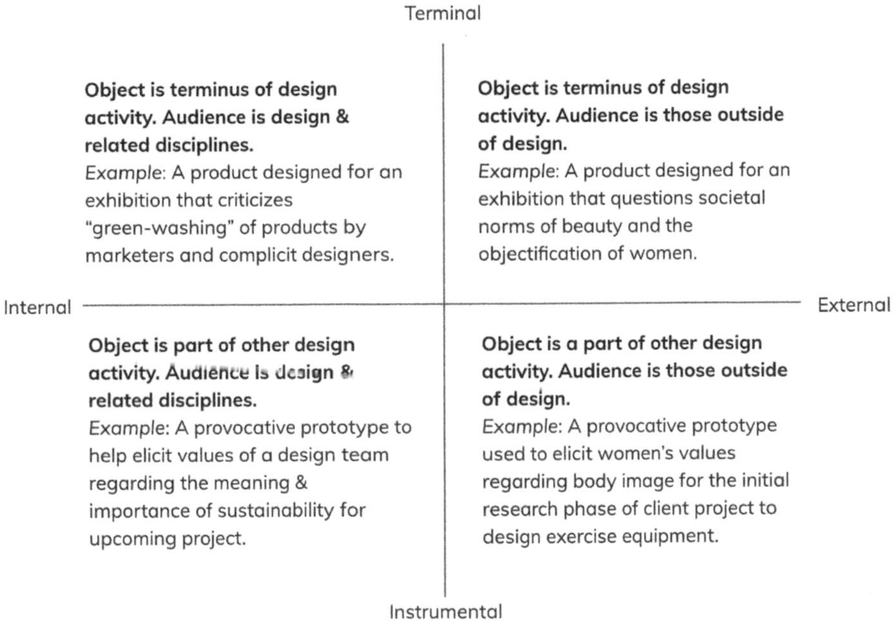

Terminal

Object is terminus of design activity. Audience is design & related disciplines. *Example:* A product designed for an exhibition that criticizes "green-washing" of products by marketers and complicit designers.	**Object is terminus of design activity. Audience is those outside of design.** *Example:* A product designed for an exhibition that questions societal norms of beauty and the objectification of women.
Object is part of other design activity. Audience is design & related disciplines. *Example:* A provocative prototype to help elicit values of a design team regarding the meaning & importance of sustainability for upcoming project.	**Object is a part of other design activity. Audience is those outside of design.** *Example:* A provocative prototype used to elicit women's values regarding body image for the initial research phase of client project to design exercise equipment.

Internal — External

Instrumental

FIGURE 9.7

Tharp and Tharp's 2x2 articulating the various applications of discursive design.

---

13 Bruce M. and Stephanie M. Tharp, "Discursive Design Basics: Mode and Audience," Nordic Design Research Conference, 2013.

In this framework, "terminal" is used to describe the design output as the final product of your design activities, while "instrumental" describes a design output that is meant to inform other activities. For use in a systems-thinking context (as well as in integrating with forms of a more traditional design approach), speculative design outputs would likely be used for instrumental purposes: as a way to affect further decision-making of some sort.

When viewed through this lens, there are a number of benefits to engaging a speculative design lens through the course of your systems-thinking work. Speculative techniques are good for asking "what if?" in a way that creates meaningful discourse.

Within the course of using speculative thinking to further decision-making, you and your stakeholders can experience multiple benefits:

- It helps you to interrogate inequities.
- It makes the abstract tangible.
- It reframes the possibilities by acknowledging context.

Interrogating Inequities

As mentioned earlier in the chapter, in Ben Passmore's graphic short story "Welcome to Tomorrowville,"[14] the illustrator describes a futuristic city where citizens are surveilled by "smart" devices. It raises the question of who might benefit from certain types of smart infrastructure (there is a character with a physical disability), and others who might suffer (people experiencing homelessness). The city is privatized and run by a corporate entity. The scenario provokes consideration of who holds power today, and who makes the kinds of decisions that will affect how everything is framed tomorrow.

This scenario is not as far-fetched as it may seem. From 2017 to 2020, Alphabet—Google's parent company—engaged its Sidewalk Labs division to build a $50 million development project on Toronto's water-front. The project included thousands of planned multiuse buildings, digitized streets, and low-income housing, and, according to Aarian Marshall in *WIRED*: "The Google sister company founded to digitize and techify urban planning would collect data on all of it, in a quest

---

14 Ben Passmore, "Welcome to Tomorrowville," in *Flash Forward: An Illustrated Guide to Possible (and Not So Possible) Tomorrows* by Rose Eveleth (Abrams ComicArts, 2021), pp. 9-25.

to perfect city living."[15] The project died due to multiple criticisms and complications, including distrust by citizens about Alphabet's potential data collection, misalignment with local governments, and disagreement over funding. On top of that, indigenous groups who had consulted on the project felt dismissed and ignored.[16]

An excerpt from Berthold Brecht's poem "Questions from a Worker Who Reads" is a good reminder of how events are typically framed when it comes to power.

> Who built the seven gates of Thebes?
>
> The books are filled with names of kings.
>
> Was it the kings who hauled the craggy blocks of stone?
>
> And Babylon, so many times destroyed.
>
> Who built the city up each time?[17]

A prompt for thinking about how you might frame future-oriented projects is: Who holds the power in this scenario, and how might you question the framing? As a designer and systems thinker, how might you ensure that diverse voices are represented in how you think about the future?

Making the Abstract Tangible

People—including your stakeholders—think about the future as a far-off place that might not seem relevant in the face of current and urgent decision-making. However it's important in the context of systems thinking to introduce discussion around long-term outcomes. Speculative imaginings can help ground thoughts around outcomes in real-life scenarios. For example, *Uninvited Guests*, the video by Superflux, helps ground viewers beyond just thinking abstractly about personal data monitors, and it actively presents an empathic picture of how using these devices might play out. Because

---

15 Aarian Marshall, "Alphabet's Sidewalk Labs Scraps Its Ambitious Toronto Project," *WIRED*, May 7, 2020.

16 Josh O'Kane, "Indigenous Group Speaks Out over 'Grossly Misleading' Sidewalk Labs Consultation," *The Globe and Mail*, October 25, 2019.

17 Berthold Brecht, "Questions from a Worker Who Reads," in *Svendborg Poems*, 1939.

it's a provocation rather than a straightforward positive picture, it can spur discussion around impact in a meaningful way.

Reframing the Possibilities

A good example of a project that reframes how systems are shaped is Thomas Thwaites' *The Toaster Project*.[18] Thwaites' objective was to build a toaster from scratch. He found that a typical, cheap, readily available toaster, upon being taken apart, had more than 400 parts made out of 100-plus different materials. Thwaite focused on just five materials: steel, mica, plastic, copper, and nickel. Throughout the subsequent nine-month process, he found he had to extract and smelt iron, attempt to create plastic from starch, and obtain water that contained dissolved copper from a copper mine. His absurd (and humorous) attempt to finally create a somewhat working toaster ended up being an interrogation of the system surrounding the inexpensive electrical goods that everyone uses, most of which, when people are done with them, or if the objects are broken, end up in landfills (see Figure 9.8).

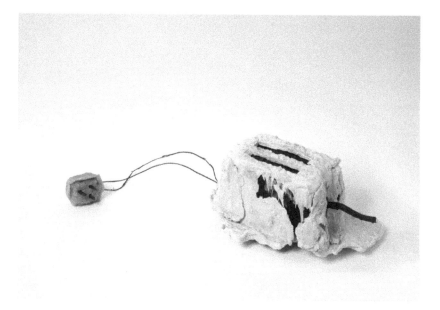

FIGURE 9.8
Thomas Thwaites' toaster actually worked momentarily, though it kind of melted on itself when it was used to make toast.

---

18 Thomas Thwaites, *The Toaster Project* (Princeton Architectural Press, 2011).

Although systems-thinking designers do not necessarily need to engage in this type of *reductio ad absurdum* project, speculative design can be a good practice for questioning the way that systems are framed. For example, if you are working in the healthcare space, it's worthwhile to consider a future in which healthcare is funded differently than it is today, or where power is held in different hands. Or you can even imagine a dark continuation of today's problems (for example, the relationship between large numbers of uninsured citizens is related to both policy and privatization of healthcare).

The act of speculating lets you not only think about how problems are solved, but also the system in which the problem-solving is taking place and the implications of those systems.

Takeaways

- Speculative design is a way to provoke reflection on the future and possibilities—good and bad—when it comes to the societal implications of design. Its relationship with systems thinking is that it typically considers context, outcomes, and impact in a way that traditional design does not.

- These types of design provocations can take several forms: physical objects, temporal storytelling, narrative storytelling, and storyboards and comics, to name a few examples.

- In order to truly engage in the criticality of speculative design, you as a designer must reflect on your own position of privilege.

- The benefits of imagining future scenarios include interrogation of inequity, making the abstract tangible, and the reframing of possibilities.

Adrienne Matthews *is a Los Angeles-born, Seattle-based visual artist, writer, and designer. She is currently a Lead Strategy Manager at Starbucks.*

How does your background inform your approach to your work?

I come from a big storytelling family. Growing up, I learned a lot about how my family members navigated their lives and livelihoods in the face of institutional barriers. This focus on storytelling drove my decision to eventually get a degree in English at Spelman College, which it is known for. Going to a school where the student body is made up of women of African descent really made me engage in intersectional thinking: considering how systems of oppression intersect and overlap, as well as how these impact how people are situated within—and engage with—institutions. This focus on critical theory helped me really use the lenses of race, gender, class, and socioeconomic status as a starting point in thinking about systems and people.

In your strategic work, how do you encourage others to also engage in this intersection between the personal and the professional?

As a strategist, in my facilitation with stakeholders, I tell people, "Let's pause for a moment to think about not just what our role is on this project, but who we are, and the identities, knowledge, and contexts we bring." In creating that moment of pause, I've gotten very different results: new connections and conversations. We're not typically prompted to reveal much about ourselves in our workplace cultures, and I try to emphasize that being inclusive is not just an idea, but something we should practice every day. This moment of "noticing" can uncover insights and/or blind spots that the team might bring to the design challenge, and can also point to whose perspective might be missing. Acknowledging this is important.

How else have you integrated this perspective in your approach to both systems thinking and design?

After I finished business school, I had some additional training in human-centered design, and this is when I started applying this lens of intersectionality into my work directly: how I frame problems, how I conduct research, and how I frame "how might we" questions that get at root-cause analysis. While I was working at the Gates Foundation, I joined a team that was responsible for designing immersive experiences to engage diverse audiences in the foundation's work to reduce global inequity. We needed to apply a systems lens to understand the broader context for a diverse audience—the relationship they might have with the Foundation, their cultural or institutional context, and the opportunities, implications, and limitations of prioritizing specific points of view. Our discussion in our design charrettes started turning toward things like, "In the experiences we're creating, how might we design for dignity?" "How might we disrupt hierarchical models of knowledge sharing?" In our empathy-building and context-setting, there was permission to pose these questions as design challenges.

That continues in my work with my current organization. Operating a retail business is a complex orchestra. Thinking about the system is something you have to consider every time you launch a new product: there's infrastructure involved, there's culture, and people—individuals with all of their complex motivations and desires. So this creates a more complex challenge than just bringing a product to market. We need to ask ourselves: how do we build a system that works?

I understand you've incorporated futures thinking into your work. Could you talk a bit about the benefit of this approach, and what are some methods that you use?

The future presents us with so many possibilities. And the last two years of the pandemic have shown us that change is constant and critical to navigate. Futures thinking can help us consider what may lie ahead, and can give us context to help create a potential future that we want to live in. As you look toward the future, what contexts might shift and impact your stakeholders, your communities, and your business model? This can help you create a more focused research plan and translate future trends into provocations to support strategic conversations.

A few approaches my teams have used in the past are futures research into social or cultural contexts, human values and behaviors, and qualitative research with diverse audiences and disciplines to understand how future "trajectories" might impact communities differently. For product design, we might also consider policy or regulatory changes that could shift the landscape for supply chain, customer behavior, and innovation. We've also used visualization prototypes to understand the potential impact of our design choices.

How do you think this approach—speculating on the future—enhances strategy on your projects or within your organization?

The process of gathering insight into potential futures can shed light on blind spots and opportunities, and which communities are already doing the work to design better systems. While we can't predict what will happen, we can pause to consider where we may want to disrupt current trends or trajectories. Where might we use our intention and resources to make a positive impact?

What are some practical ways you would recommend to designers for integrating systems thinking into their work?

I'd say that my practice has evolved through passion and curiosity. I'm always looking to bring new tools and resources to my teams, knowing that the best way to find what works is through doing. About eight years ago, I began actively seeking out HCD methods that have an equity focus, such as liberatory design, which positions HCD thinking around interventions, positionality, and systemic outcomes. I'm also influenced by concepts like theory of change, which helps teams map the connection between policy actions, design decisions, and outcomes. I'd also add that there are more paradigm-shifting frameworks and facilitation prompts from community-centered design practices, which look at restoration and repair as essential elements for innovation. Having a multidisciplinary design curiosity is helpful to expand my mindset, find collaborators in learning, and start applying the learning right away. Having context-awareness, a growth mindset, and deliberately including a diverse set of perspectives in design sprints increases the rigor and integrity of the work.

In order to build the muscle of extending your mindset, it starts with you. Embrace the power of the multidisciplinary. And remember that there's a lot of power in questions. A single question can change the course of how you do your work.

CODA

Consider the Lettuce

Buddhist monk and activist Thich Nhat Hanh once wrote, "When you plant lettuce, if it does not grow well, you don't blame the lettuce. You look for reasons it is not doing well. It may need fertilizer, or more water, or less sun. You never blame the lettuce."

I think about this quote quite often. It is a symbol of why I focus on systems thinking as a meaningful avenue for change. Understanding the problems of the world means understanding the context in which those problems sit, which allows one to consider what kinds of change will have the most impact. In a world that has deep inequities, and where the easiest path is to place the blame on those who experience misfortune, it could benefit everyone to think about how systems should change to better allow everyone to thrive. It is a form of care.

My hope is that the guidance in this book closes the gap between the desire to take on a systems-oriented mindset and the reality of engaging with it in practice. We as designers can use our power for good, to envision change. With this mindset, we can help the lettuce thrive.

INDEX

the *Blind Men and the Elephant* fable, 20–21

Blockchain Chicken Farm (Wang), 226

Borunda, Alejandra, 31

bounded rationality, 21, 108–111

Brecht, Berthold, 233

bridges built by Khasi, 36–37

Bronfenbrenner, Uri, 102–104

Bruijn, Mirjam de, 34–35, 163

bubonic plague, 186

bullet train design, 223

buzzkill, 208

C

Cameron, Mike, 109

capitalism, in causality, 38–39

Carbon Bathtub, 146–147

Carroll, Antoinette, 52

cascading effects, 123, 188

causal loops, 99, 123–134
  components of (nodes, direction, values), 124–125
  creation of, 123–130
  deep structure, as core causal loop, 131–132
  deep structure themes, 132–134
  disadvantages of, 184
  goal of a system, 130–131
  putting loops together with categories of impacts, 128–130
  types of, 125–128

causality concept in systems thinking, 38–41

cause and effect
  cyclical and linear, 17
  representation of, 99, 144
  understanding systems, 124

chain reactions of Rube Goldberg machine, 156–157

challenge mapping, 4

change. *See* theory of change

Checkland, Peter, 24–25, 153

Chew, Boon Yew, 27, 151–153

Chicago, city grid of, 14

childbirth, VBAC calculator, and race, 147–149

China, storytelling about technology and rural impact, 226–227

cholera epidemic in London, 122

Circular Business Canvas, 184

circularity and systems (cyclical thinking), 17–18, 183–184

city warrens vs. city grids, 13–14

Claveria y Zaldua, Narciso, 114–115

closed feedback loop, 128

Cobra Effect, 187

collective action, 212

colonial rule
  cobra eradication in Delhi, 187
  rat eradication in Hanoi, 186–188
  surnames imposed in Philippines, 114–115

comics, 227–228

Community category in ecological framework, 103, 166

community impact, in causal loops, 129–130

comparative stakeholder mapping, 112–113

confirmation bias, 190

constellations metaphor, 184

containers, shipping, and global shipping systems, 100–101

COVID-19 pandemic
  error of false assumptions, 190
  example of reinforcing causal loop, 126–128
  futures wheel and remote work, 200–202

disabilities
    and empathy in design thinking, 51
    "nothing about us without us," 194
discrimination in housing, and heat
    waves, 32
*Discursive Design: Critical, Speculative,
    and Alternative Things* (Tharp &
    Tharp), 218
"Discursive Design Basics: Mode and
    Audience" (Tharp & Tharp), 231
discussion guides for interviews, 85
diseases. *See also* COVID-19 pandemic
    bubonic plague, 186
    cholera epidemic in London, 122
    malaria eradication, 166
Disinformation Risk Zone, 208
Disney nature documentary, 15–16
diversity
    and "How might we?" prompts, 161
    lack of, as barrier to design work,
        193–194
    of research participants, 87
    of stakeholders in data collection, 68
doing nothing, and unintended conse-
    quences, 206–207
Doumer, Paul, 186
d.school, 4, 46
Dunne, Anthony, 217, 219, 220, 222, 231
Dutch bike, 3

E

Ecological Framework
    about stakeholder mapping, 102–105
    comparative stakeholder mapping,
        112–113
    in creating causal loops, 128–129
    levels of context in, 103, 166
*Ecological Framework for Human Develop-
    ment* (Bronfenbrenner), 102

ecological problems with invasive
    species, 62–63
Economic category of STEEP frame-
    work, 163–165
Economix (Goodwin), 132, 138
Ehrlich, Paul R., 191
Einstein, Albert, xviii
Elawa, Chris, 12
empathize phase, in design-thinking
    process, 5–6, 46–47, 48, 61, 159
empathy, role in design thinking, 50–51
England, train crashes and shift to
    cars, 41
Enter the Dragon (film), 26–27
environment. *See also* nature
    Environmental category of STEEP
        framework, 163–165
    in Tarot Cards of Tech, 204–205
equity in design and systems-thinking
    process, 161
Equity Innovation studio, 117
Erete, Sheena, 58
Eroding Goals system archetype, 136–137
error, and unintended consequences, 190
Escalation system archetype, 136–137
Escobar, Arturo, 59, 230
Ethical Explorer, 202, 208–210
ethics, in systems-thinking pluralism, 36
evaluate phase, in systems-thinking
    process, 54–55, 61–62, 157, 159
Eveleth, Rose, 227
events, in a system, 123, 128
Ever Given mega-container ship, 100–101
Exclusion Risk Zone, 208
expand phase, in systems-thinking
    process, 54–55, 60, 157, 159
expert opinion. *See* Interviews with
    Expert Designers
Eyal, Nir, 10

bridges built by Khasi, 36–37

Disney documentary, and lemmings myth, 15–16

ecological problems with invasive species, 62–63

learning from, 223–224

Mother Nature, in Tarot Cards of Tech, 204–205

Nhat Hanh, Thich, 239

nodes, as component of causal loop, 124, 128

Norman, Donald, 4

Norton, Peter, 198

"nothing about us without us," 194

Nudge: Improving Decisions About Health, Wealth, and Happiness (Thaler and Sunstein), 108

O

Odell, Jenny, 207

omafiets (Dutch bike), 3

Omidyar Group, 131

Omidyar Network, 208

Onafuwa, Dimeji, 212–214

"One Laptop Per Child" initiative, 12

OpenLearn, 41

opportunity areas, and "How might we?" prompts, 159–162

opportunity ideation in SME workshops, 89–90

orchestra causal loop map, 133–134

Organ Crafting project, Biophilia, 224

Ostrom, Elinor, 212

Otlhogile-Gordon, Pierce, 117–120

Outcomes Mapping, 170, 171–175

Outsized Power Risk Zone, 208

overreacting/overcorrecting, in Balancing Process with Delay system archetype, 136–137

P

Pacific Northwest heat wave, 31–32

Packer, George, xvii

Paris, redesign of, 14

park, postindustrial design of doing nothing, 206–207

participative principle, 26

participatory design, 58, 70, 73

Passmore, Ben, 228, 232

Patagonia, company mission statement, 196

Patel, Samir, 17

patriarchal example of Bauhaus, 229

A Pattern Language (Alexander, Ishikawa, and Silverstein), 65

Peewee's Big Adventure (film), 155

personal protective equipment (PPEs), and systems thinking by designers, 22–23

perverse incentives, 187, 191–192

Pew Research Center, 78

Philippines, colonial rule and imposition of surnames, 114–115

physical objects, as speculative design, 222

plastic hour, xvii–xviii

plausible future, as path in futures cone, 219

pluriversal design, 213

points of intervention (solutions), 123

Policy/System category in ecological framework, 103, 166

Political category of STEEP framework, 163–165

population bomb, 191

positionality, xviii, 35–36, 230

possible future, as path in futures cone, 219

postindustrial park design, 206–207

ACKNOWLEDGMENTS

B ack in 2019, I was lucky enough to serendipitously sit next to Lou Rosenfeld on a bus in Medellín, Colombia. I was there to teach a systems-thinking workshop at Interaction Latin America, and as he asked me about my perspective on the topic, I mentioned to him that I thought a gap existed because there weren't any books on systems thinking that were explicitly aimed at design practitioners. Lou asked some questions about it, and then we moved on to chatting about other things.

Fast forward to 2020. He hadn't forgotten about our conversation, and as a result, you now have this book. I can't thank Lou enough for his belief and trust in me to write about this topic, and can't say enough about the supportive environment that he provides to authors like myself.

I also want to thank Marta Justak, my kind, tough, and wise editor. She supported me when I wasn't sure about what I was doing and pushed me when I needed a push. I thought writing a book during a pandemic would be a manageable thing (I mean, I wasn't doing anything anyway, right?) but it was, in reality, incredibly difficult (it turns out it's much harder to cope with family life, work, and writing a book when everyone is home during a pandemic!). Marta recognized everything I was juggling, but her steady presence truly helped me to deliver.

To the brilliant practitioners whom I interviewed for the book, Boon Yew Chew (who also reviewed an early draft), Nicole Sarsfield, Dimeji Onafuwa, Shree Laksmi Rao, Adrienne Matthews, Pierce Otlhogile-Gordon, Behnosh Najafi, Kat Ward, and Hannah Hoffman: each of you inspires me to push my practice. Thanks so much for sharing your wisdom and methods with me.

A big thanks to those who so generously spent time reviewing and giving feedback on the book. Tyler Fox, Amy Bucher, and Jared Cole: you pushed my thinking when the book was just in draft form and helped make this book exponentially better. Brandon Schauer, Beth Kolko, David Dylan Thomas, Masuma Henry, Jose Coronado, Tracy Johnson, Hung-Hsiang Chen, and Kristin Skinner: I appreciate your thoughts and testimonials on the finished product; it helped resolve whatever outstanding imposter syndrome I had about being an author!

Huge gratitude to Kevin Bethune for contributing your brilliance as the foreword author of this book. I couldn't have asked for a better design leader and fellow author for this.

Thanks so much to Carey Jenkins and the team at Substantial for cheerleading me through the highs and lows of the writing process. I could not have had a more supportive group of colleagues as I tried to write a book while working full time as a design consultant. I also want to thank the fine administration, faculty, and students at the University of Washington HCDE program for pushing my thinking and giving me opportunities to test and share my ideas through teaching.

Thank you to my parents, Ernesto and Rebecca, and extended family—Trish, Jimmy, Soleil, Radha, Kavi, Sydney, Aimee, Simona, Sloane, and Stella—for being wonderful distractions during the pandemic and the writing process. And of course, thank you to my partner Kyle for rallying me when I didn't think I could finish this, and my kids Sofia, Dario, Dominic, and Scout, who waited patiently for me to not be writing a book on evenings, weekends, and holidays. You are the center of my systems map.

 Rosenfeld®

Dear Reader,

Thanks very much for purchasing this book. There's a story behind it and every product we create at Rosenfeld Media.

Since the early 1990s, I've been a User Experience consultant, conference presenter, workshop instructor, and author. (I'm probably best-known for having cowritten *Information Architecture for the Web and Beyond*.) In each of these roles, I've been frustrated by the missed opportunities to apply UX principles and practices.

I started Rosenfeld Media in 2005 with the goal of publishing books whose design and development showed that a publisher could practice what it preached. Since then, we've expanded into producing industry-leading conferences and workshops. In all cases, UX has helped us create better, more successful products—just as you would expect. From employing user research to drive the design of our books and conference programs, to working closely with our conference speakers on their talks, to caring deeply about customer service, we practice what we preach every day.

Please visit rosenfeldmedia.com to learn more about our **conferences**, **workshops**, **free communities**, and **other great resources** that we've made for you. And send your ideas, suggestions, and concerns my way: louis@rosenfeldmedia.com

I'd love to hear from you, and I hope you enjoy the book!

Lou Rosenfeld,
Publisher

RECENT TITLES FROM ROSENFELD MEDIA

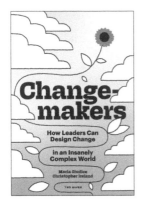

Get a great discount on a Rosenfeld Media book:
visit rfld.me/deal to learn more.

SELECTED TITLES FROM ROSENFELD MEDIA

View our full catalog at rosenfeldmedia.com/books

ABOUT THE AUTHOR

 **Sheryl Cababa** drives a human-centered design practice that is focused on systems thinking and evidence-based design, working on everything from robotic surgery experience design to reimagining K-12 education through service design. In her work with consultancies such as Substantial, frog, and Adaptive Path, she has worked with a diverse base of clients including the Gates Foundation, Microsoft, IHME, and IKEA. She holds a B.A. in journalism and political science from Syracuse University.

Sheryl is an international speaker and workshop facilitator. When she's not in the office, she can be found at the University of Washington helping educate the next generation of Human-Centered Design and Engineering students. You might also find her biking around Seattle, or talking about her most recent complicated baking project.

CPSIA information can be obtained
at www.ICGtesting.com
Printed in the USA
JSHW072036210523
42001JS00001B/1